Conscience at War

SUNY Series in Israeli Studies
Russell Stone, editor

Conscience at War

The Israeli Soldier as a Moral Critic

Ruth Linn

State University of New York Press

Published by
State University of New York Press, Albany

Printed in the United States of America

For information, address State University of New York Press, State University Plaza, Albany, NY 12246

Production by Dana Foote
Marketing by Fran Keneston

Library of Congress Cataloging-in-Publication Data

Linn, Ruth.
Conscience at war : the Israeli soldier as a moral critic / Ruth Linn.
p. cm. — (SUNY series in Israeli studies)
Includes bibliographical references and index.
ISBN 0–7914–2777–3 (hc : alk. paper). — ISBN 0–7914–2778–1 (pbk. : alk. paper)
1. Conscientious objectors—Israel. 2. Israel. Tseva haganah le-Yiśra'el. I. Title. II. Series.
UB345.I75L56 1996
355.2'24'095694—dc20 95-40640
CIP

10 9 8 7 6 5 4 3 2 1

CONTENTS

TABLES

ACKNOWLEDGMENTS

Earlier versions of the following chapters were originally published as follows:

Chapter 2 is a revised version of my article "The Claim for Moral Maturity, Consistency, and Integrity among Objecting Israeli Soldiers during a Morally Controversial War," *Journal of Applied Social Psychology,* vol. 25, no. 5 (1995), pp. 399–416. © V. H. Winston and Son, Inc.

Chapter 3 is a revised version of my article "Justice and Care Reasoning in Morally Ambiguous Situations—Examples from Vietnam and the Intifada," *Social Behavior and Personality,* vol. 21, no. 1 (1993), pp. 39–51. © The Society for Personality Research.

Chapter 4 is a revised version of my article "Morally Puzzled Individuals in a Morally Puzzled Community: Resisting Israeli Soldiers During War in Lebanon and the Intifada," *Psychological Reports,* vol. 75 (1994), pp. 423–434. © *Psychological Reports* 1994.

Chapter 7 is a revised version of my article "Holocaust Metaphors and Symbols in the Moral Dilemmas of Contemporary Israeli Soldiers," *Metaphor and Symbolic Activity,* vol. 6, no. 2 (1991), pp. 61–86. © Lawrence Erlbaum, Associates, Inc.

Chapter 8 is a revised version of my article "Resistance and Motivation—Moral, Political, or Personal? Israeli Soldiers as Selective Conscientious Objectors during the Intifada," *Social Behavior and Personality,* vol. 23, no. 1 (1995), PP. 35–44. © The Society for Personality Research.

Chapter 9 is a revised version of my article "Conscience at War and the Assessment of Credibility: Theoretical and Practical Questions," *Politics and the Individual,* vol. 4, no. 2 (1994), pp. 47–61.

I would like to thank my editor at SUNY Press, Clay Morgan, for his care and support throughout the review and publication of this book. Many thanks go to Dr. Russell Stone for his thorough review of the book and to Dana Foote for her careful editorial help. Finally, I would like to convey my thanks to Mrs. Sybil and Mr. Stephen Stone, long-term advocates of justice and peace, who were the first to encourage me to do this project.

By becoming continuous, war has ceased to exist.

—George Orwell, *1984*, p. 164

The Silenced Civilian in Uniform
An Introduction

I belong to a special generation within Israeli society, one born after the War of Independence (1948), and growing up with the hopes and illusion of their parents that in the post-Holocaust era this generation would never have to fight wars. For my generation, the Holocaust, even though not suffered directly, is a concrete event. Each of us remembers from his or her childhood the strange man or woman with a number branded on his/her arm and the mysterious, half-believed story about how his/her family had been gassed to death and had their bodies made into soap. From kindergarten age we heard the siren and stood to attention on Holocaust Day, when the theaters and the cinema were closed, and listened to the grim tales of Holocaust survivors. Some years later, these accounts on "The Banality of Evil" (Arendt 1963) became real as we listened to the reasoning of Adolf Eichmann emitted from his specially constructed glass box at his trial in Jerusalem. We heard this ordinary, well-behaved person, who had driven the Nazi extermination mill, justify his actions on the ground that he was "a cog in the machine" and "just obeying orders" (Kohlberg 1984). For those Israeli citizens who had been through the Holocaust, as well as for those who had not, the Holocaust has become a metaphor they constantly seek to understand, interpret, and respond to. Unwittingly it has become part of the daily phraseology. In army slang, for example, the paratroopers call one of their jump training devices the "Eichmann" after the gallows on which he was hanged; the more compliant soldier in the unit is often called "Soap."

Our parents' hope gave us names full of promise like Shalom (peace), Tikva (hope), and Shalva (tranquillity) as part of the illusion of "no more wars." And at night, when they put us to sleep, they would whisper that by the time we came to serve in the army we wouldn't have to fight like them.

As young Sabras (Israeli born) we were encouraged to climb the steep path to the Massada fortress, where in ancient days Jews had committed suicide rather than fall into the hands of the Romans. We were taught: "Massada will not fall again." On this site, young Israeli conscripts take an oath in which they promise to fulfill one of the most critical moral obligations a citizen of a democracy can take upon himself: the obligation to fight (kill and be killed) for one's own country (Walzer 1977). Our parents' hopes have not yet materialized. In reality, the eight-kilometer-wide state of pre-1967 Israel, with its less than three million Jewish citizens, surrounded by over 100 million Arabs, many of whom dispute its right to exist, has been engaged in a continuous struggle for survival since its inception. The somber list of military confrontations consists of the 1956 Sinai campaign (Egypt), the 1967 Six Day War (Egypt, Jordan, and Syria), the 1968–1970 War of Attrition (Egypt and Syria), the 1973 Yom Kippur War (Egypt and Syria), the 1978 Litani operation in Lebanon, the 1982–1985 Lebanon War, the 1991 Gulf War and the Intifada ("Uprising") from 1987 (official) till the 1993 Oslo agreement (though unofficially continued to these days of writing). In addition to the above list, Israel has suffered from continuous terrorist attacks on all of its frontiers, within the country itself, and against Israelis abroad (Linn 1988b).

Due to this chronic state of war, the flourishing of a culture where the army plays such a central role was inevitable. From a very early age Israeli children write letters to the soldiers along the borders, to thank them for being there and enabling them to study peacefully in school. For years we were proud to attend the military parades and felt protected when we heard the noise of aircraft. We grew up to understand that between Israel and survival there is only the Israel Defense Forces (hereafter termed as the IDF). The IDF became a living symbol and metaphor.

In the reality of "few against many," we grew up with the strong belief that our strength was a moral one, based on our right to be here in the land of Israel and to defend our democratic life here. We were proud of the IDF moral code of "purity of arms" (the obligation to minimize both casualties to innocent victims and damage to property (Hardan 1985; Gal 1986). This moral principle was epitomized in heroic stories of compulsory, career, or reserve soldiers and commanders who sacrificed their lives when trying to preserve this high moral code in the battlefield.

There was one story that was not told. This was the story of the Israeli citizen as "a soldier on eleven months annual leave." The phrase, first coined by former Israeli Chief of Staff Yigael Yadin, became an obvious reality that has no parallel in the world. The moral upheavals of this service have never been studied.

Israel's security is maintained largely by civilians in uniform (Schiff 1992). On completion of three years' compulsory military service (commencing at age eighteen) every male citizen is obliged to serve one to two months of reserve duty annually, at any location his unit is sent to, until the age of fifty-five (reduced to fifty in 1992). In times of emergency the frequency, length, and danger of the service increases. In the course of his life, the average male citizen completes a minimum of two year's army service, in addition to the three years of compulsory service. This calculation is based on the minimum period of service of one month per annum for twenty-four years served in the reserves. It excludes unexpected, prolonged reserve service of up to six months during the 1973 Yom Kippur War, two to three months during the 1982–1985 war in Lebanon, and, since 1987, the same period of two to three months during the Intifada in the Israeli administered territories.

In spite of the continuous interruptions to the individual's civilian life by the yearly routine of reserve duty and the unexpected long-term service in crisis situations, the motivation to serve the country has always been high (Gal 1986). The smooth functioning of the IDF within an interrupted civilian society (Kimmerling 1985) however, cannot reflect the high price paid both physically and mentally by Israeli reservists. It is expected that eighteen-year-old Jewish boys and girls (as well as Druze boys) will complete three years of military training (girls serve for two years) and earn the equivalent of approximately $30 a month during this period. Until 1994, no financial benefits awaited them when discharged from the army at the age of twenty-one. During their reserve service, they are compensated for their basic salary only (Horowitz 1987).

At the age of twenty-one, the Israeli male citizen may choose the army as a profession. Unlike the reservist, a career officer is paid annually for military service and often gains financial bonuses over the years. This includes free higher education, free medical care, promotions, and financial compensation when discharged after a minimum of ten years of service (Gal 1986). In fact, "the IDF career officer's pay grade is one of the highest in Israel" (Gal 1986, p. 37). Most of all, the career officers are protected from the continuous tension faced by reservists who are repeatedly called upon to leave their workplace to complete their reserve duties, and need extra time to readjust to civilian life.

Rarely does assigned annual service fall at a convenient time for the average reservist. A student may miss a whole month in his studies or alternatively, the month of the exam period, or his short vacation. A lawyer may miss a good contract, a doctor leaves behind untreated patients in the clinic and the farmer his unpicked crop. In a case of difficulty, the reservist may submit an appeal for release from service to a special committee called "The Committee for Coordination of Release from the Reserve Service" (in Hebrew, *Valtam*), which can authorize his release from the assigned service, provided the appeal is found to be justified. Rarely, if ever, does assigned annual service fall at a convenient time for the reservists' wife or children; the psychological toll on them has rarely been mentioned as a subject for inquiry (Swirsky and Safir 1991; Milgram and Bar 1993).

A possible incentive for the dedicated attendance by reservists to service is the connection they have with their buddies in their unit. As noted by Gal (1986) "the reserve units, even more than the regular units, gradually become like extended families" (p. 40). This is the result of the average reservist spending most of his service in the same unit, with the same company and often with the same commanders. "Only the wars change" (p. 40). Very often reservists will make every effort to overcome difficulties in their civilian lives and report for their assigned service so that they can complete their tour of duty with their comrades whom they can trust in emergencies and often enjoy serving with rather than spending it with unknown colleagues. Another incentive is the belief in the moral foundation of the IDF and the realization of the surrounding threat. As noted by Gal (1986): "The sense of no choice has not only been a motivational source for the Israeli soldier, it has also been the moral justification for all of Israel's wars. It was this sense of being forced by the enemy to defend himself, rather than any hatred for the enemy, that characterized the Israeli soldier's motivation throughout all times" (p. 147).

In times of war, the unique system of the reserves (*Miluim* in Hebrew) makes the IDF the largest army in the world in proportion to its population. Approximately 65 percent of the IDF's combat units are reserve forces. They are also an integral part of overall Israeli society. It had been a widely accepted norm within Israeli society that as long as there is a national consensus regarding defense issues, the reservist will make a military contribution without reservation and regardless of political affiliation (Gal 1986).

Army service becomes an entrance ticket to Israeli society in general, and the job market and political life in particular. Thus, for example, the morality of Ministers and Members of Parliament is often measured by their army service (for example, the 1988 list of the army backgrounds of the new Ministers) (*Yediot Acharonot*, 12 December 1988). Army service marks the (secular) moral identity of the average Israeli, particularly that of a male. As has been observed by Levy (1990): "The image of 'being a man' in Israel is still firmly connected with overcoming military demands and the horrors of war with flying colors, with the supposed willingness to sacrifice—seemingly without fear—the most precious essentials of life, health and sanity. . . . The military is the natural business of men" (248–249). The close bond between civilian and army life is the source from which the military draws its strength, but this same bond represents its vulnerability.

As well as the comparison between the Israeli civilian in uniform and the career officer, there is comparison with two other groups within Israeli society who are free of military obligations due to historical and political constraints. The first group consists of over seven-hundred-thousand-person Arab minorities, living in Israel, who are a priori exempt from service. At the age of twenty-one, the discharged Israeli soldier is able to start his college studies or working life, while his fellow Arab Israeli citizen has already finished a Bachelor's degree (this takes three years in Israel). After three years of army service, many young exsoldiers are required to attend one year of preuniversity classes to close the gap in knowledge and refresh them scholastically. Thus the Israeli soldier will finally commence his studies at the age of twenty-two. The more dedicated soldier, who serves as an officer, will often start a year later as he has to serve additional time in compulsory service. Throughout his studies, the Arab student will never be called upon to postpone his studies as a result of an annual reserve service or war.

The second group is the ultra-orthodox Jews who are a priori exempt from military service for conscientious reasons as long as they learn in Yeshiva (A Jewish religious academy). This political agreement is rooted in the post-Holocaust atmosphere that dominated the state of Israel in its very early years—the idea that the Jewish state would respect the wishes of observant Jews not to serve in the army if it violated their convictions (Blatt, Davis, and Kleinbaum 1975). It is important to note, however, that the IDF consists mainly of secular soldiers who nevertheless coordinate their army service in line with the religious laws (e.g., Kosher food, no military training or travelling home on Saturdays, etc.). This procedure enables most religious Jews to carry out military service. The "minority" of ultra-orthodox Jews has reached ninety thousand dissents for religious reasons (*Ha'aretz*, 4 January 1991), and when compared to the 400 known cases of secular and selective Israeli conscientious objectors in Israel since its inception in 1948, it is a significant number. When these two segments of Israeli society (Arabs and orthodox Jews) are put together, says Oren (1992), "a sizable minority, about one-fifth of the population (and growing, as these are the most fertile of groups in Israel) is found to be outside the mainstream of military service. A conscientious objector belonging to the secular Jewish majority would thus find ample grounds to feel discriminated against."

Traditionally, as stated by reserve general Mair P'ail, the IDF was "better than the nation." Once in uniform, the Israeli citizen was willing to work harder to achieve his assigned military goals than in civilian life. The short term of service with the army each year enables the reservist to remain a free-thinking civilian who is able to critically contemplate the moral issues faced by the IDF and to be its moral barometer. The contribution of the reservists to the moral atmosphere of the IDF has usually been ascribed to their civilian flavor (Gal 1986). They have often tended to bring into the army a spirit of informal discipline, as well as moral values and beliefs from their civilian lives. In their civilian lives, reservists have retained a special moral weight when protesting against injustice (Sprinzak 1977).

Despite the continuous interruption of an individual's civilian life by the yearly routine of the reserve duty and unexpected long-term service in crisis situations, cases of resistance to the draft have been rare (Blatt, Davis, and Kleinbaum 1975). As long as there was a national consensus (most apparent in self-defense and "no choice" wars), researchers tend to agree that the individual soldier had no reservations regarding military service (Horowitz 1987). He knew exactly why he was serving and what he was fighting for. Military service was an obvious need resulting from the surrounding threats (Gal 1986; Hardan 1985; Peled 1993). Since the inception of the state of Israel, there have been sporadic, marginal cases of individual criticism against the army in the form of disobedience. Serious objections emerged during the 1982–1985 stay of the IDF on the Lebanese soil, when soldiers were called to risk their life for goals whose legitimacy they questioned, or when they were assigned to military missions whose objectives they found morally confusing and/or in which they felt they could not morally win. The Lebanon war marks a dramatic turning point in the intensity, depth, and magnitude of criticism in the form of disobedience and this date serves as the starting point for this book's inquiry into the moral criticism of the Israeli soldier.

On 5 June 1982, Israel initiated a forty-eight- to seventy-two-hour preemptive strike against PLO infrastructures, which became the longest (at that time) and most controversial war in its history (Dupuy and Martell 1985; Gabriel 1984; Schiff and Ya'ari 1984; Shiffer 1984; Timmerman 1985). The short planned campaign entitled "Peace for the Galilee" was defined by the Prime Minister as a "war of choice." The Minister of Defense promised to implement a "new order" in Lebanon. And while blockading the capital city of Beirut, morally puzzled soldiers were informed by the Chief of Staff that "they were protecting the State of Israel."

With the idea of a short-term campaign, even objecting reservists joined the military efforts in Lebanon in its first phase, that is, the first two weeks of the war, or even to its (first) extended phase, until September 1982, when PLO terrorists were expelled from Beirut. However, the prolonged stay of three years on Lebanese soil triggered a growing controversy as to the moral necessity of the war (Schiff and Ya'ari 1984).

Throughout the three years of the war in Lebanon, about 165 Israeli reserve soldiers chose to adopt an unconventional mode of moral resolutions to their dilemmas about the war: they disobeyed the command to serve in the Lebanese zone when their unit was called up. They argued that such service would contradict the dictates of their conscience. At the outset, the intention of most of these soldiers was to comply with orders for general military service, but to refuse specific duty in Lebanon. Most asked to perform their reserve service within the Green Line. When their refusal was overruled and they continued to disobey their call, they were charged with a discipline offense. The objecting reservists subsequently underwent a court-martial and were sentenced to fourteen to thirty-five days in military prison, some of them on more than one occasion. The Israeli public did not know how to approach this new form of criticism. The press was quick to announce that this was a "new melody within Israeli society" (*Ha'ir*, 11 March 1983). The refusing soldiers were called "refusers"(*sarvanim* in Hebrew), a name that emphasizes the obligation they were not fulfilling, without any reference to the possible moral concerns they might have held. In spite of the growing public controversy over the war, the *sarvanim* were condemned almost unanimously as leftists, delinquents, and law breakers who were undermining democracy (*Ha'aretz*, 3 October 1983).

While not claiming to be above the law, the refusing reservists did claim to be right in disobeying their assigned reserve service in the Lebanese war zone due to the very special and perhaps agonizing circumstances surrounding that war (Linn 1986, 1987, 1988a, 1988b, 1989a, 1989b; Linn and Gilligan 1990). Some were trying to explain that their specific and selective action of disobedience was not contempt for the law, selfish, taking the law into his own hands, undermining respect for the law, self-defeating, unjustifiable when lawful channels remain open, or a subversion of the democratic process (Cohen 1971). Chapter 1 examines two main perspectives in the study of selective refusal: the "separate" and the "connected" position. The first one portrays refusal as a moral position constructed in isolation and as a form of moral separateness (Kohlberg 1984; Rawls 1971). The second one portrays refusal as a moral position constructed and manifested in connection with other people (Gilligan 1982; Walzer 1988).

The majority of reserve soldiers who objected to the war in Lebanon chose to fulfill their military obligation when called up for duty. Upon their return however, many of them,now in civilian dress, demonstrated against the war as civilians, in front of government offices, demanding Israel withdrawl from Lebanon. How would each group of objecting soldiers (the *sarvanim* as well as those protesting as civilians) justify their specific choice of action? What are the moral and nonmoral characteristics of those individuals who took a different position of criticism? Chapter 2 examines the claims for moral maturity, consistency, and integrity of both groups of objecting soldiers.

The Israeli soldiers were not given a very long time to recover from their moral confusion in the war in Lebanon. Two years after the withdrawal from Lebanon (in 1985), many Israeli soldiers found their assigned military mission—to suppress the Intifada (uprising) in the territories, as a morally problematic activity.

Whereas previously, during the war in Lebanon, the Israeli soldier had to decide how to identify terrorists and how to capture them when hiding among women and children in schools and hospitals beyond the Israeli borders, this time they had to figure out how to approach a violent mob of women and children with lethal ammunition while resisting Israeli ruling. This undefined enemy was often stationed no more than a few kilometers from the soldier's own home (Lissak 1990).

Once again, there was a wave of reservists who chose to become *sarvanim* (186 cases up to September 1993).[1] In both conflicts, one common argument against refusal has to do with the demand to exercise one's own conscientiousness in the battlefield. Is it really possible, and if so to what extent? Chapter 3 examines real-life separate and connected positions of criticism awaiting combatants in extreme ambiguous situations in the Intifada.

Similar to the war in Lebanon, not much is known of the Intifada refusers. Most of the academic books on the Intifada are political or legal analyses (Benvenisti 1992; Cohen and Wosfeld 1993; Freedman 1991; Gilbar and Susser 1992; Mishal and Aharoni 1989; Minuchin and Minuchin 1985; Schiff and Ya'ari 1990; Shalev 1990; Straschnov 1994). Selective reufsal is being discussed from legal and philosophical positions (Ben Noon 1992, Gans 1992, Sheleff 1989). The mystery remained: Who is the Intifada reservist who refuses to be the patriot, who decides to assume this unconventional position of moral critic? Chapter 4 examines the moral context in which reservists decided to assume a position of refusal in both conflicts. Chapter 5 portrays the profile of the Intifada refuser and compares it to the Lebanon refuser. Chapter 6, examines the refusal during the Intifada within the range of other forms of criticism within Israeli society.

This book focuses on data that were collected from forty-eight refusing reservists and thirty-two objecting reservists who did not refuse in the first four years of the Intifada. The writing of this book started as we were entering the sixth year of the Intifada. As of this writing (26 November 1992), the IDF spokesman reported on forty-seven Israelis who died and 5,777 who were wounded. Among the Palestinians, there have been 831 dead and 15,935 wounded, 90,000 have been detained in prisons, 11,716 have been brought to court, 133 were found innocent and 480 have been expelled from the country. Overall money paid by the national insurance for reserve service is 1.298 billion Israeli shekels. Money paid for holding Palestinian prisoners amounts to 426.6 million shekels. Overall expenses of holding IDF forces in the territories were 1.644 billion Israeli shekels.

How does this kind of limited yet prolonged and morally problematic military conflict affect the moral thinking, emotions, and moral language of the soldiers? In their attempts to solve their moral dilemmas, morally puzzled reservists often tended to locate themselves in the collective memory of their community. They often tried to generalize their experience beyond their immediate situation—to make sense of their lives in some larger perspective of the Holocaust. Chapter 7 examines the soldiers' experience and their critical use of Holocaust symbols and metaphors.

Even if the unprecedented action of selective refusal won some consensus as to the personal courage it demanded, the high level of moral maturity, moral consistency, and the like were inadequate to allay the legitimate suspicion entertained by their immediate social circle and society at large: How loyal are these critics to the society in which they want to go on living, while yet willing to let others sacrifice their lives for them? Is it possible that they are simply cowards who hide behind moral principles? How sincere is their moral struggle? When objection is followed by an act of disobedience against the law, the disobeyer's claims of moral maturity, consistency, and integrity are important and necessary but not sufficient. As has been indicated by Cohen (1971), "If in obeying his conscience another man is obliged to do what he believes—in good conscience—to be morally wrong, the genuineness of that conflict must give us a pause" (p. 212). Chapter 8 examines the refusers' motives for disobedience and chapter 9, their credibility. Chapter 10 summarizes the book by presenting psychological models of selective refusal as a separate or connected moral position. Chapter 11 summarizes the book by analyzing the action of refusal from historical, sociological, and cultural perspectives.

This book presents the moral stories of a very small sample of individuals in one of the smallest countries on the globe. In this sense, any attempt to make conclusive wide-range generalizations is premature. Yet, in spite of these limitations, the uniqueness of this group and the unique sociomoral conditions in which it functions provide the reader with a rare opportunity to examine the path of criticism in real-life, morally controversial settings. It is rare because the moral dilemma faced by the Israeli soldier has "no simple answer such as the straightforward and appropriate slogan of the American resistance 'Get Out.' The resistance in Israel faces a more difficult and intellectual moral challenge" (Chomski, in Blatt et al. 1975). This intellectual and moral challenge is the focus of this book.

Note

1. There seems to be a gap between the number of refusers as announced by the IDF and the refusers' organizations (Yesh Gevel—see chapter 6). This gap is mainly due to the differences in definition of refusers: multiple prison terms served by the same refuser are often regarded as a single case of refusal by the IDF, and therefore the army's numbers are slightly lower than those announced by the 'Yesh Gevel' spokesman.

What is the use, after all, of a silent intellectual?

—Walzer 1988, p. 148

Man does not simply "stand outside" in his subjectivity, like a critic in the theater, and look at the necessity and decide what he thinks of it.

—May 1969, p. 261

1

Refusal as a Moral Position

From Separation to Connection

In the name of science, developmental and moral psychologists traditionally detach themselves from two types of involvement. On the personal level, they most often refrain from taking a position as moral critics of real-life events. On the professional level, they refrain from studying moral critics in two ancient and very familiar social institutions: family and war. This is despite the fact that the family is considered the first school of moral development, and that war is an extreme yet frequent social phenomenon that can nevertheless reveal the noble as well as the most base examples of human behavior.

This personal (and eventually professional) detachment seems to derive from the assumption that science and social criticism will not survive without isolation. As noted by Walzer (1988), researchers may think that "political leaders must be realistic and sober, while social critics must be idealists, fierce but distant, out of touch with the complexities of real life. . . . But these stereotypes are almost certainly wrong" (p. 75).

No professional group can accept blame for the exigencies of history (May 1987). Yet, moral and developmental psychologists may serve as good examples for position taking in the face of injustice. What position, for example, did the renown Swiss child psychologist Jean Piaget assume in the face of the systematic and orderly gassing of 1.5 million children in his neighboring countries during World War II?

The actual voicing of one's own moral criticism (so it can be heard) illustrates (what I mean by) taking a position as a moral critic. Obviously, prior to this brave move, one must be capable of seeing the nature of the king's new clothes. This observation depends in turn on the position chosen. As has been observed by Burke (1965) "A way of standing is also a way of seeing or not seeing" (p. 13).

Lawrence Kohlberg, who built on Piaget's (1932/1965) pioneering work on moral development of children, embarked on his career after taking a position as a moral critic by smuggling Holocaust Jewish refugees out of Europe to Palestine. His work on moral development (Kohlberg 1984) has been one of the most significant contributions to the study of moral and political psychology. Yet his theorizing on a "just community" is freed from position taking (Power, Higgins, and Kohlberg 1989). Morality has been conceptualized as developing among peers only. Though he developed his career during the Vietnam war, Kohlberg examined the level of moral competence of only two soldiers: Eichmann's post hoc reasoning, at his Jerusalem trial for his compliance with his superiors, and Michael Bernhardt for not shooting in the My Lai massacre (see chapter 3). Not a single study has focused on the moral dilemmas, thinking, or actions of American combatants who objected that war.

These examples of detachment of cognitive moral psychologists from real-life dilemmas of war are linked by a common view of the moral self as existing and developing in no man's land. As noted by Broughton (1987):

> The heart of genetic structuralism, unfortunately, is the negation of memory. Development conceived as progressive formalization is incompatible with the maintenance of biographical integrity. Piaget's (individual) subjects have no biography; they are not only genderless and generationless but also lacking personhood. His theory no more allows for life history than it does for history. (pp. 289–290)

Assuming that the everyday world is a moral world, criticism is an inherent part of it, even if this path is chosen by few. What are the positions awaiting moral critics in general and refusing combatants in particular in times of war? What makes them choose these positions? How do they place themselves in these positions? To whom and under what premises do they proclaim and rehearse their critical arguments?

These questions will be discussed in different forms throughout the book. This chapter starts the discussion with a focus on two philosophical views of selective refusal as a position of criticism: the "separate" position (Rawls 1971) and the "connected" position (Walzer 1988). This is followed by two psychological models that portray selective refusal as reflecting universalistic morality and a separate perspective (Kohlberg 1984) or a particularistic morality and a connected perspective (Gilligan 1982). Finally, separate and connected methodologies are presented. The philosophical, psychological, and methodological views that are presented in this chapter are incorporated in the study of Israeli soldiers as moral critics.

The "Separate" Moral Position

The separate position is a hypothetical one and describes how some individuals take a stand in moral argument. It is central to John Rawls' (1971) conception of moral criticism. The separate moral critic has the privilege of taking "a point of view distanced from the controversy" (Habermas 1990, p. 162). This distance is possible if the moral concerns are voiced from the "original position" and out of the "veil of ignorance"—that is, if no one is to be advantaged or disadvantaged by natural contingencies or social change in the adoption of justice principles (Rawls 1971). The "original position" refers to a stance such that the parties who deliberate the position are rational and mutually disinterested, and there are no limits on the general information that is available to them. "Veil of ignorance" refers to making decisions without knowing one's own place in society, one's class position or social status, or one's fortune in the distribution of natural talents and abilities. Rawls believes that people seek to enhance their positions, seek activities that allow for meaningful cognitive elaboration, rather than merely hold to them.

Where would the separate critic place himself in times of war? Rawls considers war as a fertile ground for moral criticism. Theoretically, according to Rawls (1971), "the aims of a well-ordered society, or one in a state of near justice, are to preserve and strengthen the institutions of justice" (p. 131) and to achieve a just peace. If war objectives or conduct do not follow moral constraints, the individual may feel the need to give "voice to conscientious and deeply held convictions" (Rawls 1971, p. 128). He/she may take a position of civil disobedience or of a conscientious objector, both of which apparently entail some form of law breaking. Civil disobedience is defined by Rawls as a "Public, nonviolent, conscientious yet political act contrary to law, usually done with the aim of bringing about a change in the law or policies of the government" (p. 126). It is primarily based on the conflict of duties as the question is "at what point does the duty to comply with laws enacted by legislative majority . . . cease to be binding in view of the right to defend one's liberties and the duty to oppose injustice" (p. 126). Civil disobedience is political because the position is guided by political principles (the principles of justice that constitute a social institution). The civil disobedient does not appeal to the principles of personal morality, though it may coincide with and support his/her claims.

Metaphorically, this form of resistance is regarded by Rawls (1971) as a rational form of public speech (p. 127), a channel of communication that emphasizes its nonviolent nature. It is public not only because it is being addressed to the public but because it is not covert or secretive. This mode of criticism does not negate the fidelity of the critic as he is willing to accept the consequences of his actions. The person who takes this position does not deliberately seek out occasions for disobedience in order to state his case. For Rawls, conscientious objection is a position similar to that of civil disobedience but is narrower in scope, such that the critic does not comply with the law or administrative order for reasons of conscience. Rawls concedes that when it comes to actual situations, there is no significant difference between the positions presented above, and the same position may entail both dynamics. Rawls' moral critic has the right to take a stand even if injustice has not yet occurred:

> A citizen may maintain that once it is clear that the moral law of war is being regularly violated, he has a right to decline military service on the ground that he is entitled to insure that he honors his natural duty. Once he is in the armed forces, and in a situation where he finds himself ordered to do acts contrary to the moral law of war, he may not be able to resist the demand to obey. Actually, if the aims of the conflict are sufficiently dubious and the likelihood of receiving flagrantly unjust commands sufficiently great, one may have a duty and not only a right to refuse. (Rawls 1971, p. 140)

Can criticism be seen as having been constructed from a position that is not endowed with the privilege of separateness?

The "Connected" Moral Position

The connected position is central to Walzer's (1988) view of moral criticism. The connected moral critic is viewed as a person who has ties to a particular culture. His/her sense of justice emerges from shared understandings or agreements with other individuals who are aware of their historical moral selves and who form part of that society (Walzer 1988). The special role of the critic is not only to describe what is wrong in ways that suggest a remedy but also to take a stance. Otherwise the criticism has no moral value. Walzer (1988) explains:

> Critics position themselves differently in relation to their audience, adopt different linguistic strategies, make different claims to authority. They take a stand—That is what criticism requires. (p. 12)

Unlike Rawls' focus on moral reasoning and justification, Walzer views the realm of action as central to the connected position. He explains:

> Men are bound by their significant actions, not by their feelings or thoughts; action is the crucial language of moral commitment. Socrates was bound because he chose to act like a citizen in a world where citizenship was morally significant. (Walzer 1970, p. 98)

From the connected position, the only way to understand commitment to principles is to view them as commitment to other men "from whom or with whom the principles have been learned and by whom they are enforced" (Walzer 1970, p. 5). Thus, the connected moral critic would not be able to implement the ideas of a "veil of ignorance" as a guideline for his or her judgment:

> Faced with a choice between saving my own child or someone else's child from an imminent and terrible danger, I would adopt a random decision procedure. It would be much easier, obviously, if I were not able to recognize my own children or if I had no children of my own. But this highest form of ethical life is available only to a few strong-minded philosophers or to monks, hermits, and platonic guardians. The rest of us must settle for something less, which we are likely to think of as something better: we draw the best line that we can between family and community and live with the unequal intensities of love. (Walzer 1983, p. 231)

Thus, from the connected position, the moral critic is tied to the rest of the world not only by principles but also moral language, moral action, and moral commitment. The moral critic is a person who takes a position in relation to other positions. This position is fortified by moving back and forth between concrete and abstract moral thinking, "from merging the abstract and the concrete, from experiencing the abstract concretely or experiencing the concrete abstractly" (Cochran 1985, p. 4). The connected position taken by the moral critic is oriented toward moral issues to which he is bound—in the words of Cochran (1985), "To be oriented, we do not just make distinctions arbitrarily, but rather make distinctions that matter" (p. 6).

In the moral sphere, things that matter have to do with our conscience, which represents "an inner alternative to the ego, a motive beyond self-interest" (Walzer 1970, p. 132). Even though the conscientious action might be performed in individual terms, the concept of conscience is not an individualistic one; although the moral decision may be constructed in a lonely manner, "the code we almost certainly share" (Walzer 1970 pp. 130–131).

Where would the connected critic place himself in times of war? War is a fertile ground for any inquiry on connected positions: "A man has enormous debts to his native land and to his polity. He receives from them both not merely physical security but moral identity" (Walzer 1970, p. 112). To fight for one's own state is therefore one of the most serious obligations that "citizenship is usually said to entail" (Walzer 1970, p. 120), though "the (occasional) need to kill is surely the most awful of the burdens" (Walzer 1970, p. 121). Yet, it is easier to do so when the citizen is sent to fight a just war: to protect fundamental values such as national independence, communal freedom, and the lives of people, when all other means of protecting them are exhausted (Walzer 1977).

Walzer (1970) acknowledges the possibility that when a democratic country decides to go to war there will be cases of conscientious refusal by two groups of individuals:

> Those who have taken no part in the decision to go to war, and those who oppose that decision (or who oppose the conscription law that follows it), because they believe war itself or this particular war to be immoral. (p. 120)

Like Rawls, Walzer (1988) believes that soldiers are obligated to criticize potentially unjust events. This criticism, however, emerges from a connected position:

> [When] injustice is done in my name, or it is done to my people, I must speak out against it. Now criticism follows from connection. (p. 23)

Unlike Rawls' focus on justice reasoning in the dilemma of the separate critic, the dilemma of the connected critic primarily reflects a conflict of loyalties. The citizen is "obligated to obey because of his membership in a larger society, obligated to disobey (sometimes) because of his/her membership in a smaller one—(this situation) is for all its tensions, very common in history" (Walzer 1970, p. 14).

Walzer (1977) believes that civil protest and disobedience usually arise out of a community of values. But the army is an organization, not a community, and the community of ordinary soldiers is shaped by the character and purposes of the organization, not by their private commitments:

> There is a rough solidarity of men who face a common enemy and endure a common discipline . . . to disobey is to breach that elemental accord, to claim a moral separateness (or moral superiority) to challenge one's fellows, perhaps even to intensify the dangers they face. (pp. 315–316)

Within this framework, selective refusal might also be seen as a form of "moral selfishness," though sometimes it should be seen as "the only resort of the principled but lonely man" (Walzer 1968, p. 14).

For the outside observer, the selective refuser might be seen as acting from a separate position. At some point the resister will be forced to face the public and explain his claim for moral superiority, consistency and integrity (see chapter 2). However, this apparent separation is but an attempt to circumscribe the "critical distance" needed for his position—a close place to stand so his voice will be heard, but not too close, in order not to be engulfed by the audience (Walzer 1988). What is the psychological meaning of the separate and the connected positions? How can they be studied?

The Psychological Making of "Separate" and "Connected" Moral Positions

Psychological representations of Rawls' concept of the separate position are central to Kohlberg's most influential theory of the development of morality within individuals (Kohlberg 1984) and society (Power, Higgins, and Kohlberg 1989). Drawing heavily on the work of Kant and Rawls, Kohlberg's model portrays the moral critic as capable of undergoing a qualitative change in his moral potential to the point where he or she is freed from personal and societal constraints, independent of culture, and holding the capacity to examine conflicting claims of rights in a rational, objective, and detached way of thinking. This mode of thinking embodies the premise that when there is a conflict between the legal and moral domains, the moral should almost always take precedence because it represents the more objective and impartial solution within and across societies. Kohlberg's decision maker is an individual who is an implicit moral philosopher. He interprets information in terms of the cognitive structures or general organizing principles of thought that define his current stage of moral development. As the individual develops, higher stages displace the structures found at lower stages.

Kohlberg extended Piaget's two-stage model of moral development (from a primitive mode of heteronomous morality, of obedience to authority and fear from punishment, to an autonomous mode, where judgment includes the point of view of the other), to a model with six stages that develop over time and experience. The stages represent three possible approaches to any moral dilemma with respect to society's moral norms: preconventional (stages 1–2), conventional (stages 3–4) and postconventional (principled) perspectives (stages 5–6). At stage 1, the preconventional individual judges action by the likelihood of concrete punishments or rewards, while at stage 2, the individual seeks to gain tangible concrete rewards for correct behavior. In stage 3, the individual sees social approval of specific group members as more important than concrete rewards, whereas, at stage 4, the decision maker is capable of seeing the entire social system and of maintaining his conscience. Loyalty to family, group, or nation is seen as valuable in its own right, regardless of consequences. The transition from conventional to postconventional moral judgment requires introspection and moral theorizing. Individuals experience dissonance and confusion in assessing moral questions, and question social rules that were formerly taken for granted. For a stage 5 person, right is upholding the basic rights, values, and legal contracts of a society, even when they conflict with the concrete rules and laws of the group. Stage 6 marks "the final and complete triumph of reason over moral uncertainty"

(Emler 1983, p. 53). Right is defined according to principles based on respect for other people as ends rather than as means. The existence of stage 6 has never been validated empirically and thus does not appear in Kohlberg's revised Manual (Colby and Kohlberg 1987).

One way of understanding the three levels in Kohlberg's model is to think of them as three different types of relationships between the self and society's rules and expectations. From this point of view, a person at the preconventional level is one for whom rules and social expectations are something external to the self. A conventional person has achieved a socially normative appreciation for the rules and expectations of others, especially authorities, and identifies him/herself with the occupants of social or societal role relationships. The postconventional (principled) person has differentiated him/herself from normative roles, and defined values in terms of self-constructed reflected principles.

According to Kohlberg, the content of the dilemma situation or preferences may vary from issue to issue or from person to person. Yet, the structural feature of the moral thinking remains constant and defines a stage of development, a way or form of reasoning. Each individual is believed to progress through formally identifiable stages that are an invariant sequence of hierarchical, irreversible forms of moral reasoning. In the course of moral development, reasoning about fairness, justice, rights, duties, and obligations increases in conceptual sophistication, integration, and comprehensiveness and becomes more inclusive. Once the individual's stage is determined, it is possible to assess how that individual would interpret moral issues other than those on Kohlberg's test. The stages are not intended to define how one acts, but rather to outline the decision maker's structural components of moral cognitions. Yet, they may serve as good predictors of the maturity of moral action in a real-life setting (Kohlberg 1984).

The stages are identified by a standard moral interview format, structural interviewing techniques (appendix), and a standard form scoring manual (Colby and Kohlberg 1987). Kohlberg's scoring procedure involves the assignment of stage score for each match between a manual criterion judgment and a moral judgment in the interview. The scores are given in a form of moral maturity scores as well as global scores. The moral maturity scores represent a weighted average of to-issue scores and range from 100 (pure stage 1) to 500 (pure stage 5). Stage 6 does not appear in the revised scoring manual because in practice there is no difference between stages 5 and 6 (Gibbs et al. 1982). The global score consists of a pure stage (the subject's modal level) or a transitional score (e.g., 3/4) when two stages are assigned an equal number of points.

Thus, according to Kohlberg, the ideal moral critic is the one who is capable of holding a separate and objective view on the dilemma situation, if he has reached a stage of "gradual purification of the justice concept [binding duties and obligations] through its segregation from 'nonmoral' considerations" (Emler 1983, p. 59). This mature, principled moral thinker is capable of voicing his/her concerns from a pure, disconnected position across contexts because he holds a "decentered understanding of the world in which he lives" (Habermas 1990, p. 138). If Kohlberg's separate critic decided to challenge societal dictates and obligation to participate in a given war, he should be able to provide rational extralegal reasoning for his position of refusal and be able to explain the extralegal considerations that override his obligation to obey. This reasoning needs to be assessed using a scoring manual devised for real-life dilemmas of disobedience (Linn 1989a, 1989b).

Psychological representation of Walzer's (1988) conception of the connected position might be found in the work of Gilligan (1982). Gilligan conceptualized the moral critic as holding a connected and interactional self, and as searching for a unique way to conceive oneself in relation to others. Whereas the separate critic would be willing to place him/herself in a timeless and ahistorical distance from his/her audience, the connected critic would look for a place among particular individuals living in concrete historical settings. Criticism might be seen as having its source in personal feelings of connection. Even justice can be viewed as "first of all a natural sentiment, an inborn sense of our connectedness with others and our shared interests and concerns" (Solomon 1990, p. 153).

Gilligan argues that the moral critic may conceptualize and understand relationships as connected or separate. The connected or separate perspectives result in the construction of two moral orientations. These orientations are two possible ways of conceptualizing moral criticism and actions, of assessing the most important feature in the situation, or what actions are worthy of praise or blame, as well as the basis for making a moral decision (Gilligan and Wiggins 1987; Brown and Gilligan 1993). Gilligan argues that she has observed close ties between self-description and moral orientations: that different "images of the self give rise to different visions of moral agency, which in turn are reflected in different ways of defining responsibility" (p. 241). When the individual sees himself as connected to or in relation to others, it will lead to decisions based primarily on the voice of care, with the focus on issues of attachment abandonment, responsibility, and relationships. When the individual sees himself/herself as a separate, independent being, his/her decision will spring primarily from the voice of justice with the focus on issues of equality, oppression, reciprocity, and impartiality in the resolution of moral conflicts (Gilligan et al. 1990; Brown and Gilligan 1993). Like Kohlberg, Gilligan was inspired by Piaget's work but directed her studies on morality in line with his focus on real-life decision (in children's play) and the conception of morality as bound to human relationships: "apart from our relations to other people, there can be no moral necessity" (Piaget 1932/1965, p. 196). Whereas Kohlberg (1984) sees the self as being in relation to the wider society and social institution, it is considerably less interactive than the one portrayed by Gilligan.

Gilligan's conception of moral criticism reflects two lines of psychological experience to which all human beings are vulnerable: oppression and abandonment. The vulnerability to oppression may give rise to justice concerns, to the ideas of fairness, independence, rights, equality, and reciprocity. The vulnerability to abandonment may give rise to care concerns, to the ideas of loyalty, love, and relationships. Whereas Kohlberg views moral conflicts as linear, entailing a single and just moral solution (Kohlberg and Candee 1984), Gilligan views moral conflicts as negotiable, entailing the burden of consequences, and very often they are unresolved. The critic is viewed as living in a constantly changing social world. His/her audience might be real or imaginary. His thinking might be influenced by personal and or collective ties. When criticism is tied to meaningful people and not to abstract principles only, a moral decision cannot be regarded as a "discrete moment of rational 'choosing'" but rather as a "type of consciousness," that although rooted in time, is not bound by a single moment" (Lyons 1988).

Whereas Kohlberg would study the critic by using a set of hypothetical justice-focused dilemmas, by abstracting cognition from both emotion and action, Gilligan would ask the critic to talk about her/his real-life experiences of moral conflict and choice, and then would go and interpret such narratives, looking in particular for evidence of two moral voices or orientations (justice and care). This would follow an interpretive methodology based on sequences of readings with the focus on self, context, the individual's conception of morality, and moral language. Gilligan suggests a qualitative assessment of the critic's moral voice "because it is embodied, connects rather than separates psyche and body; because voice is in language, it also joins psyches and culture. Voice is inherently relational . . . " (Brown and Gilligan 1993, pp. 14–15).

Since voice should be examined in relational terms, there is no expectation to examine the highest form of moral potential but rather how one's own voice is heard by the critic him/herself as well as his/her audience. An examination in relational terms also implies the attention to the content of one's voice, not only its form. It also requires attention to the critic's use of symbols, metaphor, and moral language and what words are better heard than others.

In her voice-sensitive method, Gilligan would listen to the story the person tells: "the geography of his psychological landscape . . . to listen to the drama, the . . . who, what, when, where, and why of the narrative . . . to images, central metaphors, emotional resonances, contradictions or inconsistencies in style, revisions and absence in the story as well as shifts in the sound of the voice and in narrative position . . . [and] locate the speaker in the narrative [he or] she tells. In addition, the listening requires what we reflect on ourselves as people in the privileged position of interpreting the life events of another and to consider the implications of this act" (Brown and Gilligan 1993, p. 16).

Another focus in the assessment process is directed toward the "self": the way one defines oneself in the situation intellectually and emotionally, which parts one would want or choose to disclose about the self, as well as the role of the self in the dilemma situation of the story. Assuming that criticism is not voiced in a context-free scenario, attention is given to the why and how a given voice (justice or care) is raised, which voice is being suppressed or silenced and by whom, who is the significant audience for these moral concerns, when and how one should dare doing it, and what are the consequences of assuming such a position.

Because Gilligan's approach is constrained by a set of a priori definitions of justice and care, in this work we draw also on Tappan's (1990) methodology, which shares Gilligan's key methodological features but adopts an open-ended conception of the cognition, emotion, and action of lived moral experiences as they are represented in an interview text. In Tappan's hermeneutic approach to interpreting narrative representations of lived moral experience in interview texts, the individuals' account of their lived experience is understood in its own right; even if it may not be a direct expression and representation of what really happened, it nevertheless has a psychological reality that deserves our interpretation.

In the following study on Israeli soldiers as moral critics, the tension between the two philosophical and psychological views on, and the tension of, the separate and connected positions is discussed throughout the book. Perspectives, psychological theories, and related methodologies are utilized in different phases of the inquiry.

Operatively, four groups of moral critics are examined. The first group consists of thirty-six selective conscientious objectors from the war in Lebanon (Linn 1989a, 1989b). The experience of this group is presented as a background source for understanding the phenomenon of refusal during the Intifada. The second group is the most important one and consists of forty-eight Intifada refusers. To the best of the author's knowledge, no single psychological study has been conducted on these two groups of refusers during war time.

The third group of moral critics consists of twenty-four reservists from the war in Lebanon and thirty-two reservists from the Intifada who, even though they were against these morally controversial military conflicts, nevertheless decided to serve in one or both conflicts. Though an equally important group of moral critics, they are utilized in this research as a control group, and their experience is presented as the background of the Lebanon and the Intifada refusers. The fourth group is a heterogeneous group of soldiers and exsoldiers who voiced their moral criticism in numerous channels (media, letters, books, protests, etc.) and also serve as the background of the refusers' experience. Throughout the study I also followed Ryff's (1984) suggestion that the researcher and the subjects could in collaboration differentiate what is unique from that which is shared in the meaning of the experience.

Individuals in the first three groups underwent the same procedure of individual interviewing and testing in their homes. One part of the interview consisted of Kohlberg's test of moral development (Form B, see appendix). The second part consisted of a test of concrete moral justification for one's own action of objection. The third part was dedicated to the subject's narrative regarding his chosen position of criticism: his civilian and military experience, his conception of self, morality and moral feelings before and after his decision. Attention was given to the critic's subjective perception of his position, moral orientation, moral language and content, cultural metaphors and symbols, and his significant audience. Finally, a comprehensive demographic and attitudinal questionnaire was administered (soldiers' attitude toward the Holocaust, their reflections about the war in Lebanon, and the Intifada, their action, their punishment, and their planned future in the Israeli society, etc.).

The order of the first three parts of the interview were randomized among subjects. Each interview lasted 1.5–3 hours and was recorded with permission and later transcribed. All tests were scored blindly by the same qualified rater, who had not done the initial interviewing and was not aware of the subjects' identity. The scoring procedure of the hypothetical moral competence of the subjects followed Colby and Kohlberg's (1987) revised manual of the Moral judgment Interview (herewith MJI). The Actual Moral Reasonings (herewith AMR) was scored blindly with regard to MJI scores by the same scorer, and were computed in line with the real-life dilemma manual as presented in Linn 1989a, b. The analysis of the indepth interviews drew on Gilligan's and Tappan's narrative analysis.

Since refusers were not part of my close circle of friends, it was easy for me to approach them from a separate position. Their decision to refuse intertwined with my academic interest in the relationships between moral judgment and action.

Having raised this topic for a legitimate academic inquiry, I had to go through a long period of suspicion as to my loyalty to the state of Israel. Social researchers seem to have been influenced by the hostile atmosphere revolving around the refusers. There is no surprise that no single psychological study has been conducted on the Lebanon and the Intifada refusers *during* these two morally controversial conflicts.

One way to find the subjects was to approach the Israel Defense Forces. Yet, in order to free myself from any constraints and maintain an ideal separate position, I tried to locate these people by myself. During the war in Lebanon, the uniform response to inquiries regarding their identity was "I have no friends like that." It took eight months of searching before I came across a member of Yesh Gvul (the refusers' protest movement; see chapter 6) who held not only the entire list of refusers but was also willing to give it to me.

The first sample of thirty-six Lebanon refusers was drawn from this list of eighty-six refusers who were imprisoned during the first year of the war (1982–1983). I found this independent way of contact most helpful throughout the interview process. Many wanted me to assure them that I was not connected to the military institutions before they were willing to participate. The study group of forty-eight Intifada refusers was recruited in the same way: they were randomly sampled from a list of 165 reservists who were imprisoned during the first four years in the same way.

Whether refusal is the right moral response and resolution to the dilemmas faced by the Israeli reserve soldiers is certainly a serious question that deserves attention. However, as suggested by Hare (1981) "people can disagree about the just solution" (p. 158). The real concerns, he argues, are the knowledge of the guiding principles of those who attempt to solve the moral dilemma they face. This line of inquiry is particularly attractive when applied to anyone who may claim moral maturity, consistency, and integrity, as in the case of selective conscientious objectors. These claims are examined in the following chapter.

These people are dear to me and refusing means separating myself from them . . . I felt that I was taking myself from the womb of the Israeli society but this argument cannot serve as an adequate justification.

—An Intifada refuser

2

Refusal as a Moral Decision
From Justice to Compassion

There are two ways in which the individual soldier should judge a given war: first, in regard to the justice of the war objectives (*jus ad bellum*), and second in regards to the conduct of the war (*jus in bello*). The distinction between jus ad bellum and jus in bello consists of "two clusters of prohibitions attached to the central principle that soldiers have an equal right to kill" (Walzer 1977, p. 41); in other words: "how those victims of war who can be attacked and killed are to be distinguished from those who cannot" (p. 41). The distinction between the two sets of moral constraints is fundamental to the way we judge soldiers' moral behavior as "we draw a line between the war itself, for which soldiers are not responsible, and the conduct of the war, for which they are responsible, at least within their own sphere of activity" (Walzer 1977, p. 38). Though, theoretically, these two sets of judgments are independent, the dualism of jus ad bellum and jus in bello is at the heart of all that is most problematic in the moral reality of war (Walzer 1977).

The rule of personal responsibility for obeying a manifestly illegal order has been part of the basic moral training in the IDF since the eve of the 1956 Sinai campaign (Straschnov 1994). On October 29, 1956, Border Guard Policemen, who didn't realize that the returning civilians of the Kasem village had not been informed of the curfew, fired on them without prior warning, killing forty-nine people. From that time onward, IDF soldiers have been taught that they are obliged not to execute a manifestly illegal command as such if they sense it is inhumane in nature; the one that would deviate from the IDF tradition of purity of arms; refraining from unnecessary bloodshed and avoiding, at all cost, harming civilians in general and women and children in particular, avoiding damage to sacred buildings, and so forth (Gal 1986). This convention has traditionally been translated into actions of extra self-sacrifice in maintaining one's own moral principles on the battlefield (Hardan 1985).

On the morning of 22 July 1982, however, the Israeli public was exposed to a new form of moral thinking and action: Colonel Eli Geva, a dedicated, brilliant, young career officer who supported a limited war in Lebanon (namely to destroy the terrorists' infrastructure there) decided to assume what seemed to be a separate position of criticism in the form of disobedience. Geva's brigade had been the spearhead of the Israeli forces during their advance toward Beirut. His men performed very effectively under his daring, poised leadership. Geva's brigade was tasked with the dangerous mission of being the first brigade to enter Beirut should the order be given. Geva "found himself in painful quandary—between his military commitment to carry out his assigned mission, and his moral commitment to object to a mission he believed to be illegitimate . . ." (Gal 1985, p. 538). His moral reservations finally outweighed his military obligation, and he requested to be relived from this particular assignment and become a tank driver. He further clarified that, should his request be denied, he would not disobey any order he might receive. He argued that it would be morally unjustified to expose his people to such a mission, and morally unjustified to destroy and kill many innocent others on the opposing side. Geva's position resulted in great confusion among the high-ranking commands and created a public controversy regarding his right to take such a position.

One of the major themes of this controversy was the question of whether his concerns were voiced from a separate or connected position. Given the the ideal portrayal of the Israeli-born "Sabra" whose integrity is manifested in his "talking straight" (Katriel 1986), many agreed Geva may have expressed some sort of moral integrity and consistency even if his action implies detachment and separation. Others argued that his criticism and action manifested his connection. More confusion revolved around the question of whether indeed his concerns reflected a mature form of moral thinking, or whether these argument were just a cover for fear, distress, or fatigue. Many were yearning to understand his care-focused behavior: can an officer neglect his soldiers on the battlefield for moral reasons?

Geva was immediately dismissed from the army, losing his career and pension. The IDF, however, dropped its plan regarding Beirut. Geva did not view his position as a separate one. He further insisted through various interviews that a soldier should not refuse military service: "We have no choice . . . but to work against the war through democratic means . . . [refusal] will undermine the basis of the army's existence, which is vital in our case" (*Ha'aretz*, 15 January 1983).

Some commentators argued that while Geva cared about the moral deterioration of the war, Geva did not refuse any order, and had he done so, he would have been court-martialed. This was also the perception of the IDF's judge-advocate General, who was ordered to look into the possibility and found no ground for prosecution (Oren 1992). Geva's attempts to assume a connected position by asking to join the reserves (he could have served another twenty years) have been rejected by army officials to this day. It is important to note that Geva's criticism was voiced and operationalized during the official period of the war (until the withdrawal of the terrorists from Beirut), when most soldiers were serving under emergency rule (Code 8) and resistance could have led to severe punishment.

Geva's act remains the lone extraordinary protest of a high-ranking career officer. Though the refusal of reservists to perform their month-long active duty call-up when it involved service in Lebanon followed this historical opposition, the link between the two phenomena has never been studied (see chapter 4). Simple facts such as the prolonged and unexpected stay in Lebanon (1982–1985), the war's morally controversial nature, the growing, fierce attacks by local guerrillas in the area, and reservists being called to serve beyond their normal tour of duty seem to have served as a psychological moral trigger for the refusals. Some Lebanon refusers fought the war as compulsory service soldiers. Others as reservists. Due to the length of the war, many compulsory service soldiers had the opportunity to serve also as reservists during its "occupation" period (Linn 1986).

Yet, in spite of the heavy physical and moral load of service, the majority of reservists served. Some of the more publicly objecting reserve soldiers (such as those who were affiliated with a large protest group called "Peace Now" that called for withdrawal from Lebanon) argued that objection did not imply that the reservist would not fulfill his military obligation when called up for duty. Upon their return from the reserves, many of them donned civilian dress and went out to demonstrate against the war as civilians, in front of government offices. They proclaimed that their right to voice their moral concern was in line with the IDF moral code of purity of arms: their dedication to and their fulfilment of the hardship of military obligation.

The moral dilemmas of the individual soldiers discussed in this chapter are dual in nature. The first dilemma is with the moral objection to the war itself. Though they ended up pursuing different actions, refusing and nonrefusing soldiers held a common definition of the injustice of the war. The following statement by a spokesman of the Peace Now movement describes their dilemma regarding the war, which is identical to that presented by the refusers' movement ("Yesh Gvul" in Hebrew, meaning "there is a limit"; see chapter 6):

> The Lebanon war is primarily a war . . . in which people had no faith . . . even from the outset. This is the first time the Israeli soldier had been obliged to find in himself the willingness to fight and be killed in a nondefensive war. This is the first time that the question "where is the limit" has so vividly been raised. (*Ha'aretz*, 23 September 1983)

This chapter, however, confines itself to the secondary dilemma facing the two groups of objecting soldiers: What was the morally preferred action in the face of moral objection to the war?

This question touches upon one of the most intriguing yet unexplored issues in the field of moral and political psychology: the relationship between hypothetical and concrete moral knowledge. As has been admitted by Kohlberg, "From the point of view of cognitive developmental theory . . . the development of judgment to action is something to be studied and theoretically conceptualized" (Kohlberg 1976, p. 46).

A comprehensive account of morality demands a knowledge of both judgment and action as "understanding guides the action and determines its specific meaning, while action brings moral understanding to its natural completion" (Blasi 1983, p. 178). Several studies have documented that stage 5 moral thinkers are more often affiliated with left-wing orientations (Emler, Renwick, and Malone 1983; Rest 1979), and stage 4 is associated with the endorsement of more conservative beliefs and actions. As individuals progress on Kohlberg's justice scale toward a complete separate position they become less conservative in their actions choices and may advocate a position of civil disobedience. Kohlberg and Kramer (1969) reported an association between moral competence and an individual's thinking on political issues, such as the Vietnam war and the draft. Studies on student activism have shown a similar pattern: consistency between types of actions and principled moral thinking (Kohlberg and Candee 1984). Haan Smith and Block's study (1968) examined three groups of activists: (1) students who had been arrested at the Free Speech Movement during the 1964 sit-in at Berkeley; (2) a group from San Francisco state colleges who belonged to organizations that supported direct action; and (3) a control group of nonactivists from a variety of organizations at colleges in the Bay area. The students were asked to complete a moral reasoning protocol (this differed in procedure from our study). Activism was found to be associated with stage 5 moral competence. The study by Fishkin et al. (1973) on the Kent State incident suggested that stage 4 moral thinkers were more in keeping with a conservative form of activism. Leming's (1974) study of the involvement of high school students with a protest against the invasion in Cambodia suggested that these students were associated with stage 5 moral competence whereas stage 4 moral thinkers were not direct action supporters.

Yet, none of these studies explained what constitutes the nature of the relationships between moral reasoning and activism. Nor did the actions studied entail a direct risk to one's own life or to the lives of close others. Moreover, the actors were not members (nor soldiers) in the institutions where they manifested their objection. And finally, their activism did not stand in contradiction to their moral obligation to defend their own country, nor was it conducted among individuals with whom they would have a long-term affiliation and commitment. All of the above make the study of objecting Israeli combatants a theoretical, as well as a concrete, venture.

As selective conscientious objectors, the refusers claim to experience a clash between their conscientious claims and the demands of a state that professes to believe that it is fighting to protect social values and ideals (Scheissel 1968). Most often this clash is neither accidental nor irrational. Yet, particularly when their action involves disobedience to a legal law, we cannot take for granted the individuals' claim that they are acting conscientiously, or their sincere belief that what they do is right. Indeed, "while not claiming to be above the law or exempt from it, they do claim to be right in disobeying it in very special and perhaps even agonizing situations" (Cohen 1971, p. 192). Moral disobedience thus requires extralegal reasoning for breaking the law, as well as the ability to show that these nonlegal considerations override their obligation to obey. In Kohlberg's term, this claim for moral superiority is most likely to be heard from principled moral thinkers. The latter are more likely to manifest consistency in their thinking across context.

The search for consistency between hypothetical and concrete justice structures is of particular interest in the case of the selective conscientious objector, whose overt moral conduct of resistance to the military is not a way of life. So is the search for moral integrity—a consistency between the actor's judgment concerning the morality of a given choice of action and the performance of the action. This search provides some understanding about the content of the subjects' reasoning, why it was relevant for the actor to act in a certain way within a given situation, how the action contributed to his sense of self-consistency, and, above all, why it was necessary for the actor to be involved with both situations and action (Blasi 1983, p. 198).

The extent to which the acting self is involved in the dilemma and controls and initiates the resolution of the conflict was not thoroughly investigated by Kohlberg. The refusers may differ in their subjective perception of themselves as having "active" or "passive" control over their performed actions (Linn 1989b). These attitudinal factors need to be taken into considerations when their claim for moral integrity is being assessed.

The study presented in this chapter examines the three major claims that are raised by selective conscientious objectors: the claim for moral maturity (or superiority), for consistency, and for integrity. The three claims are operationalized in this study as follows:

1. The claim for moral maturity—the extent to which each objecting soldier succeeded in justifying his action from a principled moral stage.
2. The claim for moral consistency—(a) Personal stage consistency—the extent to which each individual (in the two

groups, refusers and Peace Now) succeeded in justifying his action in correspondence with his hypothetical moral competence (as measured by Kohlberg's Moral judgment Interview, MJI score). (b) Between groups consistency—the extent to which the Actual Moral Reasoning (AMR) scores and the MJI scores in the two groups, refusers and Peace Now, were comparable.

3. The claim for moral integrity (Blasi 1983)—the extent to which the action performed by each group of soldiers corresponded with the content of their judgments concerning the morality of their action.

The Study

Subjects: The study examined two groups of objecting soldiers: The first group consisted of thirty-six reserve soldiers who had refused to serve in Lebanon and were sentenced from fourteen to thirty-five days in military prison. A few have been imprisoned more than one time when refusing additional drafts. This sample was randomly selected from a list of eighty-six refusers who refused to serve within the first year of the war. The other group consisted of twenty-four Peace Now soldiers who were randomly selected at the time of the study from a list of activists from the three main cities in Israel.
Procedure: Individuals in both groups underwent the same procedure of interviewing and testing in their homes (see description in chapter 1).

Results

Demographics: Refusers: The age of the refusers ranged from twenty-three to forty-six years (mean = 31, mode = 28). Sixteen were currently married, five were divorced, and fifteen were single. Twenty-three had academic degrees, including four Ph.D.s and three doctoral candidates (mean = 14.9 years of study). Seven (20 percent) were officers and twenty-nine (80 percent) were soldiers. The refusers were attached to the paratroopers, infantry, engineering, armoured artillery, and medical units. Twenty-two (61 percent) had military experience in war prior to the Lebanon conflict. Thirty subjects (83 percent) were the only refusers in their unit. Twenty-six subjects (72 percent) decided to refuse after having already served in Lebanon. In terms of political orientation, three were Communists, eighteen were left wing, and fifteen with the Labor Party (center left). They had spent between fourteen and ninety-nine days in a military prison. Thirty subjects (83 percent) asked to return to their unit upon their release from prison. In terms of military role, medics made up the largest homogeneous group (7).

Peace Now: The age of the soldiers who defined themselves in accordance with Peace Now ideology ranged between twenty-four and fifty-two years (mean = 33, mode = 36). Eighteen (75 percent) were married and six (25 percent) were single. Eight (33 percent) were officers and sixteen (67 percent) were soldiers. They were attached to the paratroopers, infantry, engineering, armoured artillery, and medical units. Most of the activists (16 = 67 percent) had served from twenty-eight to ninety-five days in Lebanon. Their level of formal schooling ranged from twelve to nineteen years of studies (four Ph.D.'s). Seventeen subjects (71 percent) had previous war experience. In terms of political orientation, six (25 percent) ranked themselves as left wing, fourteen (58 percent) as Labor Party, and four (17 percent) as right wing.

The Claim for Moral Maturity and Personal Consistency

Table 1 presents the MJI and AMR global stage score distributions of the refusers and Peace Now soldiers. The table suggests that both groups consisted of individuals who were in various stages of

Table 1. Moral Judgment Interview (MJI) and Actual Moral Reasoning (AMR) Global Stage Distributions of Refusers (N = 36) and Peace Now (N = 24)

Stage	2/3	3	3/4	4	4/5	5
			Refusers			
MJI	3(8.3)	1(2.8)	10(27.8)	6(16.7)	8(22.2)	8(22.2)
AMR	3(8.3)	2(5.6)	6(16.7)	12(33.3)	3(8.3)	10(27.8)
			Peace Now			
MJI	1(4.2)	3(12.5)	9(37.5)	3(12.5)	3(8.3)	6(25.0)
AMR	1(4.2)	3(12.5)	6(25.0)	14(58.3)	0	0

Note: The numbers in parentheses indicate percentage.

moral development, from transitional stage 2/3 to stage 5. Both groups, however, managed to justify their action from a relatively mature point of view (stage 4 moral logic).

The Pearson correlation between the refusers' MJI and AMR was significant, r = .89, p<.001. Paired t-test was not statistically significant. Similarly, Pearson correlation between the Peace Now's MJI and AMR was significant, r = .74, p<.001, and the paired t-test was not statistically significant for within-subject comparison in the Peace Now scores. In both Peace Now and refusers groups, the data thus indicate consistency in achievements in MJI and AMR scores. Table 2 provides a cross tabulation of MJI and AMR global stage scores for the refusers.

Table 2. Cross Tabulation of Refusers' MJI by AMR (N = 36)

AMR	2/3	3	3/4	4	4/5	5	total
MJI							
2/3	3						3
3		1					1
3/4		1	3	6			10
4			3	2	1		6
4/5				4	2	2	8
5						8	8
	3	2	6	12	3	10	

For nineteen refusers, the global score achievements in the MJI and AMR dilemma situations were the same. For seventeen refusers,

Table 3. Cross Tabulation of Peace Now MJI by AMR (N = 24)

AMR	2/5	3	3/5	4	4/5	5	total
MJI							
2/3	1						1
3		3					3
3/5			5	4			9
4			1	2			3
4/5				2			2
5				6			6
	1	3	6	14	0	0	

the scores were different. The direction of the differences in stage of reasoning in the two interviews was not consistent—eight had AMR scores at least half a stage lower than their MJI scores and nine had AMR scores at least half a stage higher than their MJI scores. Table 3 provides a cross tabulation of MJI and AMR global stage scores for the Peace Now soldiers.

For eleven Peace Now soldiers global score achievements in the MJI and AMR dilemma situations were the same. Nine subjects experienced a stage loss, at least half a stage, (i.e., their AMR score was lower than their MJI scores). Four experienced stage gain (i.e., their AMR score was higher than their MJI scores).

The Claim for Stage Consistency (between groups)

There was no statistically significant difference between the mean of the MJI stage scores of the Peace Now score (391.7) and of the refusers (404.2). However, the mean AMR of the Peace Now score(368.8) was statistically different from the mean AMR of the refusers (405.6, $t = 2.369$, $p = .01$). The refusers manifested a statistically significantly higher mode of actual moral reasoning than the Peace Now soldiers.

Multiple linear regression analyses with MJI scores as the dependent variable for the refusers suggested that the number of years of education was the only statistically significant predictor of MJI scores ($p<.00001$). This has been previously reported (Linn 1987). Interestingly, similar multiple linear regression analyses, with MJI scores as the dependent variable for the Peace Now group suggested that the number of years of education was an important predictor ($p<.006$). For each year of education, expected MJI increased by 16.4 points. However, being an officer (vs. others) was the strongest predictor for this group, increasing the expected MJI by 112.4 points ($p = .024$). Having a commanding position (vs. other rank) increased the expected MJI scores by 76.8 points, but was not statistically significant ($p = .072$) at the 0.05 level. Also, being active vs. passive (Linn 1987) could contribute 17.2 points to the MJI scores, but the coefficient was not statistically significant at the 0.05 level ($p = .072$). Other variables were not independent predictors of MJI either for the refusers or the Peace Now group.

A multiple linear regression analysis with AMR as a dependent variable indicated that both education and being active (vs. passive) were predictors of the refusers' AMR scores. A change from passive to active involvement in the dilemma situation was found to contribute forty-two points to the AMR scores, while each year of studies contributed fifteen points (Linn 1987). Years of education were important independent predictors of the AMR scores among the Peace Now interviewees as well. For each year of education, expected AMR among the Peace Now group increased by 9.2 points ($p = 0.044$). Being an officer (vs. other ranks), having a commanding position (vs. others) and being active (vs. passive) and other demographic variables were not statistically significant.

The Claim for Moral Integrity

Ninety percent of the refusers viewed the Peace Now action as noneffective. At least thirty subjects were the sole refusers in their respective units. In terms of political orientation, three defined themselves as Communists, eighteen as leftists, and fifteen as close to the orientation of the Labor party. Fifty-four percent of Peace Now soldiers argued that refusal was not justified. Eighteen (75 percent) viewed refusal as very effective, and six (25 percent) viewed it as noneffective. Eleven (46 percent) subjects argued that they appreciated refusal but did not agree with this stand. Though eight (33 percent) admitted they had thought about refusal, sixteen (67 percent) did not consider that option at all. Eleven (46 percent) subjects argued that they did not have the courage to disobey, even if they found it justified.

Discussion

The Claim for Moral Maturity and Consistency

The demographics suggest that both groups of subjects consisted of dedicated soldiers. The refusers participated in previous wars and must be regarded as selective conscientious objectors rather than pacifists as they advocated a "qualified acceptance of violence" (Scheissel 1968, p. 20). Yet, they "refuse to commit themselves to any absolute principle (but) cling tenaciously to their right to judge (morally) each situation, each war" (Scheissel 1968, p. 22). Were they more morally mature than those who refused to refuse?

The MJI reasoning of the objecting soldiers in the two groups ranged between transitional stage 2/3 to stage 5 with a transitional modal stage of 3/4 for both groups. It further shows that in the hypothetical context, 22 percent of the refusers and 25 percent of the Peace Now soldiers were fully postconventional, with an additional 22 percent of the refusers and 8 percent of Peace Now soldiers falling into the transitional 4/5. In real-life context, 36 percent of the refusers and none of the Peace Now soldiers fell into stages 4/5 and 5.

Refusers seemed to construct their action out of the minimum understanding of stage 4 moral logic (ability to differentiate between moral and legal law, and the appreciation of the greater validity of the former). Peace Now soldiers presented the reverse picture. Their actual moral reasoning could not break through stage 4 moral logic. This trend is reflected in the justifications of this Peace Now activist:

> I have two moral concerns. First, those of my soldiers who immigrated from Arab countries and hate the Arabs more than anybody else. If I am not there with them then they may not behave with any restraint when they deal with the civilians. Second, if I leave them then they will find an excuse not to serve in the army. They do it because of me.

The significant difference in the AMR stage between the two groups could reflect two different conceptions of the morally preferred action, rather than a low level of actual moral competence. For the refusers, the right to refuse seemed to emerge directly from the unjust situation in which they found themselves. The Peace Now soldiers, while sharing the refusers' thoughts about the unjust nature of the war, viewed refusal as a dangerous luxury, as this Peace Now soldier explained:

> I believe that there is no difference between our concern for human lives and those of the refusers. If he is moral he should be in the system. We will always be forced to fight for our lives and therefore we cannot consider refusal as an option. . . . I see no justification in abandoning the democratic rules in order to achieve justice as long as no violation was intentional.

The gap between the levels of moral judgments in the real-life context might point toward two modes of moral thinking where the Peace Now soldiers give priority to the notion of "collective security" (Emler 1983, p. 65), to which Kohlberg's scale is not sensitive in its more mature form of justice. Nor is the scale sensitive to interpersonal loyalties, or commitments to other members of society, or the "possibility of cognitive affective regression" (Vine

1983, p. 41). Thus, though the Peace Now soldiers held an original postconventional moral competence, their failure to maintain a practical mature mode of moral reasoning, and their adherence to stage 4 social order moral logic, seems to reflect some sort of "realistic appraisal of the situation" (Locke 1983 b, p. 166).

Assuming there are no scoring difficulties, the widespread stage consistency among the refusers is rather anomalous where both conventional and postconventional hypothetical modes of moral reasoning lead to a unified experience of solitary refusal. The Peace Now soldiers adopted a conventional mode of action within Israeli society, that of group protest as civilians (Sprinzak 1977). They were primarily geared *toward* prevailing social attitudes, and were therefore less likely to break through transitional stage 4/5 "moral anarchy" by which they would express their rejection of the adequacy of the existing system (Candee 1976). Thus, if the major concern of the Peace Now soldiers was to protest *within* the system, then they were less likely to present Kohlbergian principled thinking, a kind of "prior to society's" reasoning. This type of postconventional mode of reasoning "may be luxuries that only persons in privileged or carefully protected circumstances can afford" (Brown and Herrnstein 1975, p. 325). By setting themselves apart from society, the refusers created (in an artificial way) these luxurious conditions. Other lawbreakers, such as striking physicians, for example, did not manage to sustain Kohlberg's mode of stage consistency when they acted as a group form within the system (Linn 1988a).

The data does not suggest that the level of moral competence of the refusers was higher than that of objecting soldiers who decided not to refuse. Yet the refusers seem to be unique in their ability to maintain moral consistency in their action, mainly due to some nonmoral intervening factors such as the "courage to be alone" (Fromm 1981, p. 24) or "personal strength" (Linn 1988a). This courage seemed to stem from three major factors:

Personal predisposition of isolation in the resolution of the dilemma. I have always been an individual decision maker—I was always willing to tolerate social condemnation for my own choice—that is how I make decisions. . . . It felt good that I could solve this problem on my own.

Lack of formal attachment to a military unit. The ideas about refusal were with me and in my political environment before the war, and

I guess will remain with me in regard to the territories when we get out of Lebanon. I guess the refusal to serve in the territories, which existed among few before the war, reflects the real dilemma. I was all alone with my ideas during the reserves, and I had to cope with it all alone since the people around me did not share it. It was finally, with the backing of other people outside my unit who felt the same, that I made up my mind to act upon my own conscience.

Previous experience of successful solitary action. We were facing the Syrians and I said to myself *I do not know what I am doing here,* and I planned that if there was a sudden attack, I would crawl out of the side of my tank and not take part in the fighting . . . but then I knew that if it happened I would not have the determination to do so . . . the social pressure in war is sometimes irresistible. . . . The decision to refuse was my second hardest decision. The first was my divorce. . . . They were two recent and close decisions, and they gave me the felling that I had the inner strength to do what I feel is right . . . even if the rest of the world does not share my ideas.

The data suggest that the refusers' moral decision-making process, which involved breaking the law, was more closely related to their loner tendencies, or their conviction in standing alone, rather than their moral reasoning. The fact that 83 percent were the only refusers in their unit suggests that the action of refusal was constructed in an individualistic fashion. The refusing soldiers reported also on loose connection and detachment from their units; some because they had no friends in the unit and some because their military role led them to be transferred from one unit to the other. The large proportion of medics (seven out of thirty-six) in this sample is one example of this. The role of these soldiers leads them to be transferred from one unit to another according to the army's needs. Other refusers who had a unit of their own did not consider themselves attached to it, either due to their extreme ideological stand or due to the fact that the Lebanon war was the first reserve service with their unit. For others, refusal matched their tendency to adopt detachment or self-control as a mode of resolution for personal and moral dilemmas.

The type of courage (to stand alone) was not seen as a contributing factor to consistency across stages among the Peace Now group. Forty-six percent of the Peace Now soldiers indicated that they did not have the courage to disobey. They seemed to believe that protests made by reservists who have fulfilled their military duty are valued more by the Israeli society.

The Claim for Moral Integrity

To what extent did the action taken by each group of objectors correspond with their judgment concerning the morality of their action? The data suggest that the two groups of objectors viewed their action as a moral one. The Peace Now soldiers seemed to hold two sets of moral precepts: (a) it is morally right to demand withdrawal from Lebanon, (b) it is morally wrong to enforce this change via refusal or any other nondemocratic ways that involve law breaking. Both concerns led the Peace Now soldiers to experience self-consistency (Blasi 1983) when abiding by high moral principles, even when they experienced moral turmoil in the war. Their military rank seems to have served as an important contributor (after education) to their actual moral competence. Interestingly, Peace Now soldiers were not as hostile to the refusers as was the general public (they were able to empathize more closely with their concrete moral struggle as to how best to manifest their moral concerns about the war). However, 75 percent of the Peace Now soldiers did not hide their belief that refusal was an effective mode of action though not necessarily justified given the fact that none of the refusers was ordered to perform a flagrantly illegal command—an inhumane act to which they were obliged to refuse. Forty-six percent of the Peace Now soldiers, as has been reported before, even argued that, when screening their potential choices, they did not have the courage to choose refusal as an option.

The refusers, however, viewed their action as just (though painful) and essential for their personal tendencies to resolve moral dilemmas in a linear and individualistic way:

> I felt good that I was giving my personal answer to the war in Lebanon. Before, I demonstrated, I signed petitions . . . but in refusing, there was a possibility to prick the balloon myself.

Peace Now soldiers seem to create a sense of moral harmony from the variety of acceptable moral actions that they considered available, and the fact that their action represented a variety of people with a plurality of opinion and political orientations:

> In Peace Now, there were people whom I knew, I respected their opinions and I knew we could *work together* . . . There are many

> ways you can act with people and this variety of opinions under one umbrella is our strength . . .

The refusers' linear judgment-action relationship is reflected in the moral attitude they manifested in their response to Form B of Kohlberg's Moral judgment Interview. In this interview they were asked whether Dr. Rogers should report Dr. Jefferson after seeing him perform a mercy killing, which is illegal. A refusing soldier argued:

> You ask me if Dr. Rogers should report Dr. Jefferson. But I do not understand your question! I think that if Dr. Jefferson decides that the right action is to give the woman the drug, he should *stand up and report it himself* personally and not wait to be reported. He should explain his just motives for this action even though it is against the law. . . . I see the refusers in the same way—if you decided that serving in Lebanon is not justified, don't find physical excuses but stand up for what you think.

The Peace Now soldiers presented a different course of action, for example:

> Should Dr. Rogers report Dr. Jefferson? I think not—I think that my conscience is primarily directed *toward people not toward rules*—I would certainly not report him but primarily would consider the idea of thinking of protesting on his behalf.

In spite of the individualistic nature of the action of disobedience, most refusers tend to admit at one point or another in the interview that they did not dare to be the first refuser. Paradoxically, the courage to individually link judgment with action seems to have been inspired by the existence of a protest movement that they themselves created, called "There Is a Limit" (see chapter 6). Thus, though the refusers acted individually, they nevertheless benefited from the *group* as a moral frame of reference even if only temporarily. One refuser clarified this point: "I see the protest movement 'There is a Limit' as a bus that I stepped on because it stopped at the right stop when I needed it. But when it changes I will get off."

Moreover, although the refusers detached themselves from their unit, they nevertheless hoped to return to it upon their release from prison. This attitude indicated a desire to serve with their long-term comrades in the event of a future war they considered morally justified. As already noted by Walzer (1988), "though the critic sometimes finds it hard to surrender his specialized and solitary role . . . they also need commitment and support" (p. 23). The following refuser seemed to confirm this thesis:

> I had the feeling that something was wrong in this war but I didn't know how to change things, I tried to talk to friends around me, to send letters, to demonstrate, and then I realized that I wouldn't solve my problem until I refused—but I couldn't do it to my friends—not because they wouldn't like me after that (they really understood me), but because they trust me and needed me as well as I needed them—the biggest punishment for me would be to be removed to another unit—I can count on them to be around in times of a (just) war . . . and we would have such times.

Conclusion

Both groups of soldiers were geared toward an action of moral criticism of their society, a society in which they live and for which they are called upon to sacrifice their lives. Within the Israeli society, the refusers were a priori assigned to a separate position by the public. The hesitancy of the Peace Now activists to protest at the outset of the war but rather later on may hint that they feared the exclusion awaiting those who objected while soldiers were still spilling their blood for the country. To some extent, this hesitancy was part of some refusers as well when they decided to postpone their wish to refuse at the beginning of the war. This hesitancy, however, might be the function of the (yet unknown) severe punishment awaiting the reservists if they decided to refuse at war situation (unlike reserve service).

In this chapter we have traced the nature of the relationships between moral competence and action when examining the distinct position each group of individuals chose to take: Peace Now soldiers viewed inclusion as the moral foundation of their action, whereas the refusers viewed inclusion as a necessary by-product of their action (that is, the action will tie them back to their society). Nevertheless, this is a vague distinction, as one could identify refusal as emerging from the same sense of inclusion (Walzer 1988), as this refuser concludes:

> I am close to forty years old and I have taken part in all the wars since I was eighteen years old. I could easily be transferred to another unit where I could serve in an office and not on the bat-

> tlefield. I am not going to do so since I feel that it would be an escape to close my eyes and say to myself—I am okay, I got out. This is wrong because in this way I solve my problem and I let my friends in the unit do the work. I want to return to my unit upon release from prison since if I continue to serve and remain part of the unit, I buy myself the right to criticize, the right to shout.

These findings lead us to broaden our inquiry far beyond the question of moral maturity, consistency, and integrity. It calls for further attention to the question of moral inclusion in the sphere of criticism. How far can an objecting individual follow his right to shout while in the turmoil of war, when decisions must be made in the face of sudden changes in the social reality of the situation, in the face of sparse authoritative information, and in the absence of an opportunity to reason about the situation beforehand (Brown and Herrnstein 1975; Milgram 1974)?

The following chapter attempts to analyze obedience to authority in extremely morally ambiguous situations in times of war. Extreme military situations as such often reveal the most noble as well as the most base examples of human behavior. Thus, we move into the study of refusal during the Intifada through the study of the possibilities awaiting morally puzzled soldiers in the field. Kohlberg's (1984) pioneering analysis of the My Lai situation and its resistance serves as the framework for this analysis. The following chapter employs the recent documentation of the My Lai situation by Bilton and Sim (1992) in an attempt to assess separate and connected positions awaiting moral critics in the battlefield. This presentation is followed by two extreme cases of obedience to authority during the onset of the Intifada.

The culture of war . . . does not compel troops to commit atrocities, but it creates the circumstances in which atrocity is possible, maybe probable, but not inevitable.

—Bilton and Sim 1992, p. 18

3

Refusal in the Battlefield

From Passive to Active

What does the combatant's moral competence tell about his moral action in general and while under pressure in particular? Kohlberg (1984) believes that one does not act directly on principles, but rather on specific content judgments engendered by those principles. Moral judgments serve two psychological functions that he deems necessary for moral action: "The first is a denotic decision function, a judgment of what is right. The second is a follow through function, a judgment of responsibility to act on what one has judged to be right" (p. 517). Thus, the definition of moral action, according to Kohlberg, includes the actor's perception of right action and his judgment of responsibility to perform the action.

However, laboratory experiments show that, in situations involving authority, an individual's perception and sense of responsibility do not lead the moral thinker into his prospective action so smoothly. For example, in Milgram's (1974) famous study on obedience to authority, naive subjects were recruited to "shock" an innocent victim under the guise of studying the effects of punishment on memory. Milgram argued (and proved) that in authoritative situation there is a pressure for all subjects to enter an "agentic state of mind," and therefore they tend to not question the legitimacy of authority. Once in this mode, individuals no longer evaluate the morality of their actions by themselves, but rather see themselves as agents carrying out the commands of their superiors. Kelman and Hamilton (1989) suggested three social processes that seem to weaken moral inhibitions among actors in the field: (1) authorization—the situation becomes so defined that the individual is absolved of the responsibility to make personal moral choices; (2) routinization—the action becomes so organized that there is no opportunity for raising moral questions; and (3) dehumanization—the actors' attitudes toward the target and toward themselves become so structured that it is neither necessary nor possible for them to view the relationships in moral terms.

Kohlberg brought some hope to Milgram's 1974 study by showing that nearly all subjects at the highest moral stage (which is now regarded as at least stage 4) were able to resist authority and quit the experiment early (87 percent). Milgram also reported that subjects who quit the experiment seemed to relinquish their sense of responsibility considerably less often than did subjects who were obedient. Kohlberg than moved outside the laboratory situation to the My Lai situation and examined Bernhardt's sole refusal to shoot civilians in the terrible massacre there. This chapter follows Kohlberg's line of inquiry and takes the My Lai situation as a setting where moral action can best be studied.

This examination, however, is based upon data from Bilton and Sim's (1992) book and from their documentary film (Yorkshire Television) on the My Lai situation. This is followed by an examination of obedience and resistance to authority during extreme situations at the onset of the Intifada. By no means do these comparisons imply that the situations are similar, as the My Lai situation is a unique case of massacre and, as emphasized by Walzer (1977), can only be compared to a massacre. Still, the focus is on similarities and differences in the separate and connected positions of moral criticism that await combatants in extremely ambiguous situations in the battlefield.

The My Lai Situation: Why Did Kohlberg Fail to Interview Thompson?

On 16 March 1968, an American infantry company was ordered to attack Vietcong guerrillas in the Vietnamese village of My Lai. The soldiers were informed that the inhabitants were supposed to be outside the village on the day of the attack. The advance on the village was not met by any hostile fire. Within four hours the soldiers of this Company had murdered, raped, burned, and mutilated four to five hundred innocent victims.

The men of "Charlie" company had arrived in Vietnam from Hawaii in December of 1967. Their age ranged from eighteen to twenty years old. Nearly half were blacks and few had higher education. They were later described as a typical cross-section of American youth assigned to most combat units at that time, in that place, and in that war. Originally, they were supporters of the war in Vietnam or lacked the social resources to avoid participation in it (Kelman and Hamilton 1989). The soldiers were promised they would find only Vietcong in the village and were not instructed what to do with the innocent local population if they encountered them. The ambiguous orders left the soldiers with the "feelings" that all the people in the village were the enemy (Bilton and Sim 1992). Researchers on this case (Bilton and Sim 1992; Hersh 1975; Kelman and Hamilton 1989) share the idea that the men in Charlie company were in a mood of revenge following the loss and wounding of the unit combatants by booby traps, mines, and snipers in the weeks leading up to the My Lai massacre. There was also a growing frustration regarding the distinction between who was a Vietcong and who was a civilian. A year later, Ronald Ridenhour, an American soldier who was not present in My Lai, heard about the massacre from a soldier who had participated and informed the authorities. No copy of the original command was found. Lieutenant Calley was the only person from the unit who was convicted. He was accused of 109 cases of murder in cold blood. He argued that he followed his superior's orders (Captain Medina). Calley ended up serving three years under house arrest in his apartment and was granted parole on 10 September 1975. He viewed himself (and was viewed by many others) as a victim of the political system.

Kohlberg asserted that in the My Lai situation "we may reasonably argue that all ethical principles would define *not killing* civilians as the *more* moral action" (1984, p. 570). Bernhardt's moral behavior of not shooting became a subject for Kohlberg's moral inquiry:

> Bernhardt sets a priority on human life, but was also able to see that life is valuable regardless of the social categories into which an individual falls. This reasoning meets the criteria for substage B (hierarchy, prescriptivity, and universality), at least at the stage 4 level. (1984, p. 568)[1]

Kohlberg (1984) was convinced that Bernhardt's ability to single out the right moral action serves as a manifestation of his high level of moral competence since "Persons at each higher stage of moral reasoning acted more consistently in the direction of supporting rights and acting responsibly both in the laboratory setting and outsidc the laboratory" (p. 564).

As has been argued by Linn and Gilligan (1990), Bernhardt's passive nonaction of not shooting and not reporting might well be judged as a manifestation of moral indifference. In fact, it was the solitary moral stand of *nonaction* that enabled Bernhardt to be consistent with his principles across contexts, as he explained to Kohlberg: "When I thought of shooting people I figured: 'Well, I'm going to be doing *my own war,* let them do their own war' [emphasis added] (Kohlberg 1984, p. 549)."

Bernhardt was praised by Kohlberg for resisting (the temptation of) shooting. Bernhardt's presumed "moral selfishness" (Walzer 1968, p. 14) led him to conceptualize the right action as *not acting,* that is, as refraining and hesitating from activating his moral self. Did Bernhardt's high level of moral competence provide him the opportunity to discern other moral action alternatives? Locke (1981) doubts this, saying: "the more sophisticated our moral understanding, the more difficult it may be to resolve conflicting moral claims" (p. 177). Moreover, if human lives are equal across nations, why did Bernhardt make no attempt to save the lives of innocent Vietnamese even if he had to threaten the life of the one American who gave the order to shoot them ? Is *not shooting* the only morally right response? In what way is this view constructive in preventing the evil in this situation? Is there another way to determine what constitutes moral action in such circumstances? Is it accidental that Kohlberg never interviewed Hugh Thompson, a helicopter pilot circling the My Lai site who rescued several Vietnamese by threatening Calley? Is there a possibility that Thompson's reasoning for his action would not be in accord with the explanatory power of Kohlberg's theory (Broughton 1978) and therefore his case was overlooked?

Thompson's "physical distance from the authority" (Kelman and Hamilton 1989, p. 158) must be emphasized. He was not under Calley's orders. As an outsider to the unit it was easier for Thompson to challenge Calley's authority. Yet, this challenge could have been exclusively passive as well, such as reporting to higher authorities about the event without risking his own self on behalf of others. Thompson's reasoning seems to suggest that his incentive for an active mode of action emerged from a scale of justice that was geared toward the particular rather than the abstract. In an interview filmed by Yorkshire Television (Bilton and Sim 1992), Thompson asserted:

> During the mission, we kept circling around, we saw a lot of the bodies . . . and started to wonder . . . we weren't receiving any fire . . . we didn't like it. There were too many casualties there and how they were located. . . . The artillery couldn't do this.

Thompson's radio messages to higher commands were ignored. When Thompson saw GIs advancing on another group of defenseless women he ordered his crew to turn their guns on their fellow Americans, as Lauren Kobran, Thompson's gunner, attested:

> Warrant officer Thompson was desperate to get those people, whom he believed to be civilians, to a safe area. He realized that what he was trying to do to help the people on the ground was not getting done. He was convinced that the ground forces would kill these people if he didn't get to them first. He landed the aircraft between the American forces and the Vietnamese people in the bunker. He got out of the aircraft, and went and had words with the Lieutenant as to how he could get these people out of the bunker. Calley said the only way he knew was with hand grenades. So when Warrant Officer Thompson came back to the aircraft he was furious and he was desperate to get those people out of the bunker. He told us he was going over to the bunker himself to see if he could get them out. I don't even think he took a rifle with him; besides side arms, he was relatively unarmed. He told us: "If the Americans open fire on the Vietnamese as he was getting them out of the bunker, then *we should return fire on the Americans.*"

When he cognitively defined the situation as immoral, Thompson activated his decision by inspiring the entire crew to join him in a collective action. By redefining the situation (the Americans are the enemy), he reduced the notion of disobedience as a deviant action (Gamson et al. 1982; Kelman and Hamilton 1989). Unlike Bernhardt, Thompson seems to have redefined the situation from a moral dilemma revolving around claims of rights to a dilemma where he has a conflict of responsibility and connection; from a moral dilemma that calls for resisting one's own temptation (to comply, to withdraw oneself from the immoral situation, to preserve one's own principles in isolation) to a moral dilemma that calls for altruistic action, for reaching out to people, for embedded selves (Linn and Gilligan 1990). In constructing his decision

Thompson seems to have replaced hesitation as the emotional ingredient of the proposed action with spontaneity, as he told Bilton and Sim :

> When [I] instructed my crew chief and gunner to open fire on *them* if they opened up on any more civilians I don't know how I would have felt if they would have opened [up fire], but on that particular day I didn't give it a second thought, they were the *enemy* at that time I guess. They sure were the enemy to the people on the ground.

Unlike Bernhardt, Thompson did not necessarily manifest stage 4 moral thinking:

> While flying around we came across a ditch, full of bodies—a lot of women and kids. I remember thinking, how did these people get to be in the ditch and I guess I finally thought about the Nazis, marching everybody to the ditch and blowing them away. And we are *supposed* to be the good guys with white hats. It upset me.

Thompson's refusal to become a Nazi marks the historical dimension of his moral self that Kohlberg never takes into account (Broughton 1987). Thompson seems to have voiced his concern from a connected moral position, where the moral action constructed did not necessarily free the actor from further moral dilemmas:

> One time as we were flying around we noticed some movement in the ditches. Andrew Arder, who is my crew chief, saw a child moving around amongst the bodies. We landed the aircraft next to the ditch and got out with the gunner standing on one side and me on the other while Andrew Arder went down through the bodies and brought back a child. By then it was obvious how these people had got into the ditch. We got the child on board and out of there. *There were more we could probably have saved* but we couldn't carry them. We flew the child to a hospital . . . it was a very sober flight. I looked at the kid, trying to figure out her age. I thought she was about three or four. I had a son at home the same age, *you think it could be your kid.* Later I found out through investigation that it was a girl. We could hardly tell, we checked arms and legs, there were no bullet wounds. It breaks hearts to think about things like that [emphasis added].

With the help of larger helicopter gunships, Hugh Thompson and his crew succeeded in airlifting to safety some old men, women, and children. It seems quite clear that Thompson performed a moral action, an action that might be rated even as more effective than the 'nonintervention' action of Bernhardt. Thompson's action was based on paying attention to the parameters of the situation (the threat posed by Calley), inventing an effective response (threatening Calley so that he would not interrupt him while taking out survivors from the ditches), and on recruiting the other members of his crew to sense the "moral pain" he was experiencing. Thompson's action implied that he discern that Calley might respond to threat, that he discovered an effective way of threatening Calley, and that he drew on his knowledge of Calley, the situation, and of his relationship with Calley (as well as perhaps knowledge of himself and of what actions he was capable of taking). Thompson's action reflects a form of a connected morality, what "ordinary people—not philosophers—call justice" (Solomon 1990, p. 289).

Kohlberg does not consider special ways of approaching or experiencing or imagining relationships (as webs of connection, rather than as hierarchies of inequality or balanced scales) as morally mature logic. The same is true for the special way of experiencing and conceiving oneself in relation to others as connected and therefore interdependent (attached), rather than as separate and therefore capable of objectivity (and objectification). Bernhardt's reasoning regarding the report on the event seems to question the notion of morality as an exclusive conflict of rights:

> When the time came to do it (to testify, R.L.), I was asked to get specific about who did what. I was asked to point the finger at certain individuals. I really didn't feel comfortable with that, after all, I'd spent a lot of time with these people. Even though they did all of that—I also knew their other side. We spent a long time over there—it was not one long string of abuse of Vietnamese, murdering Vietnamese civilians. Most of the time we did soldiering stuff, fighting and sweating and bleeding, just like soldiers do. Besides by then, I was with another military unit and when you point the finger at some of your former comrades, these men you are now with begin to wonder about you too.

The Beita and Hawarra Situations: Where is Thompson?

Planned or spontaneous, the Intifada commenced on 7 December 1987.[2] What surprised Israeli officials was that what they assumed to be a local and sporadic demonstration, following a car accident in the Gaza strip, spread to the West Bank. Within days, the demonstrations became extremely violent, including throwing of stones and bricks, stabbing, throwing of lethal metal objects, setting fire to cars, throwing petrol bombs, spreading oil and spikes on roads, blocking roads with stones, wounding and killing Israeli civilian drivers by throwing petrol bombs into their cars, and stabbing Israeli citizens shopping outside and inside the Green Line (pre-1967 borders). The uprising found many individual soldiers unequipped (morally and militarily) to fight an undeclared war that was often led by women and children who used "cold," though very often lethal, ammunition. The inability of the high-ranking command to visualize the impact and the scope of the demonstrations was reflected in the official definition of the event as *hafarot seder* (disruptions of order). This definition eventually resulted in assigning the soldiers to policing work (for which they were never trained) to restore "order" and "quiet." Army officials were reluctant to exercise conventional military power, even when the lives of the soldiers were at stake. Very often soldiers found themselves alone against a violent mob, unable and forbidden to shoot, and obliged to find their own solution to the situation. During this period, the soldiers deployed in the territories were mainly in compulsory service (ages eighteen to twenty-one), and obviously less experienced and morally mature than the reservists.

Most notable are the first two months of the Intifada known in army slang as "the black two months" (*Ma'ariv,* 10 November 1989). Soldiers stated that within these two black months "There was absolute uncertainty as to what was allowed and disallowed. . . . There was a deep sense of frustration among the soldiers . . . they felt helpless, because they had no way of responding to the villagers' provocations. The villagers were well aware of the orders (not to shoot) . . . if they throw stones. . . . There was not a single soldier without 'black and blue marks' incurred by stone throwing" (*Jerusalem Post,* 2 April 1990). The confused high-ranking command issued unclear orders in an attempt to avoid the use of "live" ammunition on violent civilians. Most notable is the policy of beating during the black two months (*Chadashot,* 22 September 1989). This policy was issued by the Minister of Defense, Yizchak Rabin. Rabin asserted in various forums (the media, to senior officers, to soldiers) the need "to break the bones" of the rioters. When talking to soldiers he insisted that "no one will die of a beating" (*Ma'ariv,* 6 July 1990), "it will hurt but maybe they will stop" (*Chadashot*, 22 June 1990). The stated rationale of this policy was that hitting (rather than shooting) "will look better (morally) in the eyes of the world." He ordered senior officers to "do the job" promising that he "will take care of the media and the politicians" (*Ha'aretz*, 21 June 1990) "and lawyers" (*Chadashot*, 22 June 1990). In a television broadcast he gave assurance that he was responsible for the policy.

On 19 January and 21 January 1988, Colonel Yehuda Meir, a career officer who was commander of the town of Nablus prior to the outbreak of the Intifada, ordered compulsory service infantry troops to arrest twelve rioters from the village of Beita who were suspected of incitement following violent demonstrations and to break their bones. The rioters did not resist the arrest and were assembled according to a list provided by the Secret Service. When the company commander, Ben Moshe, protested that the above orders to break their bones, despite lack of resistance, were immoral, Meir said they were in keeping with new IDF policy and must be followed, and then he left the area. Ben Moshe later testified:

> I remember that I was shocked. I didn't know how to swallow this. This was a new command. It was not detached from the context or reality of those days. But those days in Nablus will be remembered by me as an abnormal time in my life. This was a command that arouses some immediate resistance in you. It is hard to do such a thing. Yehuda Meir told me that the prisons were full and this was the reason for this command. I gave the soldiers the opportunity not to obey the command since I, the commander, could not do so. I felt uneasy. While the order was being carried out I was in the bus, or near the bus, except for one time when I could not hold back. I ran to one group of Arabs and then to the second. I ordered the men to take their Identity cards and release them. . . . When we came back to the base I gave an order not to go to bed. I talked with the officers, then with the soldiers. I shared with them my dilemmas and my feelings. I don't know if I had the right to do so. I tried to clarify to the soldiers what we had done. I did not try to make excuses. . . . This was more of an emotional discussion than a logical one. I told them that what we had done as representatives of the IDF was not within the IDF moral norms and not the way the IDF resolves problems. All the time during our stay in Nablus I worked hard to control the soldiers although we were provoked all the time, but here I felt that the ground was falling away under me. On that day I went to Meir and complained. He mocked me and said: You paratroopers are "shooting and cry-

> ing" but here in the Infantry we are "doing" (the work) and "laughing." (*Ha'aretz*, 13 April 1990)[3]

> The next day we were ordered to do the same thing (in the village of Hawarra). Meir insisted that we should not strike any parts of the body other than the arms and legs, and to let someone go back to the village and inform the villagers. I resisted the command. I talked about the moral side, my education in the IDF, the potential legitimization that the order gave to the soldiers. Meir didn't try to convince me. He told me that it was an order. I answered that if it was an order I would do it but first I wanted to talk to the divisional commander. After a short discussion with him I got the feeling that the order was okay. (*Chadashot*, 13 April 1990)

Ben Moshe described his moral decision after this meeting: "From my point of view the decision was made but the argument was not over" (*Ha'aretz*, 13 April 1990). Unlike Calley, Ben Moshe seemed to be aware of the inappropriateness of the commands. He tried to protest. When he failed, he permitted his soldiers to carry out these commands depending on their conscience. Ben Moshe did not take part in the beatings but sat in the bus. At some point the bus driver was asked by Ben Moshe to race the engine to drown the screaming (*Jerusalem Post*, 19 January 1990). All together, twenty youths were beaten. Some of them required medical treatment afterward. Some clubs were broken. Though the unit that carried out the action might not be regarded as an elite unit within the Israeli army, it was portrayed by the Israeli press as a good company (*Ha'aretz*, 17 May 1990). After this event, Captain Ben Moshe, who originally planned to be a career officer, decided to leave the army. Unlike Bernhardt, who did not initiate a complaint about the event, Ben Moshe complained to the Human Rights members in the Israeli Parliament.

A reservist who happened to serve in the area and witnessed the event further brought this story to the public's attention. The story became known to the public on 4 May 1989, a year and three months after the event. Fearing that a public trial would open a Pandora's box, the army tried to persuade Meir to resign and suppress the story but he refused (Straschnov 1994). The Association for Civil Rights in Israel petitioned the High Court of Justice, demanding that Col. Meir be court-martialed for ordering soldiers to commit a flagrantly illegal command. They further argued that letting Meir off without a trial, while lower-ranking soldiers are court-martialed for similar offenses, violated the IDF's principles of purity of arms and responsibility of commanders. This petition was also signed by "concerned parents of IDF soldiers," a group of soldiers' parents protesting alleged excessive use of arms in the occupied territories (*Jerusalem Post*, 29 May 1989). In June 1990, the army was instructed by the Supreme Court to prosecute Meir. No copy of Meir's order was found (*Jerusalem Post*, 4 November 1990). A special military court sentenced Meir to demotion to the rank of private, and he was dismissed from the army. In an interview to the press prior to the trial, Meir said, "I am a victim of the system" (*Ma'ariv*, 30 March 1990).

Meir's defense lawyer argued that the policy to beat for the sake of punishment was originated in instructions by the Minister of Defense in January 1988, and this "illegal command when beating not in the course of an arrest . . . had spread like lighting throughout the troops" (*Jerusalem Post*, 4 November 1990). Colonel Meir testified that there was an unrealistic gap between the policy of beating, as dictated by Defense Minister Rabin, and the command to use "reasonable" force:

> There was no way the leading rioters could be caught. In the first line there were children, in the second line there were women, and only later the leaders. (*Chadashot*, 22 June 1990)

Meir argued at his trial that he resisted Rabin's policy, and indicated that he routinely reported to his superior about his activities and the beatings, and that there was nothing special about it. This was part of the "norm" (*Ha'aretz*, 24 June 1990).

Could a reservist behave better in a similar situation? One reservist who served during the "black two months" reported:

> We were called to reserves for training . . . and suddenly we were moved to the West Bank—under an emergency rule (Code 8). It was very cold, and we were sent without equipment. It was very chaotic, but the critical thing is that during the night all the battalion had a meeting with a brigadier, and the battalion commander. I don't remember the details, but basically the message was that if we were stoned, it was necessary for us to catch the stone throwers and break their bones so next time they won't throw stones at Israeli soldiers. There was no discussion on the legality of the action, or as to whether it was a manifestly legal or a manifestly illegal command . . . the truth of the matter is that I was already considering refusal at that time, but (since things were not clear to me) I believed first of all I should check what was happening in the field, and then reach a decision. I said to myself:

"this is all theory, I'll go and see what's happening first." In one case (after forty-eight hours without sleep following a frustrated encounter whereby the villagers trapped us and we weren't allowed to shoot) we came across a mess . . . there was a curfew and we heard that a Golani unit had captured seventeen stone throwers. The arrestees were brought to the main road. They were bound, hands tied behind their backs. They were laid face down on the road, then a Golani soldier went berserk. He took a club, and hit them hard. His action opened a Pandora's box. Suddenly other soldiers joined him. I tried to stop them. "What are you doing?" I asked. "These people are tied up!" But the soldiers were too hysterical to listen. The Golani company commander did nothing. Our battalion commander said only one thing: "Don't hit their heads!" When he saw that me and some other reservists were trying to prevent the beatings, he ordered his deputy commander to remove us since, "they haven't got the guts to digest it."

The hitting continued. I couldn't understand how this could be happening. I decided that I wouldn't join my unit any more, not in a passive way, nor in an active way in the territories since I'm not willing to be part of it. For ultimately, if I am there I am also responsible . . . before taking them back to the village there was more hitting. The next day we were due to be released. Another battalion arrived, but our departure was postponed for more than half a day. Why? So General Mitzna (a former critic of the Lebanon war, R.L.) could come and give us a final speech. His most important comment was that all that we had seen and heard during this service was *military equipment* and so we were not allowed to take it out. The fact that General Mitzna, who was very busy, delayed an entire battalion in order to make such a comment says it all . . . [suggests that] he tried to silence us.

It was clear to me that I was going to defy the General, since I wasn't willing to be silenced. The next day I went home and talked to a Member of Parliament. I wanted this event to be studied. I know that till today nothing has been done. Another reservist came with me . . . eventually it appeared in the *Jerusalem Post* but nobody did anything. I am not going to serve in the Intifada any more . . . everybody tells me that if I am politically oriented to the left then I am obliged to be in the Intifada in order to report—I reported! I reported to the most legitimate authorities in this country. And what was done? However, I will go one more time, and I will talk one more time, and then they will distort and whitewash what I say!

It is now two years since I witnessed this event. It is my word against the word of the career battalion commander. I am only a

> private, thirty years in the IDF as a reservist, but what is the weight of my word as compared to a (career) battalion commander who is also a lieutenant colonel? Today I think maybe I should have lay down with the arrestees, or maybe I should have shot in the air, or said to the battalion commander: stop this immediately, [I do not care if] you arrest me [for this], or put me in jail.
>
> Now I understand I lacked the courage, and I don't know if I would be braver today. Would I have enough courage to actively intervene instead of merely not taking part in such an atrocity. I am forty-nine years old, I am not a little child, the thought of serving time in prison for thirty-five days is not pleasant, but I don't see any other choice. (Rosen and Hamerman 1990, pp. 206–217)

Discussion

The My Lai situation marks a clear case of a massacre and it can only be compared to a massacre. Given this reservation, this chapter made an attempt to compare the positions of criticism awaiting combatants in the turmoil of war. These events were extreme. They were chosen as a subject for comparison because of the ambiguity in which the decision makers were forced to construct their choice of action. No less important is the political ingredient of these settings. Kohlberg (1984) argues that nonlaboratory situations such as My Lai are also "political situations" in the sense that they are "made by one group of people in relationship to another" (p. 564). These relationships are seen by Kohlberg as a mediating force between the individual moral judgment and action:

> While we have seen that each individual's perception of a moral situation at My Lai differed due to moral stage, the decisions were not made solely by individuals acting alone. Moral decisions in real life are almost always a group norm or group decision-making process. Moreover, individual moral action is often the function of these norms or processes. For example, in the massacre at My Lai individual American soldiers murdered noncombatant women and children. They did so partly because as individuals they were subject to a series of obligations and quasi obligations that allowed them to, at least in part, justify what in other circumstances they themselves might have considered immoral behavior. The reason that these soldiers were able to justify actions that they might normally not have done is that My Lai was essentially a group action taken on the bases of group norms and hierarchical authority. The

> moral choice made by each individual soldier who pulled the trigger was embedded in a larger institutional context of the army and decision-making procedure. Their decisions are dependent in large part upon a *collectively shared definition of situation* and of what should be done about it, in short, the group "moral atmosphere" [emphasis added]. (Kohlberg 1984, p. 571)

Given the fact that the average moral stage of a young adult is a conventional one (thus making him susceptible to situational and personal influences on his actions), it is important to question what constitutes the moral atmosphere in which the moral action was constructed, and what were the binding factors that prevented the decision makers from resisting authority or behaving in a Thompsonian way.

Neither event was defined as war. Given their previous experience as victimized soldiers, the orders they were given could have been interpreted as "reasonable." In both cases, the high-ranking command spoke with two voices: they demanded an assertive performance of action as well as restraint, courtesies, and respectability. In both cases a clear order was given, though no written documentation existed. In both cases, combatants performed their mission with more "dedication" than expected. As has been documented by Eilam (1991): "In many cases, the executors are those individuals who originate the command in the field" (p. 138). Kelman and Hamilton (1989) reached the same conclusion saying that "apparently no written orders were ever issued" in the My Lai case, on all levels. Thus, they conclude "Whether Calley himself had been ordered by his superior to 'waste' the whole area, as he claimed, remains a matter of controversy. Even if we assume, however, that he was not explicitly ordered to wipe out the village, he had reason to believe that such actions were expected by his superior officers. Indeed, the very nature of the war conveyed this expectation" (p. 17). Whereas there have been a few other atrocities at the level of Beita and Hawarra in the quelling of the Intifada throughout the years, particularly in the Gaza Strip, the vast majority of the IDF units have acted in line with high moral standards in the sometimes confusing circumstances of the conflict (see chapter 6).

At some point, both Bernhardt and Ben Moshe, viewed the nature of their military command as contradicting the dictates of their consciences. They both decided to take a stance of "nonaction" and "let them do their own war." While not at peace with his "nonaction," Ben Moshe allowed his soldiers to selectively object to the mission. Ben Moshe materialized his care orientation as a secondary line of action: he intervened on behalf of the victims after some time. He further on talked with the soldiers. In order to regain a sense of moral self, Ben Moshe decided to perform a post hoc action of resistance—first by leaving the army with protest and then initiating a publication of the event.

Cognitively, both actors preserved some form of "critical distance" (Walzer 1988). Can it be considered a "triumph of moral principle over moral reality" (Walzer 1988, p. 71), even though their critical thinking was not directed primarily toward critical intervention in the field? Whereas they seemed to understand the immorality of the action, they did not find in themselves the "lonely" courage to resist (face to face) the existing authority (Fromm 1981). Nor did they have the courage (different from the courage to disobey) to form a collective backing for an altruistic action as Thompson managed to construct (with the luxury of not having the same situational "binding forces") (Milgram 1974). While having the cognitive sophistication to reason hypothetically from the perspective of the oppressors as well as the victims, their failure to implement justice rationally, even in the sphere of mere disobedience, questions the explanatory weight of Kohlberg's stages as well as the overall idea of real-life decisions as stage related (Steenbarger 1991).

Both decision makers tried to manifest mature justice thinking, for which detachment is considered the hallmark. Both decision makers found it easier to define and redefine the morally ambiguous situations in justice terms (probably due to the nature of army and war that revolves around obligations, commands, and effectiveness). But justice, sometimes, creates a distance between self and others, and carries with it the danger of objectification, the ability to treat others as objects and feel no connection to them: "In the absence of co-feeling one cannot know what others are feeling, and therefore one may live in egocentric ignorance dangerously prone to rationalization" (Gilligan and Wiggins 1987, p. 291).

When guided by universally impartial principles of justice that exclude individual differences, even the mature decision maker may be maneuvered into a position of "nobody" (Benhabib and Cornell 1988). He may end up in subjectivity, as "the more strenuously he tries to be 'purely objective' about his data and his work, the more he is caught up in subjectivity, deny it though he may" (May 1979, p.12).

Thus far we are left with some unanswered questions that deserve further inquiry: Is it possible to view resistance to authority as motivated by care orientation? Can altruistic behavior be regarded as morally superior to disobedience? On what scale? Can both types of reasoning be regarded as having been voiced exclusively from a "connected" moral position? How does the "moral reality" of war shape the individual's decision to refuse?

Assuming that refusal is not the sole product of an individual's moral character but is performed within a given context, in a community to which one is committed, its understanding requires the examination of the character of the community as well as the relationship that exists between these two (Walzer 1977). These relationships are discussed in the following chapter.

Notes

1. Kohlberg doesn't seem to differentiate between mature moral thoughts and credibility (see Linn 1989b). He always refers to Bernhardt as the only soldier who did not shoot in My Lai. When Colonel William G. Eckhardt, JAGC, who was chief prosecutor in the case of the senior army command on the ground at the My Lai incident, was asked by the author about Kohlberg's claim he responded: "everybody was shooting in My Lai, I don't know that Bernhardt didn't shoot" (personal communication, 22 January 1987, U.S. meeting, Washington, "Morality in and out of war: Professional conduct on the battlefield"). Nevertheless, in this chapter I refer to Bernhardt's testimony to Kohlberg as credible.

2. Different sources give different dates. The Bezelem organization, for example, sees the ninth of December as the official start of the Intifada.

3. Following the 1973 Yom Kippur War, Israeli troops were sent to disperse demonstrations by youths in the occupied territories, with tear gas. In a letter of protest sent to the press, they described the insoluble moral conflict of their service as a situation where they were "shooting and crying."

I don't think it moral to flatten a house and even if I simply stand by, I am a passive participant . . . so by my passive involvement I am actually active. . . . If I weren't in the field it wouldn't be possible to destroy the house . . . I think that the impact of my action (refusing) is more significant than the actions of those who remain in the field—the ones who shoot and cry. . . . The intransigent attitude of society toward refusers suggests that the refusers are having an impact on Israeli society.

—An Intifada refuser

4

Refusal in Context
From Vietnam to Algiers

Service in the army is one of the most serious moral obligations of the Israeli male citizen. Refusal to serve in the IDF in order to protect a soldier's own moral integrity, and/or effect change in society, has no legal status. Objection on conscientious grounds by secular combatant soldiers has been very rare, consisting of a few individuals whose sporadic challenges to military service have hardly claimed public attention (Blatt, Davis, and Klienbaum 1975). On several occasions (most notably 1970, 1978, 1987), groups of high school graduates sent letters with clear (hypothetical) indications to refuse. Most famous is the 1970 letter. Following a publicized note from Dr. Nachum Goldman that the Israeli government had refused a peace initiative by Egyptian president Nasser, about 100 high school graduates signed a letter addressed to Golda Meir, then Israel's Prime Minister, which stated:

> Until now we believed that we were going to serve and fight three years because we had no choice. After this event . . . we are wondering why we should fight in a repeated war which holds no future. . . . People are broken psychologically. . . . People think it is easier to win in spirit. Our country is becoming militaristic and in the schools there is an atmosphere such as: "Here I am going to get killed." And jokes like "See you on the memorial board." (*Ma'ariv*, 1 August 1987)

Within the moral atmosphere of the seventies where the Arabs refused the proposal of "peace for land," military service as well as reserve service was still taken for granted and these critics were dismissed easily. Nearly all of the signatories ended up serving in elite units during their compulsory service.

The second wave of warning letters of refusal by high school graduates materialized in 1978 prior to the visit of the Egyptian president, Sadat:

> Our brothers fell in four wars knowing that they had no option but to fight. But how do you expect us to go to war when we are not sure whether the road that leads to war is just? . . . If the Prime Minister will not sign peace treaties with other nations, our hands will have blood on them—the blood of those who died.

The third wave of letters with threats of refusal came from high school graduates during the Intifada and were directed at the Minister of Defense, Rabin. In one letter, 280 high school graduates objected to the emotional breakdown that awaits soldiers who are obliged to serve in the territories against their conscience (*Ha'aretz*, 4 December 1989). A pilot study on this group of potential refusers suggests that unlike the high school signatories during the seventies, many got out of military service by various pretexts (Hetsroni and Holtz 1992).

The most famous case of concrete refusal to serve prior to the war in Lebanon is found in the case of Gad Elgazi. Even as a high school student Elgazi had refused to go on day trips across the Green Line. After his conscription, he served with distinction in his unit until he was ordered to serve within the territories. He refused on five separate occasions for which he was punished with a total of 120 days in the camp lockup. When again refusing, he was given a full court-martial (January 1981) and was sentenced to a year in prison (and eventually served nine months). The prosecutor in the case said in his summation that the IDF would not be able to function if every soldier were free to act according to his conscience, however exalted his beliefs. On the contrary, highly moral soldiers like Elgazi were badly needed in the problematic areas such as the occupied territories.

The act of refusal was completely foreign to Israeli society at that time and Elgazi imprisonment caused little public uproar. Not only was refusal considered by the public as an extreme separate position, but also the fact that Elgazi's parents were active members of Rakach (the extreme communist and anti-zionist political party).

The other case of individual objection emerged during the war in Lebanon with the request of Colonel Geva to serve as a simple soldier (see chapter 2). Even though Geva came from a zionist and patriotic family, his action was regarded primarily as foreign to the moral spirit of the IDF since his action implied separation from his soldiers. It took the three years of the war in Lebanon and its 165 cases of selective refusals for society to come to terms (if at all) with this form of criticism (Dupuy and Martell 1985; Gabriel 1984; Schiff and Ya'ari 1984; Shiffer 1984; Timmerman 1985).

Assuming that conscientious refusal is not solely the product of an individual's moral thinking, but rather a function of the character of the community, as well as the relations that exist between them (Walzer 1970), this chapter discusses those contextual factors prior to and during the war in Lebanon that paved the way for refusal and enabled the reservists to challenge one of their most serious obligations as Israeli citizens—to serve in the IDF in line with its moral code.

The repeated orders for reserve service in the Lebanese war zone gradually made it clear that the burden of service in the extended conflict was not shared by all (*Ha'aretz*, 11 April 1985). It became "a war in another place" (*Ha'aretz*, 10 August 1984) conducted in a "lost country" (*Ha'aretz*, 23 September 1983) where the "IDF soldiers are stuck in the mud" (*Yediot Acharonot*, 28 December 1984).

When sent to fight an 'optional' war (as opposed to a war of no alternative), to control civilian population without success and to decide the impossible task of differentiating between terrorists and innocent civilians, a growing number of Israeli soldiers gradually and painfully started to question the meaning of their service. When the war stretched beyond the familiar notion of time, space, and moral criteria, it generated a split between the army and the nation, as well as between the reservists and the career officers who recruited them, a split that paved the way for refusal. A fighting artillery man describes this split:

> We were bombing Beirut all the time. A man from the TV came after we had finished shooting. He waited and waited and nothing happened. So finally he said: "If you don't shoot I'm leaving—I need a programme for tonight!" One of the commanders requested permission to shoot. That shocked me. My commander returned that evening from leave and I told him that I would do only the minimum, no more. That was my first step toward refusal.

Those soldiers who fulfilled their duty could not always share their experience with all the people around them. Most notable was the discouragement of some fighters from kibbutz, the traditional source of IDF officers; every soldier from a kibbutz is regarded as the "son" of this collective:

> A son comes from the war in Lebanon, and he is not welcomed by the member who might have said: "We are proud of you" but rather "Are you crazy? Haven't you got better things to do?" (*Ma'ariv*, 17 May 1984)

Though the war in Lebanon was the first war that was brought to each citizen's living room through the color TV screen, not all the citizens participated, or even cared. Dedicated soldiers reported their experience as being "the cannon fodder of the people in the hinterland" (*Yediot Acharonot*, 24 September 1984). Questions about the moral necessity of the war and its conduct were inevitable, and the growing feeling of detachment from those who sent the soldiers and the soldier themselves intensified the split. A refuser explained:

> I reached my decision after a long and bitter debate with myself and after being a long time in Lebanon . . . here I am being taken into prison by this officer, who sits in a small car, and all the way I am thinking whether I am being fair to my comrades who are now on their way to Lebanon, and whether my action will have the right impact. I felt that for those army officers and clerks in the car who were doing their routine work of processing us, i.e., the paperwork, we were just an additional burden. They could not know that we refused not out of the hatred of Israel, but rather as a result of heavy thought and care. But they, of course, never served in Lebanon and treat us as a burden.

With the deteriorating economy (up to 400 percent inflation), the army-nation split turned into a living paradox, as explained by this refuser: "My boss is a major in the army. Nevertheless, he asked us very seriously *not* to go to reserve service no matter what we do."

There was also an ideological split: as the Lebanese war was fought after over a decade of ruling Palestinians, for some the prolonged stay in Lebanon implied another form of ruling of an Arab population. Some of the Lebanon refusers already had difficulties with the service in the territories. Refusal, thus, was a logical result of these concerns. One refusing reservist explained:

> After serving in the occupied territories, where we had to enter houses and search for terrorists, I knew that I had two options: either to complain and try to change the behavior of the soldiers, or to take the personal option of not taking part. I reached an

> agreement with my commander whereby each time my unit went to serve in the territories, I stayed and cleaned out emergency vehicles. When the war broke out, it was mutually understood that the agreement was cancelled and that I ought to go to Lebanon. Then the question was not whether to go or not, but whether I should evade or refuse. I had a kidney complaint and my commanders and myself knew that I could get a complete release from military service.

On this ground of alienation, history has known many types of conscientious objectors (Scheissel 1968; Walzer 1988). Yet, for the Israeli reservist, refusal was more complicated given the daily physical threat regarding the survival of his state, as well as the realization that within this given context the army was a necessity.

With these reservations in mind, most objecting reservists tended not to consider refusal as the first and most preferred mode of moral resolution to their dilemma about the war in Lebanon, as this refuser explained:

> At this point [the beginning of the war] I didn't think of refusal, I felt that I and a few others served as a sort of brake. At least we drank from tin cans and not from the finjans (ornate copper containers) from the luxurious Lebanese villas. Perhaps that is my only excuse for not refusing right then.

With the prolonged stay on the Lebanese soil and with the growing need to fight guerrilla resistance on top of the frustrating search for terrorists, the reservists were no longer confident that they were fighting a just war. Their ability to find a just meaning for their involvement in the war gradually diminished. This was accompanied by their inability to overcome the natural fear of death as this Lebanon refuser observed:

> I am a paratrooper. It is a very scary job—I always fear the jump from the airplane . . . but here, in the Lebanon war, I could not find the power to overcome my fear. I think I just didn't want to.

It seems that for the first time in their fighting history, the Israeli reservist could directly sense the intimate connection between justice, inner strength, and the ability to overcome fear, as this refuser explained:

> I am not naive. I don't think that across the borders there are people waiting for us with open arms. I believe that this is a terrible enemy. It is simply for this reason that I believe that we need to be

> even stronger and more just. The moment we stop being just, we have no business there. I truly believe that with things like justice, you cannot play with soldiers.

Regardless of the growing moral emotions of care for their own army and democracy, refusers were not granted the understanding of their position as a connected one, not even by their objecting buddies. More than that, selective refusal was not a familiar form of moral distress as this Lebanon refuser related:

> I talked to the people around me [while at a civilian memorial evening for my commander who had been ambushed and died], telling them that I was considering refusal and they just didn't understand what I was talking about. It is not because they were *against* refusal, but because they didn't realize that it was possible for them to do so. Indeed, if you had met me a year before and talked about refusal, I would have laughed at you as well. I was awaiting harsh responses . . . but there were some who shook my hand. Others were negative.

Even though the grave mistake of the Lebanon war had gradually been rectified, the justice position of the refusers was regarded as detached and indifferent. It seems that the demands of the refusers to not only preserve their moral principles but also to appeal for Israeli citizens' understanding of their position as a connected one were premature.

Two years after their withdrawal from Lebanon (in 1985), which was often regarded as the "Israeli Vietnam" by the public (*Davar,* 20 January 1989) as well as by the refusers (Ben Noon 1992; Minuchin and Minuchin 1985), the Israeli soldiers were drawn into a different, morally complicated military involvement that resembled the battles over Algiers (*Chadashot,* 13 January 1989). This time it was a "small war" (Inbar 1991), an Arab uprising (Intifada) in the territories headed by a violent mob consisting of women, children, and youth using "cold" yet deadly weapons. While some of the rioters demanded self-determination, others wanted the annihilation of the Jewish state (Benvenisti 1992; Gilbar and Susser 1992; Mishal and Aharoni 1989; Schiff and Yaari 1990; Shalev 1990). No in vain, the IDF Chief of Staff decided to give high-ranking officers the book " The Savage War for Peace" (Horne 1977).

The moral complexity of the Intifada was needed to broaden the community's understanding that just as there are varieties of moral complexities, so are there varieties of moral responses.

Apparently, the Intifada occurred in a familiar setting. For twenty years some reservists could have viewed themselves as serving in the administered territories rather than the occupied territories. They could have regarded the service as a lawful and moral obligation of a temporary occupying force. This force was intended to maintain the military stronghold and care for the welfare of the local inhabitants until a peace agreement was achieved. It took the eruption of the Intifada to bring forward the anomaly of the situation, whereby a temporary occupation had extended to a permanent one. This corresponded with an already growing erosion in the willingness to serve in the territories prior to the war in Lebanon (Linn 1986, 1987, 1988a, 1989b).

For a relatively long time the Intifada was regarded as a temporary disorder. Unlike the war in Lebanon, this time it was hard to argue that the Intifada occurred beyond the borders when many events took place a few kilometers from Tel Aviv. Unlike the war in Lebanon, service in the Intifada was not participation in a planned invasion, nor the making of a new order. It was a routine (though problematic) tour of duty in face of an old political arrangement about which the reservists could have protested as civilians long before.

Unlike their sudden assignment to the war in Lebanon, the potential Intifada refusers had the opportunity to reason about the situation beforehand—which is an important factor in moral decision making (Brown and Herrnstein 1975). Unlike the Lebanon refusers, many of the Intifada refusers escalated their resistance to a political level, to the point where they questioned the legitimacy of the IDF. This protest manifested itself in the specific demands that the Intifada refusers allowed themselves to ask for; from resisting the IDF wearing uniforms to increased demands of refusers as to where, when, and what type of reserve service they were willing to do (such as not to take a commanding position, not to be sent to protect settlers, not to have contact with the local population, not to go beyond the Green line, not to guard prisons). Whereas the moral predicament regarding Lebanon existed beyond the border, the moral dilemmas during the Intifada passed within the green line. Thus, for example, some soldiers argued they would refuse to guard Kziot prison camp (filled with Intifada rioters) though it was located within the green line. Some refused to escort prisoners from the Megiddo prison in which they were serving (within the Green Line) to the courts in Jenin (beyond the Green Line).

Though it was no longer a precedent, refusal as a mode of moral resolution was still rejected by the public, and its existence was denied by high-ranking officials. The first fifty cases of refusal during the first year of the Intifada were regarded as "insignificant compared to the 1.5 million days of reserves in the territories" (*Ha'aretz*, 2 April 1989). More than two years later, the growing number of refusers (more than 100) were still regarded as low by officials, who considered them an "insignificant minority" (*Ha'aretz*, 21 February 1990). In the beginning of the fourth year, the number of refusers stood at 160. By the end of the fifth year, 170 soldiers had been imprisoned, of them nineteen were compulsory service soldiers and the rest were reservists (*Ha'aretz*, 12 December 1992). Most Israelis preferred to accept the low numbers as factual, even though for each "white" (deliberate and public) refuser there could have been ten more "gray" (evasion of service due to various excuses) refusers (see chapter 6).

The Intifada refusers did not escape the hostile public attitude the Lebanon refusers had received. In spite of the growing consensus regarding the need for a political rather than a military solution to the Intifada, refusal remained an unaccepted position and one that would prepare the ground for a potential right wing resistance (*Ha'aretz*, 19 November 1992).

Whereas the refusal in Lebanon emerged within the context of a right wing government, the Intifada refusers were called by their left wing oriented government to suppress the uprising. Most illuminating is the moral confusion among members of Knesset affiliated with the Human Rights political party (Ratz) regarding the refusers. Since the outbreak of the Intifada, this left wing party had implicitly supported the left wing government with the ideology of "moral suppression," claiming soldiers should serve in the territories regardless of their moral dilemmas for they are obliged "to pay the moral price for the sake of political agreement which is soon to come" (*Chadashot*, 8 June 1990).

Ratz never gave public support to the Lebanon refusers. However, on 17 February 1989 its leader, Shulamit Aloni, argued that she saw in the Intifada refusers "divine souls" (*Ma'ariv*). This, however, did not represent the opinions of the other three members in her party. Dedi Zuker argued that if the refuser "sits at home, he is even so responsible for what is going on in the West Bank and that nobody can save his soul by refusing." Ran Cohen argued that if the refuser is indeed "a divine soul—let him serve there!" (*Ma'ariv*,

17 February 1989). Most interesting was the reaction of the fourth MK, Yossi Sarid, who was one of the main objectors to the Lebanon war from its outset. Sarid chose to volunteer and fulfill his reserve service in Lebanon—in order to show it was possible to live in a schizophrenic political reality, that though you are against the war it is illegitimate and anti-Zionistic to refuse. His objection to the occupation, however, did not result in his volunteering to do his reserve service in the territories. In the eyes of one Intifada refuser:

> Yossi Sarid, as well as Uzi Landau [a Likud party Member of Parliament who volunteered to serve as a reservist during the Lebanon war] knew why they did not volunteer [for reserve service in the territories]. No matter what the soldier does—whether he shoots at a child who is about to throw a block on someone's head, or whether he lets it happen—he will be doing the wrong thing.

According to Sarid, the role of the left was to fight within the army: "We are the last dam. If we advocated refusal, the army is ruined, in terms of morale and morality. So far there is no guarantee that we do not have other enemies who respect our moral norms such as Sadam and Asad."

The attitude of army generals toward the Intifada refusers was frequently hostile as well. In an interview with the press, a former Lebanon general, Yanush Ben Gal, said:

> Refusers? Kill them. The refusers are not hurting the army's morale, nor harming the dedication of those soldiers and commanders who are dealing with the war, because there is a consensus in the nation that the Intifada is a national threat that must be removed. There is a need to fight it, even if it tires us. And we must win. We despise the refusers. I see them as traitors serving time in prison . . . nobody has the right to decide where he wants to serve . . . this is the beginning of anarchy. I think that a citizen who refuses to serve in the territories should be stripped of all his rights as a citizen (*Ha'aretz*, 19 May 1989).

At the same time, the Chief Education Officer (Brigadier General Gross) asserted that "The IDF holds no magic medicine to the moral dilemmas that service in the territories raise" (*Ha'aretz*, 16 January 1990).

Paradoxically, attention was given to the moral excellence of the soldiers regardless of the moral dilemmas they were forced to face. A former chief psychologist of the IDF wrote in a book on the

Intifada: "The activity of the IDF during the Intifada became, in my opinion, one of the nicest challenges for the IDF commanders" (Gal 1990, p. 143).

In spite of some similarities between the moral dilemmas experienced by some soldiers in both conflicts (Lebanon and Intifada), refusal during the Intifada was not accepted as a mode of personal moral resolution in face of the unbearable growing moral anarchy in the field. The moral ingredient of the refusers' action was not addressed as a serious concern. Yoram Dinstein, an eminent professor of law, wrote to the press:

> The refusers are involved in a political struggle. The refuser is ready to risk his life in order to draw media attention to the cause he is fighting for . . . the greatest defeat for him is a lack of interest by the general public. I think it is in the interest of the government to present the refusers as a small-scale phenomenon. (*Yediot Acharonot,* 23 May 1989)

Only a few officials stated that refusal was a manifestation not only of the individual's moral crisis, but also of a moral crisis permeating the entire IDF. Professor Martin Van Kreveld, a military historian, declared:

> Rabin [the Minister of Defense], Shomron [the Chief of Staff)] and Mitzna (Central Command)—these commanders are simply sending the soldiers to the casbah (the market center in Nablus) without giving them the possibility to protect themselves, and when the soldiers shoot the wrong bullet or the wrong child, they put them on trial without giving them backing. No organization can exist in this situation, The IDF is being torn to pieces and what is left are gangs trying to protect their own lives and later remove the evidence from the media and the commanders. . . .
>
> Refusal, doesn't harm the army . . . this is the only way . . . the fact that the refusers are coming only from the line of the reservists and not from the career officers, reflects badly on the career officers—it proves that they are dedicated slaves to their rank and salary—and that they don't understand what is going on outside this . . . the elite of the nation is founded among the refusers. (*Ha'aretz,* 12 May 1989)

When attempting to understand refusal in its own terms, various private individuals and officials drew public attention once again to the case of of Colonel Eli Geva (see chapter 2). One Intifada soldier wrote to the press:

> Unlike the Lebanon war, there is no high-ranking career officer who will stand up against what is going on in the territories—this gives the state officials extremely valuable and precious time [for political or nonmilitary arrangements] . . . but it is doubtful whether this time is being used effectively by them. (*Ha'aretz,* 21 February 1990)

A brief note in the press in June 1990 revealed that a lieutenant colonel who was in charge of the Jebalia region (a violent refugee camp in the Gaza Strip where the Intifada started) decided to retire from the army because he could not cope with the moral dilemmas raised in his sector. He became depressed by the continuous need to clash with the native population and despondent whenever a Palestinian was killed in his region. His friends viewed his reaction as similar to that of Eli Geva (*Chadashot,* 18 June 1990).

The Human Right, MK Sarid, used Eli Geva as a frame of reference in assessing the efficiency of resistance within the system. Sarid stated:

> The members of "Yesh Gvul" (the refusers' protest movement) cannot claim that the war in Lebanon was shortened even for one day because of them. . . . One Eli Geva shook the entire system more than hundreds of refusers. (*Davar,* 10 February 1988)

Geva also became a moral landmark for the Intifada refusers. Some soldiers who did not agree with him during the Lebanon war found themselves viewing his ideas differently during the Intifada. Some commanders in particular tried to follow in his footsteps during the Intifada by asking to serve as private soldiers prior to their refusal.

Many morally distressed soldiers continued nevertheless to serve in the Intifada. Refusal remains a difficult position to take, even if this option exists more openly. Thus, when on 7 December 1992 three reservists were killed in their vehicle by terrorists near Gaza from a car overtaking them, forty of their comrades in their unit bitterly complained to Prime Minister Rabin that during their reserve service in the territories they had been transformed by the IDF into "moving targets." Yet, these same unit members assured the Israeli public that "if we are called again to serve in Gaza, we will not refuse" (*Yediot Acharonot,* 1 January 1993).

Who is the Intifada refuser? How is he different from the Lebanon refuser? The following chapter examines these questions.

I think that the decision to exclude yourself from the main stream is a very serious one . . . you have to be in deep distress to refuse . . . and for those who experience this distress refusal is inevitable . . . you must realize that the only difference between people involved in the conflict is the depth of the distress, its level of authenticity, and their spiritual independence.

—An Intifada refuser

5

Refusal in Action
From Precedence to Option

When deciding to detach themselves from the shared moral meaning of the army, the Intifada refusers suggest that this action was the only way in which they could be true to their moral selves, and that there was no other way in which their conscience could remain intact. The validation of this deliberate moral choice is not only the responsibility of the objectors but also our duty: Refusers may have to stand alone and defend their personal integrity against their fellow citizens: "But this is hard to do, and we ought not to pretend that it is (morally) easy. Nor ought we make it easy" (Cohen 1971, p. 130). It is important to note that the decision to refuse military service might be divided into two phases: the first is the process prior to the overt declaration of refusal; the second starts from the declaration up to the adjudication of the claim. Both phases require some form of lonely courage. Fromm (1981) argued that, in order to disobey, one must have the courage to be alone. Kohlberg (1984) favoured the concept of "ego strength." Walzer saw moral disobedience in the military as a form of "moral selfishness" but sometimes it is "the only resort of the principled but *lonely* man" (1968, p. 14). What are the personal and societal resources that might be associated with this lonely decision to disobey?

Even though refusal in the Intifada was more of an option than the Lebanon war, the number of refusers within its first four years of existence, namely 165, does not suggest that the process of refusal was easier on the individual reserve soldier than it was in Lebanon. Once again, refusal was regarded as a separate position of criticism and required some form of personal strength. This chapter examines the civilian, military, personal, and experiential sources of this strength among forty-eight refusers during the first four years of the Intifada.

Civilian Background

Table 4 presents the demographics of the refusers' civilian lives.

The data presented in this table suggest that the Intifada refuser is a secular, thirty-year-old Ashkenazi Israeli male, who lives in a

Table 4. Civilian Background (N = 48)

Ages		
21–49		Mode = 34
Background		
Ashkenazi	44(92%)	
Location		
City	44(92%),	7(15%) ex-kibbutz members
Kibbutz	4(8%)	
Status		
Single and divorced	17(35%)	
Married	31(65%),	29(60%) with children
Education		
High school	10(21%)	
Higher education (B.A.)	15(31%)	Mode = 15
Higher education (M.A.)	16(33%)	
Higher education (Ph.D.)	7(15%)	
Occupation		
Liberal professions	44(92%)	
Sons of Holocaust Survivor	12(25%)	
Being Abroad before Refusal	14(29%)	
Place of Birth		
Israel	33(69%)	
South America	11(23%)	

Political Orientation	
Communists	15(31%)
Left	27(56%)
Peace Now	5(10%)
Right wing	1(2%)
Activity in Protest Groups Prior to Refusal	25(52%)
Membership in "Yesh Gvul"	
Prior refusal	16(33%)
After refusal	29(60%)

city, is married with children, is highly educated, and is a member of the liberal professions. He has a record of solitary and opinionated decisions: Among the Israeli born, there were large numbers of exkibbutz members in the sample (15 percent). In their interviews, these exkibbutz members often pointed out their ability to construct unconventional and lonely moral decisions while under stress—similar to what they had undergone when deciding to leave the cohesiveness of the kibbutz setting where they grew up and were expected to stay. Twenty-five percent of the refusers were sons of Holocaust survivors. Twenty-three percent of the refusers in this group had immigrated (very often without any family members) from South American countries. They had developed a growing sensitivity to excessive use of military power and potential harm and control by military regimes in their home countries. Interestingly, fourteen subjects (29 percent), were abroad prior to their decision to disobey. All reported that this experience of separateness enabled them to adopt a more individualistic view of themselves as key players in this situation.

The Intifada refusers appear to be political individualists. Whereas during the war in Lebanon even some refusers had initially supported a short and limited campaign against terrorists advocating the right of any democracy to defend itself against terrorists (Linn 1988b; O'Brien 1986), most of the Intifada refusers were already politically opinionated to some degree regarding the status and future of the territories prior to the onset of the Intifada: 87 percent of the refusers had leanings toward left-wing political parties. Moreover, 52 percent of the Intifada refusers were already active in protest groups prior to their refusal (as compared to 30 percent during the war in Lebanon). It is important to note that 31 percent of the Intifada refusers affiliated themselves to Communist parties with a clear-cut objection to the occupation on their program (as oppose to less than 1 percent during the war in Lebanon).

In sum, the Intifada refuser may be portrayed as an individualistic decision maker who had long been concerned with the political goals of continual occupation and who, prior to refusal, tried to respond to what he regarded as a form of injustice. He involved himself in protest groups and with political parties that had definite agendas regarding withdrawal from the territories.

Military Background

Table 5 presents the demographics of the refusers' military lives.

Table 5. Military Background (N = 48)

Rank	
Soldiers	35(73%)
Officers	13(27%)
Units	
Artillery	10(21%)
Engineering	
Civil defense	7(15%)
Medical	15(31%)
Infantry, armored	16(33%)
Roles	
Fighters	33(69%)
Nonfighters	15(31%)
War Experience	
1967	1(2%)
Attrition	3(6%)
Missions	6(13%)
Yom Kippur	15(31%)
Lebanon	24(50%)

Time in Lebanon	
Days	4(8%)
One month	5(10%)
Two months–year	15(31%)
Service in Territories	24(50%)
Service during Intifada	8(17%)
Connection to the Unit	
Low	29(60%)
Average	8(17%)
Strong	11(23%)
1–15 Years in Unit	23(48%)
No Core Unit	25(52%)
Consulting with Soldiers	10(21%)
Consulting with Commander	9(19%)
Good Connection with Commander	11(23%)
Lebanon Refusers	9(19%)
Knowing other Refusers	37(77%)
Reasons for Refusal	
Not wanting to be part of an occupying force	33(69%)
Fear of having to execute a flagrantly illegal command	15(31%)
Most Stressful Aspect	
Encountering population	37(77%)

The Intifada refusers came from various units in the IDF. They appear to be experienced military officers (27 percent) and soldiers (73 percent) who were dedicated to the army, had participated in previous wars in combat role (since 1967), and had spent at least one stint of reserve service in the war in Lebanon and/or the territories prior to their decision to refuse. These data leave no doubt about the selectivity of their action. Unlike the Lebanon sample of refusers, the sample of the Intifada refusers includes two combatant majors (one of whom retains his position of battalion commander). Though there was one major among the Lebanon sample, he was not a combatant and did not hold a commanding position.

The military background of the Intifada refusers presented in table 5 provides some information regarding the availability of a lonely path toward refusal. Twenty-nine (60 percent) of the refusers reported loose connections to their core unit. Fifty-two percent of the refusers did not have a core unit of their own; their refusal did not involve the need to detach themselves from a cohesive unit. To this, one should add the fact that thirty-seven (77 percent) had no close affinity with their commanders. About 80 percent of the refusers did not feel free to consult with them or with their fellow soldiers.

In terms of military role, during the war in Lebanon there was a large percentage of combatant medics among the refusers. This fact was explained in two ways: first, very often combatant medics in the IDF do not have a battalion of their own. They are transferred from unit to unit according to the army's need. Thus, combatant medics have no chance to develop stable interpersonal connections while serving in the IDF, nor are they bound by the unit cohesiveness or commitments. Second, there is some selection bias in the population of the medics in the IDF; almost 50 percent of the medics in both conflicts indicated that when they were drafted at age eighteen they had presented their objection to a combatant position, either because of their political orientation or their low motivation. They often asked for or accepted the humanistic role of a medic, which fitted their nonmilitaristic aspirations.

Medics also do not have a permanent battalion commander. In this sense their separate position is similar to the other two groups of detached soldiers identified during the Intifada. The first of these is the engineering unit. Like the medics, the soldiers in some engineering units were not a cohesive group nor did they have a battalion commander who guided them through military life and could handle the refuser's case. For example, the only soldier in the sample who was imprisoned five times in a row came from the engineering unit. In his words: "this would not have happened if I had had a direct commander, a father-figure, who can sometimes find an alternative solution for you." The second example of separateness is found in the Civil Defense units. These units were not only characterized sometimes by the lack of a direct and permanent commander, but also became a harbor for those low-motivated combatants who would have liked to be transferred to a unit that was not sent to the war zone. Many of the Lebanon refusers were sent to such units. Paradoxically, due to the nature of the military conflict in the Intifada (an encounter with a civilian population), it became one of the units that was most frequently assigned to the territories.

Unlike 61 percent of the Lebanon refusers, who completed one tour of duty in the war zone before refusing, only eight (17 percent) of the Intifada refusers had served in the territories during the Intifada prior to their refusal (though quite a few had experienced a difficult tour there even before the Intifada broke out). Three major explanations seem to exist for this mode of a priori refusal during the Intifada: (a) During the war in Lebanon, a number of refusers felt the need to legitimize their claim to refuse. In Israeli society, reservists' moral claims are given a special weight due to their obligation fulfillment. Thus, refusers who wanted to gain some legitimacy for their refusal often chose to serve one time in the war zone before deciding to refuse (Sprinzak 1977, 1986; Sprinzak and Diamond 1990). (b) Unlike the war in Lebanon, refusal was a familiar form of action during the Intifada as 77 percent of the refusers knew other refusers prior to their decision (c) Service in the territories prior to the refusal was not needed as many refusers were familiar not only with others who refused but also with the exact nature of the service in the territories. Unlike the Lebanon war, the Intifada refusers had the opportunity to reason about the situation beforehand. It was therefore no surprise that many of them had already been concerned with the objective of this conflict (jus ad bellum) long before its conduct (jus in bello). Whereas soldiers may be responsible only for their moral behavior in the battlefield (Walzer 1977, 1988), these refusals might be seen reflecting the soldiers' moral and political concerns as civilians who saw themselves as responsible for the objectives of the conflict as well as for its conduct.

The major reason, cited by 69 percent, of the Intifada refusers for their refusal was rooted in their reluctance to be part of an occupying force in the territories. Some argued that they did not want to wear uniforms: "automatically it makes me part of the occupation." Others argued that "over the Green Line many undemocratic things are being done and I would have to do them in the name of democracy."

The second reason for refusing, alluded to by 31 percent of the subjects, was the fear of finding themselves in a position where they would be induced to perform an immoral action. One refuser explained:

> I refused to go to Gaza in an IDF uniform. I had been there twice as a civilian to repair electricity at a time when people were afraid to be there. I did not want to be an oppressor. I was not afraid that I would have to use my rifle, only of the direction I would have to shoot in.

When asked to rate the most stressful factor in the the service, 77 percent of the subjects cited the encounter with the population:

> I refused because I realized I could no longer stand the situation. The confrontations with the population. To look into the eyes of the frightened children, knocking on doors at night and going into houses when everyone is asleep. I felt that this emotional burden would stay with me all my life.

For the Intifada refuser, refusal meant one or more forms of protest:

> *Protesting the inability to make a moral change while in the field.* In Rafiah I was ordered to enter an area that was densely populated at a critical time. I found the situation to be one that was potentially fermenting. I tried to defuse the situation, and so in some small way I think I do have an influence, but on the larger scale I am oiling the machine that I don't approve of.

> *Protesting the indifference during the "Israeli Vietnam."* During the war in Lebanon I served on the eastern front. When I went back to Tel Aviv on the bus, riding down the main street I suddenly realized that this was not like any other war. In the previous wars all the country had been at war, this time it was only a minority that was involved in the war and people in the hinterland did not realize that there was a war going on. Nowadays it is the same.

> *Protesting the existence of victims in both sides.* There was a person in jail who had killed a Palestinian, and he had taken it very hard psychologically. He thought that the punishment that he received, two months in prison, was too light. *He was okay and acted in line with the regulations,* but instead of shooting in the air, he screamed first, then knelt down and directed his shots at the legs. The Palestinian was shot in the neck and killed.

> *Protesting the moral burden of the intifada.* When I came back from service there, the experience stayed with me for months and ever since I received this draft two months ago the feeling returned. I told myself I do reserve service twice a year and for three months

after that I would be in distress, which adds up to five months a year. That doesn't leave much time and I prefer to be disturbed for one month in prison, knowing that things are clear, rather than the alternative.

Protesting the possibility of burn out. I am in the middle of my life—I have another twenty years of army service ahead of me. I want to live in Israel, but in order to live here I also have to live in prison.

Protesting the vanishing identity of the Israeli soldier. For a long time I made concessions to myself, because I was offered alternative services by my company commander. In my civilian life I am active in creating communications between Israelis and Palestinians. It is less a feeling that we are against them and they are against us, more a feeling that we are in the same mud. I wanted to refuse before but things were not as clear as they are now. It is not some external force but rather a function of my maturation. Suddenly it was clear to me why I was refusing. From the point of view of the Palestinians, I try to see how the Israeli soldier looks to them—I think they look quite miserable and pathetic.

Protesting alienation. The Lebanon refusal was a luxurious refusal because the refusers knew it would be over in one or two years, both for those who refused and those who went there. With the Intifada nobody knows when it will end. I think that the Lebanon war proved to the Israeli people that the country no longer cared for its citizens . . . they can serve forever as long as they don't bother the establishment.

In sum, the data on the military experience of the refusers portrays them as dedicated soldiers with military experience, who individually considered the possibility of selective refusal in the territories even before the Intifada. Their activism and political awareness, as well as previous military experience prior to that conflict, seem to have broadened their vision regarding the long-term impact of selectively protesting military life in the face of morally controversial wars.

The Experience of Refusal

Table 6 gives another indication of the lonely manner in which refusal was constructed.

The table shows that the largest group of refusers in this sample emerged during the first year of the Intifada. Even though refusal was more of an option during the Intifada than in Lebanon, 79 per-

Table 6. The Refusal Experience (N = 48)

Single Refuser in the Unit	38(79%)
Time of Refusal	
Before Intifada	4(8%)
First Year	24(58%)
Second Year	6(13%)
Third Year	5(10%)
Fourth Year	5(10%)
Commander Invested Time	29(60%)
Wish to Return to the Unit	32(67%)
2–5 Refusals in Intifada	13(27%)
Removed from the Unit	27(57%)
Tried by Own Commander	13(27%)
Being Abroad before Refusal	14(29%)
Hoped to be Released without Prison	38(79%)
Refusal as a Protest	37(77%)
Refusal in Lebanon	9(19%)
Tried to Evade Service	13(27%)
Convincing Others	28(58%)
Affected by the Holocaust	31(65%)

cent of the refusing soldiers were the only refusers in their unit. Even when the soldier was not attached to the unit or to the commander, in 60 percent of the cases the commanders invested a great deal of time in trying to persuade the potential refusers not to refuse, and looked for an alternative to imprisonment. This factor could have contributed to the desire of 67 percent of the soldiers to return to their original unit.

It seems that even when the refusers chose to resolve their moral dilemmas during the Intifada in a lonely manner, inclusion remained an important factor for their sense of self. Commanders who were angry with their soldiers for letting others serve, and carry the burden of the refusers' conscience, tended to add another form of punishment to the refusing soldiers by not allowing them to return to the unit after prison. Other forms of severe punishment were the threat (and implementation) of repeated jailing.

Thus twenty-seven refusers (57 percent) were removed from their unit in addition to their imprisonment. A few were demoted. It is hard to know whether these responses that were supposedly aimed at detaching the refusers from the military setting, simply reflected the hostile atmosphere regarding refusal. It is possible that this response reflected the alienation between the commanders and the refusers, given the fact that 63 percent of the refusers were court-martialed by commanders who were new to them. Alternatively, it might be argued that, while the commanders were willing to invest time and listen to the refusers' claims, they seemed to be less tolerant in terms of concessions.

It is important to note that the tendency of the commanders to remove the refusing soldier from their unit was unique to the Intifada. During the war in Lebanon, many commanders viewed the moral refuser as a moral asset to the unit and wanted him to return to the unit after prison (Linn 1989b). It seems that the Intifada commanders were not as certain of the refusers' motivation. Perhaps related to this, they were not as willing to become better acquainted with the refusers. Given the fact that the IDF has never studied the refusers' claims and personal characteristics, nor informed the Intifada commanders about this phenomenon, it is questionable what kind of knowledge was available to the frustrated commanders during the Intifada.

From the refusers' comments during interviews, it looks as if the commanders during the Intifada tended to view refusal more as a tactic than a manifestation of moral distress. This view does not imply that the commanders were not considering the moral distress of the soldiers. Like most Israeli citizens, they were well aware of the morally problematic tasks faced by the IDF soldiers who were sent to suppress the Intifada. The question at stake for these commanders was not whether the soldier was experiencing moral distress but rather the question of moral commitment: given that the service was morally problematic for many, should the reservist have the right to assume some sort of morally superior position and leave the work to others?

The table shows that 79 percent of the refusers did not originally want to disobey, but rather wanted to serve elsewhere. This fact is most interesting given that 77 percent of the Intifada refusers viewed their refusal as a protest. About one-third of the refusers tried to evade service. The claim for having been motivated by personal reasons (Linn 1995b) thus gains another dimension with these data. It might be suggested that this inclination toward personal motivation for refusal (as compared with moral and/or political; see chapter 8) was a sign of a society without hope, a society whose citizens no longer wanted to exercise their lonely courage for suffering the consequences of the desire to preserve their own principles or to change state policy in times of a morally controversial war with no end in sight. Instead, by presenting mainly personal justifications (assuming they have the ability to view moral and political issues that are at stake) the refusers were making a kind of double protest. They were willing to be punished for assuming a separate position in face of injustice, and at the same time disregarded their society as deserving their moral or political claims. Interestingly, 27 percent of the refusers argued that they unsuccessfully tried to avoid service using various excuses such as illnesses or job difficulties (as compared with 8 percent of Lebanon refusers who tried to avoid service in the war zone by such means). Though they did not actively preach refusal, 58 percent of the refusers admitted that they tended to advise their morally puzzled friends to do so.

Nine (19 percent) refusers were already Lebanon refusers. Since 50 percent of the sample had served in Lebanon, one may argue that refusal during the Intifada was fueled not only by moral despair or noncompliance with the missions and the political policy of the government, but also by frustration regarding the effectiveness of public and straightforward refusal in the face of their previous experience in Lebanon. Thirty-one (65 percent) refusers referred to the Holocaust when reflecting about their decision-making process.

To summarize, the Intifada refuser might be portrayed as a realistic refuser, an experienced soldier who, unlike the Lebanon refuser, knew the personal price of refusal and its doubtful public effectiveness. He was motivated to refuse in order to avoid serving in a military force whose legitimacy in this given situation was questionable in his eyes. The refuser did not wish to be drawn into a situation where there was a likelihood that he would be forced to commit a flagrantly illegal command in the course of his service by having to shoot at a violent mob of women and children. Being more realistic than the Lebanon refuser, it seems the Intifada refuser did not fear the appearance of his action; he was less likely to seek external legitimization for his a priori refusal.

The Impact of Refusal

Table 7 presents demographics that describe the impact of re-fusal. The apparently blurred distinction between the army and civilian life obviously has its strengths, but it also has its worrying moments. Table 7 suggests that only 46 percent of the subjects dared to reveal their refusal in the work place. Only four refusers expected positive support. In a country where 70 percent of its industry is geared toward security products, a refuser might find himself an unwanted worker. Thus, it was surprising to find (for the subjects as well) that following their decision 44 percent of the refusers won a modicum of support or even admiration in their workplace, and even more so (77 percent) in their military units. Whereas refusal could be seen primarily as a protest, as thirty-seven (77 percent) of the refusers claimed it was, the fact that many (79 percent) hoped they would get away without prison seems to serve

Table 7. The Impact of Refusal (N = 48)

Voluntarily Told Workplace	22(46%)
Expected Positive Support	4(8%)
Postaction Positive Support	21(44%)
Received Admiration of Courage	37(77%)
Returned to the Reserves	43(89%)
Punishment Was Justified	24(50%)
Thinks the Severity of Punishment is Fair	35(73%)
Serving in the Reserve	43(89%)
Will Refuse to Fight against Syria	12(25%)
Justify Refusal Only in Intifada	17(37%)
Service Integral Part of Identity	23(48%)

as a partial explanation for the numerous pragmatic reasons for refusal raised by the subjects when asked to justify their action (see chapter 8).

On the whole, most (89 percent) returned to serve in the reserves and might be regarded as dedicated, though frustrated, soldiers. The credit for this seems partially due to the commanders, who often made great efforts to understand the refuser and give him a fair trial. The prison terms seemed to have increased the political awareness of the refusers, a fact that resulted in double the number of refusers becoming affiliated to the refusers' protest movements (60 percent) compared to the war in Lebanon (see table 5).

Retrospectively, regarding their action in the context of a legal system they supported, 50 percent of the refusers acknowledged that their punishment was justified and 73 percent thought that the length of punishment they received was just. Some of the Intifada refusers were also Lebanon refusers. Of those who were not, some were too young to refuse, others did not dare to. Most regarded the idea of refusal during the war in Lebanon as justified. Finally, unlike the myth regarding service in the army as an integral part of the Israeli male identity (Lieblich 1989), these data point toward some possible change in the construction of the moral identity of the Israeli male in which army service has a decreasing function: twelve (25 percent) of the refusers would not even have had faith in the order to join a war against Syria (the most aggressive and feared enemy of Israel at that time), and only twenty-three (48 percent) refusers considered the service in the IDF as an integral part of their identity.

Conclusion

The Israeli Intifada refuser tended to be an experienced soldier who had almost been brought to the brink of refusal by a previous morally controversial war. The refuser tended to be distressed by the need to encounter the civilian population as a soldier, by the prospect of having to perform illegal commands in a situation characterized by new moral codes, and by his overall lack of pride in being part of an occupying military force. His detachment from the unit, and probably his individualistic personal tendencies, helped him to translate his reluctance to serve into a factual position of refusal.

As we will see subsequently, the Intifada refuser seems to develop his criticism based on the precedence of his comrades during the war in Lebanon. Though refusal was an option during the Intifada, it was not a simple option. This option needs to be examined against a variety of other forms of criticism that prevailed during the Intifada. Some of these forms of criticism emerged from more connected positions than others. In describing these forms in the next chapter, attention is given not only to the construction of the position of criticism, but also to the probability of its success within a given system: should the objecting individual voice his concern within the system, or should he "exit" from this system and "voice" his criticisms outside it? The following chapter borrows the terms *voice* and *exit* from Hirschman's (1970) model of response to pressure for the analysis of the "critical distance" assumed by various separate or connected critics.

Of course someone may come and argue that I should protest as a civilian and not as a soldier if I want to advance a political cause. But you have to understand the fact that serving for one month a year in the army does not make me a soldier. Even when I am in the army I have the head of a civilian and I do not think I can act any other way. Israel is proud of the fact that the army is the nation's army but this is also our limitation, we are all involved and the involvement is deep.

—An Intifada refuser

6

Forms of Criticism

From "Voice" to "Exit"

This chapter tries to locate the action of selective refusal during the Intifada within the range of moral criticism during this conflict. For the sake of analysis, we choose to (partially) borrow the concepts of 'voice' and 'exit' from Hirschman's (1970) model of response to pressure in the world of business. In Hirschman's model, "loyalty," "voice," and "exit" represent three modes of response to declining participation in a social organization; the dissatisfied customer can select a course of action from one of these three basic options. "Loyalty" means choosing to remain silent, placing self-interest or commitment to the organization above the accountability of the event. "Voice" means choosing to speak out about the problem identified in the situation. It is an attempt to change rather than escape from the situation, and is seen as a political action par excellence. "Exit" means the act of leaving the organization; it is seen as an option of last resort.

This chapter, however departs from the model by regarding selective refusal of military service within the Israeli society during a war situation, as a form of exit rather than a form of voice as the conventional research of civil disobedience would indicate (Ben Noon 1990; Gans 1992; Sheleff 1988). We will argue that within the psychology of moral connection and given the unique Israeli setting, it is possible to view exit as and extended form of voice (Linn, 1995c).

According to Walzer (1977), resistance to participating in a given war might be seen as minimizing one's own danger at the expense of others: "To disobey is . . . to claim a moral separateness (or moral superiority) to challenge one's fellows, (and) perhaps even to intensify the dangers they face" (p. 315). Thus, the study of selective refusal is primarily a study of the decision to separate oneself from the shared understanding of that society as a form of "moral selfishness" (Walzer 1968, p. 14), or the study of exit as a moral position. Walzer's claim of moral separateness is particularly applicable to the Israeli society with its emphasis on a collective moral orientation along the life cycle of the individual (Levy 1990; Linn and Gilligan 1990, Peleg 1990, Student 1991; Sobel 1986). We argue that fearing to lose their moral identity (which they constructed in a connected form) dissatisfied Israeli reservists would be inclined to assume various positions of criticism before they choose to exit themselves from an instituion (the IDF) that enjoys the highest consensus in the country (Gal 1986). We would argue that the Israeli reservist would prefer channeling his protest in the form of voice before assuming a position of exit, since the position of exit is an extremely (morally) painful one that some decision makers would try to avoid. The forms of criticism under review are presented as following inner developmental phases:

I. Voice
Ia. *Primary Voice*—direct protest of reservists
A. Protesting the physical burden of the service
B. Protesting the moral burden of the service
  i. protesting the nature of the commands
  ii. protesting the alienation
  iii. protesting the duty in morally problematic sites and military roles
  iv. protest movements
  v. protesting Holocaust symbols and metaphors (see chapter 7)
Ib. *Secondary Voice*—individual and group protest on behalf of fighting soldiers

II. Exit
IIa. *Internal Exit*—refusal of military service
  i. 'White' refusal (see chapter 4)
  ii. 'Gray' refusal
IIb. *External Exit*—rejection of life in Israel
  i. Emigration (in Hebrew *yerida*—literally *descent*)
  ii. Suicide

Analysis

I. Voice

Ia. *Primary Voice*—direct protest of reservists

A. Protesting the physical burden of the service

> When the load is easy to bear, the inequality in the division of burden hurts your sense of justice, but does not bother you too much. If two people have to carry a load of two libras together, one of them will be able to carry it alone. But if the load is 400 libras, there is a need to divide the load equally, otherwise, the person who has to carry the load by himself will collapse and the mission will not be performed."

These words, by Louis XVI's Minister of the Treasury, uttered 216 years ago, appear in a detailed letter sent by 100 fighting reservists during the Intifada who complained about the burden of reserve service. It was organized by Chaim Mendelson, a reservist, who was an artillery major in Northern Command and a lawyer in civilian life. "As long as the State of Israel is in a state of peace," writes Mendelson, "the burden of the reserves is not high. Its weight is like two libras, and even if it is not distributed equally, it does not bother anyone too much. However, when the State of Israel is in the position of participating in a 'small war' as in Lebanon or the Intifada, there is a need for more reserve units to discharge the current security duties. Mendelson was surprised that the majority of people are quick to raise their voices against the ultra-orthodox and the way they evade service, but few talk about "gray" refusers (those who evade service through the employment of a variety of counterfeit excuses). The above letter was sent on 5 June 1991 to the Minister of Defense, Moshe Arens. His response was to inform Mendelson that his unit was doing the same reserve service as any other reserve unit. No response came from the Chief of Staff. On 20 January 1993 it was reported by the newspaper *Chadashot* that "the Chief of Staff is still reading the letter."

Ron Shamir, a second-year electrical engineering student at the University of Tel Aviv was an excellent student prior to the Intifada. Two months after the start of the Intifada (December 1987) he was called for a month of reserve service, which coincided with the exam period in the second semester. As a reserve major who was a company commander in the armoured division, he wanted to continue his studies as well as maintaining his moral obligation as a citizen (i.e., to accomplish his reserve service and/or not to refuse service):

> Of course I could have applied to Valtam (the IDF committee for coordinating a release) but my "(morally) twisted" perception of the world prevented me from doing so. I am a company commander. Under my command there are sixty soldiers. They all come to me with problems and ask to be released. How can I refuse their requests on the one hand and release myself on the other? This would not be moral. This was not simply a routine reserve service. It occurred during the hardest part of Intifada. This is not a period of war in which each person fully sacrifices himself, but a period associated with hard inner emotional dilemmas. I cannot see myself sending my soldiers for a month of reserve service while I am sitting at home. (*Chadashot,* 25 December 1988)

During the term of service, Ron took one day of vacation, wrote the exams, and miraculously passed all but one of them. During the following semester he was again called for duty and once more his term of service fell during the date of his exams. This time he failed and had to temporarily abandon his studies, forfeiting his course fees. When he wrote to army officials, their response cynically questioned why he had not applied to Valtam. Ron reflects on the event:

> There is no equal share of the burden when only 2 or 3 percent of the population perform this amount of reserve service. I do not ask anybody to salute me for doing it, but I think that they could have some consideration. The simple thing to do would be to leave the service at the front line and become a driver in the rear. Then I would be able to apply to Valtam without any feelings of guilt. I feel like I am in a Catch 22 situation. Everybody says: "Apply to Valtam." I did not apply and consequently I am thrown out of my studies. (*Chadashot,* 25 December 1988)

Ron describes the feeling of alienation as follows:

> I wanted to ask the Dean if he had ever done reserve duty. He gave me the impression that he did not know what I was talking about. I wonder what percentage of students do reserve service . . . the only source of encouragement that I had was from my fellow reservists at my rank who were stuck in the same mud. (*Chadashot,* 25 December 1988)

The increased service demands since the 1982 Lebanese war (not taking into account the moral dilemmas they entailed), resulted in mounting questions among the reservists as to the necessity of reserve duty and its nature. One reservists wrote to the press:

> How long must Israeli citizens be exposed to unlimited army service until the age of fifty-five? And all without taking into account the tasks the citizen is obliged to perform; the lack of privileges that he has as a reservist and more recently his transformation into an officer who is routinely called to serve the occupation. (*Ha'aretz,* 26 April 1988)

An adult education teacher wrote to the press:

> I see my students miss three months a year when called upon to attend two tours of reserve service a year. They hardly catch up with their studies. (*Ha'aretz,* 30 January 1990)

The interference of reserve service in individual civilian life has been well known, although never systematically studied. Naturally, prolonged service seems to affect those who are dissatisfied with reserve duty more than those who are not. The resulting vulnerability of reservists is barely discussed in the military life of the Israelis. For example, on 11 September 1988, the IDF discovered some medical officers who discharged potential reservists who wished to avoid service. One reservist was quick to write to the press about his temptation to avoid service:

> If the army were sensitive to the professional needs of the individual, less soldiers would ask for release . . . not necessarily from the daily difficulties, economic or family problems, but the feeling that you are not needed in the system and are being thrown into the gutter of the IDF. (*Chadashot,* 22 September 1988)

One example of this insensitivity can be found among others in the recent use of reservists as building inspectors for expensive villas being built for career officers near Tel Aviv (*Yediot Acharonot,* 4 April 1992). But even those who usually find fulfillment in their service are not immune to the harm done by the excessive service demands or the time needed for readjustment from service to civilian life, particularly if the duty was a morally problematic one. A reservist wrote to the press during the Intifada:

> I wanted to study to be a technical engineer . . . but I was afraid it would be complicated. This is my seventh tour in the territories (starting in 1988) . . . and I have a family with two children. . . . I would become a refuser if it would not hurt my family and my

> studies. I would become a refuser not only due to the wrongdoing in the territories but also because the reserve is ruining my life—my studies have been so prolonged because of the reserves, twice already my tour has been during exam time. It is true that sometimes you get a day off in order to do your exams, but who has a head for studying for exams between *gas and stones* [emphasis added]. (*Chadashot*, 2 April 1990)

The unequal share of the burden bothered the reservists in Lebanon (Linn 1989b) but became an issue of protest during the Intifada. Reservists and their wives formed an organization they named "Netel Miluim Savir" (NMS), which yields a double meaning in Hebrew: phonetically it sounds like NIMAAS meaning "we've had it," while its literal meaning is "reasonable load of service." In their appeal, the reservists and their wives indicated that service in the territories was an emotional burden more than a physical one and that they would be happy to serve the country on other frontiers as well as the Intifada. They also argued that their complaints regarding their load of service were rejected with official responses like: "You are needed by the army" (*Ha'aretz*, 10 November 1989).

The physical burden increases the reservists' realization of the discrepancy between those who serve and those who (for unknown reasons) do not serve. For example, soldiers and officers from a reserve unit who served 135 days (four rounds) within the territories and were later ordered an additional twenty-two days, anonymously wrote to the press:

> We have a feeling that the Intifada is being approached by a few battalions taking turns, dealt with whereas most of the other units in the IDF and men in Israeli society continue to live their lives as usual . . .

One of the commanders added:

> I work for a company where, in my judgment, there are 240 workers who are eligible for reserves. I see only fifteen who are called up for reserve duty at this excessive rate. (*Ha'aretz*, 18 June 1989)

Not long after, two armoured companies protested, campaigning in favor of a balanced burden of reserve service, defining themselves as "career reservists" (*Ma'ariv*, 9 April 1990). Acknowledging the heavy load, the Chief of Staff suggested reducing the tax burden for those who serve long periods (i.e., over forty-five days a year). This suggestion was turned down by the treasury, which argued that this move would cost 8 million Israeli shekels per year (*Davar*, 21 September 1989).

The decreasing motivation of the reservists to serve cannot be dissociated from excessive terms of service. This load is twice that for reservists with special family needs even if called to serve within the Green Line (*Ha'aretz*, 25 May 1990). Not surprisingly, when fighting for their rights, reservists give the situation of the ultra-orthodox as their moral frame of reference. Thus for example, the former adult education teacher mentioned above asked why the Treasury allocated six million shekels to raise the army compensation pension for the ultra-orthodox, who had never served in the army, instead of lowering the soldiers' taxes (*Ha'aretz*, 30 January 1990). One reservist observed:

> In the long history of our country, not all Israeli people have taken an equal share in the extraordinary burden of national security . . . why doesn't the comptroller examine how many people are not part of the effort that many believe to be the central backbone of the building of our nation? (*Yediot Acharonot*, 24 June 1990)

The dual roles of the Israeli reservist is a familiar fact for the Arabs in the territories. Their rationale for throwing stones at civilian journalists is this: "Today you are a journalist and tomorrow you will be doing reserve service" (*Chadashot*, 13 December 1989). The Intifada has become "the reservists' war of attrition" (*Jerusalem Post*, 3 February 1989) due to its heavy physical and moral burden. Interestingly, this label was shared by the Arabs. In the words of one of their leaders, Kadumi, through this "war of attrition . . . it is hoped to change the mentality of Israel" (*Ha'aretz*, 6 May 1990). The Arab Intifada activists were well aware of the moral vulnerability of the Israeli reservists, as one of them stated to the press:

> Our role is to have your army stay in the area all the time. . . . There are now tens of thousands of soldiers in the territories. . . . So you will need the reserves. And the reserves means an economic collapse of the civilian market, horror stories and accumulation of bitterness. Time is on our side. (*Chadashot*, 4 March 1988)

Research findings seem to support the Arab's observation. In a study on Israeli "burn out" during the Intifada (Pines 1990), 72 percent of the officers who had direct contact with the rioting population described themselves as stressed by it. One reservist supports these findings as well:

> Reserve duty means burden, often a heavy one and sometimes very heavy. Sometimes it is made more burdensome when soldiers are not treated as they would like to be treated. So I suggest that you do not casually call it "The nation's army" . . . sometimes it is not so. (*Yediot Acharonot*, 24 June 1990)

The accumulation of service may take its toll on the readiness of the underpaid long-term reservists. When scolded by a career officer for not being on alert in Gaza, a reservist responded: "How many years can you hold your hand onto the rifle butt? Ten years? fifteen years? The hand is tired" (*Yediot Acharonot*, 12 December 1990).

B. Protesting the moral burden of the service

The most notable measure of Israeli reservists' moral commitment and motivation was traditionally found at international airports in times of war—reservists competing over seats in the Israeli airlines in order to return and join their fighting units before the war was over. This was the case during the 1967 and 1973 wars. Few returned during the first phase of the war in Lebanon and no one is known to have returned to fight in the Intifada.

Within the Israeli chronic state of war, Peace activists were regarded as political altruists (Hertz-Lazarovitz 1993). Before the 1967 war, public criticism of the army was a nonsignificant issue. Those few soldiers who refused to serve in the army prior to the Lebanon war were mostly regarded as (and often were) political activists, extremists, communists, or insane (Blatt, Davis, and Kleinbaum 1975). Even during the 1967–1970[1] long and forgotten war of attrition, criticism of the army was not done in a direct form. In spite of the long service, lack of equipment, and, partially, in face of indifferent high-ranking command, to the general public it was clear who the enemy was. The only outlet to the frustrating situation of heavy casualties and stagnation in the political sphere awaiting the reservists was found in the form of loyalty: the decision of experienced reservists (known as "tigers") to take upon themselves an extra load of service. They joined the commanders along the Suez Canal in order to help them in their hard task of sustaining the military line. No massive demonstrations occurred when Israeli jets systematically bombed the Egyptian cities along the Suez Canal. Soldiers were led to believe that they were stationed for long periods in the bunkers in order to help the government gain political strength for when the Arabs would be ready to negotiate peace for land. Life in Israel continued as usual while far away along the Suez Canal death was a daily event. No award was ever given by the army to those who were fighting this war (which was not termed as a war). Though the toll of that war exceeds the toll of the Six Day War, it became the least remembered and least documented war in Israeli military history. The lack of criticism from the Israeli side throughout the War of Attrition was one of the signals used by the Egyptians when trying to assess whether the IDF was on the alert on the eve of the Yom Kippur war (Heikal 1975).

The first wave of public criticism against the army, emerged following the 1973 surprise war attack from Egypt and Syria. Combat reservists protested the government ineptitude. They demanded and succeeded in forming a committee of inquiry about the war and brought about an eventual change in government (Sprinzak 1977). The public voicing of criticism during the 1982 war in Lebanon, while it was still going on, seems to reflect also the accumulation of moral distress among soldiers since the 1973 Yom Kippur war. This distress was heightened in light of the peace with Egypt, when the possibility of conflict resolution in other means than war was seen, for the first time, as possible—though not simple. The timing of this criticism (the ongoing war) and its target (not only the government but also the army as well as Israeli society at large) suggest that the critics considered their audience resilient enough to be exposed to their words without lowering their morale or ability to fight.

Being "neither a guerrilla war nor a terror campaign" but rather a small war (Inbar 1991) the Intifada primarily needed policing work for which the average Israeli reservist was not trained. The immediate response to this new type of pressure was in the form of loyalty. Mature reservists from all walks of life initiated a group of Intifada "tigers": they took upon themselves an extra load of service, joining the young commanders in their confusing missions. They were later asked by the IDF to quit fearing the politization of the army. The new tigers left, but the moral burden remained. With time, the moral complexity increased. It resulted in various forms of moral protest:

i. Protesting the nature of the commands

The surprised and confused military chain of command viewed the Intifada as sporadic demonstrations. Soldiers were instructed not to harm the civilians but to use tear gas in order to disperse the demonstrations. After this stage, they were allowed to use rubber bullets, plastic bullets, and then live ammunition if rioters refused to disperse. Most morally problematic was the encounter with violent women and children who were used as the spearhead of the riots, and who often held deadly devices (such as petrol bombs or heavy blocks, axes, etc.). The IDF regulations were changed daily. Soldiers were instructed not to use regular bullets but plastic ones (less harmful but also less accurate at a range of over fifteen meters), and to fire only at the legs of rioters; live ammunition was to be used if rioters appeared be over the age of sixteen and over a distance of seventy meters, and then only if the bullet was directed at the legs.

To this confusion one must add the factor that the Minister of Defense issued a policy of beating (see chapter 3) and assured the soldiers that he was responsible for that policy (*Yediot Acharonot*, 29 January 1988). Yet he refused to admit his responsibility for this policy in the trials of soldiers who transgressed (known as Givati A and B military trials, see Straschnov 1994). He later admitted that he failed to estimate the depth and magnitude of the phenomenon (*Ha'aretz*, 29 November 1990). After he left office, the Chief of Staff argued that he would be pleased if a new law were enacted that would prevent the prosecution of soldiers who were caught acting in a deviant manner (or even when literally obeying the commands) during the first "black two months of the Intifada" (*Ha'aretz*, 19 October 1990). The "black two months" were followed by new updated regulations by the Chief of Staff:

> IDF soldiers are obliged to act decisively and with self-control, sensitivity and reservation that would fit the highest moral standards according to which the IDF and its commanders are obliged to behave. . . . It is forbidden to use force after the accomplishment of the task, after dispersing demonstrators, or when there is no resistance to our forces. (*Yediot Acharonot*, 24 February 1988)

The ambiguity of commands as well as the unrealistic new regulations have taken their toll among the best of the soldiers: if they do not respond to the violent mob they may lose their own life and if they respond, they may (most likely) hurt innocent Arabs, which is morally and legally wrong. Not knowing with any certainty whether the person he is facing is the (official) enemy, the soldier's growing fear of misjudgment often results in his cynically claiming that he cannot serve without an "attached lawyer." Although there have been recurrent demands to define the Intifada as a war after each bloody incident (*Ha'aretz*, 20 February 1989), but to this day it has never officially been regarded as the "seventh war" (Gal 1990; Lissak 1990; Peri 1993).

For example, on 3 May 1988, the reserve company of sergeant Arev found itself involved in a massive, violent demonstration in the village of Beni Nai, near Hebron. The career colonel commanding the area said to the reservists in Arev's unit, "Here we have a war" (*Yediot Acharonot*, 20 October 1989). The soldiers of the unit had live ammunition as well as rubber bullets. The company commander ordered them to act "without live bullets," which some heard as "with live bullets." Arev killed two Arab rioters while chasing them when another section of the company was trapped; he was subsequently charged, since he killed Arabs who were fleeing from him, not ones who were threatening his life. Arev was convicted by a military court and sentenced to one and a half years in jail. For the first time in the country's history, infantry reservists who served in the territories demonstrated against the Minister of Defense on the grounds that "the orders were ambiguous." They argued that the orders did not specify the conditions for shooting and that "it is not possible for soldiers to be indicted when their commanders give orders only to withdraw from them later" (*Ha'aretz*, 26 October 1989). Lacking definitions, training, and backing, the reservists (who came from all political parties) protested:

> When we wear our uniform we place the army before everything. We forget politics . . . we are betrayed soldiers. We have done what we were obliged to do and now we pay the price for the politicians. (*Yediot Acharonot*, 20 October 1989)

The protest did not help. Arev's appeal was not accepted (*Ha'aretz*, 9 January 1992). The career colonel was dismissed from the army. The hesitancy of individual soldiers to use live ammunition, even in life-threatening situations, reached its peak on the eve of the Hebrew New Year, September 1990, when a thirty-year-old reservist was burned alive by Arab rioters following a car accident in the Gaza Strip.

To the ambiguity of the commands one must add the confusion of the high-ranking command, as reported by this reservist who returned from the Gaza Strip:

> The mission as detailed to the soldiers is not to overpower the Intifada but to lower the degree of the violence. How do you

lower the volume of the violence? How can the unit know if it has succeeded in following the mission successfully compared with the previous unit when the only measure available is the level of nervousness of the lonely soldier in a lonely alley who is facing a ten-year-old child who curses the soldier's mom? . . . The pockets of the commanders are becoming cracked from the stockpile of commands in them. The folders of information written by the Chief of Staff are interspersed with the instruction pages of the brigade commander . . . There is a special booklet regulating how to open fire and how to deal with women. New regulations are being substituted and replacing old ones, and every few weeks new regulations are being distributed. Commanders have in their pockets lists of names of rioters, together with replacement Identity cards for every person whose Identity card is taken from him. Finally, there is a command that authorizes closure of the area cordoned off by the division commander. To all of these, one must add the dozens of verbal regulations and commands that override the written commands. New soldiers who arrive in the territories go through hours of instruction until the mind refuses to absorb any more information. The main issue is that everything is covered and nothing is forgotten. If there is an inquiry committee, no one would be able to argue that things have not been said and that soldiers have not been warned. The logical decision has remained intact and the soldiers guided by fear and fatigue. (*Ha'aretz*, 12 December 1990)

ii. Protesting the alienation

It is important to remeber that unlike some other soldiers in the world the Israeli refuser is "faced with two additional constraints prior to his personal ability to translate his objection to a specific war into the action of refusal. One is related to the daily physical threat regarding the survival of the state of Israel . . . the other is the realization that the army is a necessity and life in Israeli means reserve service as a primary civil obligation" (Linn 1989b, p. 137). Yet, since the war in Lebanon, the Israeli soldier seems to dare not only to question the validity of these constraints, but to do it publicly rather than in private (Katriel 1985). Thus for example, when asked by the media about their feelings, some paratroopers during the long and forgotten war in Lebanon answered using a play on words of a children's song, "Come over to our airplane and take our coffins to Sharon (the Minister of Defense during the Lebanon war)" (Shinhar 1989). Similarly during the Intifada, one televised reserve paratrooper stationed in Nablus told the Prime Minister that "It is not possible that you know what we are going through if they (the career military commanders) *do not know*" (*Yediot Acharonot*, 18 April 1989). The reservist was later rebuked by Major General Amram Mitzna, head of central command (although himself a known critic of the Lebanon war). In a letter to the press, this reservist further explained the long-term impact of his alienation:

Shooting and Defecating

> One of the saddest experiences for someone returning from a stint of army service in the territories is to see how many friends and relatives simply don't want to hear what you saw or did there. At first you see the blank look in the eyes, you understand that your story isn't sinking in, and you think that maybe there's something wrong with the way you're telling it. It takes a while to realize that the blank look appeared the moment you began your story. It is not from lack of sympathy or understanding on the listener's part; it is simply an obstinate refusal to know—a generalized refusal that is possibly the worst casualty the Intifada has inflicted on this country.
>
> On January 17, Prime Minister Yitzhak Shamir came to Nablus for a short visit. After taking a look at the city from a nearby hilltop and being briefed by his generals, he dropped in for a friendly chat with soldiers serving in the area. The most surprising thing about that meeting between the Prime Minister and the paratroopers was that Mr. Shamir seemed genuinely surprised by what he heard there. Stark reality had suddenly struck him in the face, and the anger and impatience that could be seen in his eyes and hands were as much a result of the words he was hearing as of the fact that for several long minutes he was forced to listen and to know.
>
> During the previous evening, when we were told that the Prime Minister would be arriving the following morning and that he would probably be coming to see us, a few men had joked about what they would tell him should the opportunity arise. Next day we were given that opportunity, and some of us got up and spoke.
>
> There were many things I would have liked to tell Mr. Shamir on that sunny morning in Nablus. I would have liked to tell him about my democratic values and what compulsory military service in an occupied city can do to them; I would have liked to speak of how the Palestinians are getting stronger day by day, morally and

spiritually, while we are getting weaker, and I would have liked to scream and cry about how our army is being sullied, corroded and undermined by the impossible task the government has given it.

In the end, having only a couple of minutes at my disposal, I only said that as far as I could see, there was no way that he and the men around him could know what is really happening in the field, when even battalion and company commanders have no way of knowing exactly what soldiers are doing when they are out on patrol.

Now, however, I can sit at home with time to spare and fantasize for a while on what I would have told Mr. Shamir, had I been granted a few minutes more of his time.

To begin with, I would have explained that when I said he and his men don't know what is actually going on in the area, I had two things in mind. The first is that no one can really know what the whole thing is about until he personally goes there, puts a helmet and a visor on his head and goes out to see and feel the place for himself.

You can read the papers, watch the news on television, and you can even do your best to imagine what the soldier and the Arabs are going through. But until you see a three-year-old girl crying hysterically simply because she sees you approaching down the street; until you see a grown man literally shaking all over just because you've asked him for his ID card; in short, until you see and smell and hear the fear and the hate and the anger, it all remains abstract and distant and not too urgent.

The second thing I had in mind was that the daily reality of the occupation is immensely complex, being made up of tens of thousands of individual encounters between thousands of soldiers and thousands of Arabs at check points, in demonstrations, and on the streets and alleys of villages, towns, and refugee camps.

The exceptional results of each day's encounters are known to us all: we read the statistics of dead and wounded in the press. But these are only the newsworthy exceptions; the fuller picture, which never reaches any of us, would appear as follows: two Arabs dead, five wounded, 154 kicked, 256 slapped and 97 made an example of and humiliated.

Having a citizen's army means that all kinds of men reach the territories; far too many of them arrive there with problems and frustrations that they find all too easy to vent on the local population. Naturally, when these Rambos return to their base, they see no reason for reporting their actions to their commanding officers.

Another issue I would have liked to raise with Mr. Shamir was the use and abuse of plastic bullets against young stone throwers.

The orders we were given in this regard were very explicit: every stone-throwing incident must end either in an arrest or in a stone thrower with a plastic bullet in his leg. At the same time, we must do our best not to kill anyone; the army has finally understood that every time an Arab is killed, it is they and not we who have scored another point.

Yet carrying out these orders is not as easy as it may sound. Catching children and teenagers who are playing against you in their home court can be almost impossible, and hitting a running youth at 70 meters with a plastic bullet under the knee (those are the regulations) is extremely difficult.

The plastic bullet is much lighter than its steel-coated cousin and therefore, although it is not as lethal, it is far less accurate. Nevertheless, in spite of these difficulties, during the twenty days we spent in the Casba in Nablus, we did exactly as we were told: we killed no one and we hit seventeen Arab youths in the leg with plastic bullets.

These seventeen kids, and the men who shot them, deserve a few comments. The first is to repeat that all these youths and children were hit in the leg, most of them under the knee. To put this accomplishment in perspective, it should be noted that during the past few months, more than forty people have been killed by plastic bullets, while hundreds more have been seriously injured.

Had only three or four people been hit by our unit, one could contend that our accuracy was a stroke of luck. Seventeen woundings, however, without even one serious injury, cannot be attributed to mere chance, and the army should check case by case, with lie detectors if necessary: why is it that so many people have been killed by plastic bullets? Is it because our troops don't know how to shoot—or is it that some of them can shoot all too well?

In addition, the politicians at the top should know that today there is a blatant contradiction between the oral order given in the field—to shoot or arrest every possible stone thrower—and the written order to shoot in the air before you fire a plastic bullet.

The trouble here is that by shooting in the air before you shoot plastic, you can make things difficult for yourself. In order to hit these kids, you must stalk and ambush them, and the shot in the air, which may scare them away (as was intended by those who wrote the order) can become an irrelevant nuisance.

This contradiction is often resolved by having someone shoot in the air while someone else fires a plastic bullet; the main thing is to be legally "covered." The third and final comment is that none of these seventeen youths was shot in self-defense: they were all shot as a punishment for throwing stones. The moral implications of this fact are there for everyone to reflect on: we did our best to obey orders, we kept the city quiet, but in the process we intentionally wounded seventeen people who never really endangered us.

One of the remarks that was repeated over and over in the meeting with Mr. Shamir was that while we are getting weaker, the Palestinians are getting stronger. I think this contention is especially important for convincing the rational rightists among us that the time has come to leave the territories.

In this country, there are two kinds of people who define themselves as right wingers. There are those for whom the Land of Israel is sacred and must be kept under Jewish control at any cost, and there are those for whom holding on to the West Bank is simply a matter of security.

With the former group there is nothing to talk about; with the latter, on the other hand, one can have a discussion on their own terms. These are people who understand that Israel's security rests primarily on its military force. Should the army be considerably weakened, "strategic depth" and "natural borders" would not count for much.

In spite of this, the armed forces are now forced to spend millions of dollars on a lost war instead of investing in new weapons systems. Unfortunately, this is not all. Money, material and training are undoubtedly important, but if an army marches on its stomach, it stands on its discipline and morale. And today the army's discipline is being attacked on two fronts.

On the one hand, too many young recruits are left for long days with too much freedom and too much power in their hands, without being supervised by their commanders. Anyone who has served in the army will understand how potentially catastrophic this can be: orders to young soldiers are almost meaningless if they are not supported by the observant eye of noncoms and officers. On the other hand, too many soldiers have seen their own officers openly disregarding or even disobeying the army's laws. In regular fighting units, where officers are often regarded as semi-divine, nothing more destructive could be imagined.

The end result of this overall situation is that the best and the brightest young officers now serving in the army will gradually opt out of a career in a demoralized, inefficient, and undisciplined force. Who wants a career with an army that has been involved in a petty civil war for four out of the last five and one-half years?

The last point I would have raised with the Prime Minister, in the hope that he could have done something about it, is a mere trifle compared to all the above. Everyday, several observation

> points are set up on various roofs in and around Nablus. The soldiers who man these posts usually stay out from sunrise to sunset. They eat there, they watch the city awake and trade and work, and sooner or later they also have to defecate. But there are no toilets on the roofs of these buildings, and so the soldiers have to make do with landings, rooftops and abandoned rooms. The results can be appalling.
>
> On one building where I was stationed for a few days, large areas of the roof was covered with a coat of excrement and used toilet paper. Unfortunately, the building's tenants have to hang their laundry on that roof. Believe me, Mr. Prime Minister, it's not a pretty sight to see a middle-aged woman from a good family making her way through piles of feces to reach her laundry.
>
> When we asked the brigade commander in charge of Samaria if anything could be done about this problem, we received the usual answer: "no money for chemical toilets."
>
> The trouble of course, is that if the woman in question had been Jewish instead of Arab, no one would even have thought of using her roof as a public lavatory. (*Jerusalem Post*, 21 February 1989)

Two weeks after this dramatic meeting with the reservists in Nablus, the Prime Minister came to observe IDF military exercises. Soldiers in compulsary service were asked to raise questions. None of them dared to do so in spite of encouragement from their commanders (*Ha'aretz*, 9 November 1989).

iii. Protesting the service in morally problematic sites and positions

Since the war in Lebanon, prison guard duty became the military role that evoked the most frequent and strongest objections. During the war in Lebanon, the PLO prison camp, Ansar, built by Israel on Lebanese soil, became a symbol of moral paradoxes and recorded the largest percentage of refusals (Linn 1989b). Kziot, the Intifada rioter prison camp in Israel inherited the name Ansar as well as moral paradoxes. It reached the point where some reservists required medical treatment when they mentally collapsed during service there (*Chadashot*, 17 January 1992). For many Israeli soldiers, service in prison and as prison guards was more morally distressing than any other, due to the heavy cultural load of the Holocaust (see chapter 7).

The Gaza Strip became a major site on which there was a growing consensus of objection that cut across political affiliations. For example, a group of twelve paratroopers who completed seventy days in one year as reservists during the Intifada (including one month in Gaza), wrote to the Prime Minister as follows:

> Dear Prime Minister,
>
> Issue: The presence of the IDF in the Gaza Strip.
>
> We are a group of officers who have just finished our reserve service in the Gaza Strip. We want to protest as citizens of this country who represent various political opinions, against the deployment of the IDF in the Gaza Strip. According to our assessment, there is neither a logical, economic or military basis to rule 750,000 inhabitants in the area. This control increases the tremendous hatred between the nations involved and there is no solution. We ask that IDF forces be removed from the Strip, as a unilateral action on the part of Israel. (*Ma'ariv*, 7 December 1990)

Another protest letter was sent by thirty-two reservists from an armoured unit. One of the signatories, right-wing in his political ideas, argued in an interview following this protest:

> We did not kill anyone (during our service in Gaza) . . . We did not break any heads. But when you are stationed there for a whole month you start to understand why there are so many infringements that bring people to court-martial.
>
> This is a frustrating reserve duty. I want to be sure that the person who sends me there knows what he wants me to do there, apart from my being a moving target to the Intifada Forces. (*Yediot Acharonot*, 7 December 1990)

A career officer who responded to the complaint signalled the growing detachment between the army official and the reservists:

> Your protest touches upon a political problem and therefore I cannot answer it. History tells us that armies that were caught in similar situations fell apart. I am glad to say that this phenomenon has not happened to the IDF. (*Yediot Acharonot*, 7 December 1990)

iv. Protest movements

The initial attempt to escape the "Lebanon Mud" (*Chadashot*, 10 February 1989) was manifested in the construction of protest groups. This infrastructure already existed for those who decided to publicly voice their moral or political concerns during the Intifada, and provided an incentive for the emergence of new protest groups. The following are those protest movements that were directly organized by reservists (primary voice). In the next section the protest movements that were organized on behalf of reservists will be discussed (secondary voice).

The Committee against the War in Lebanon—Originally founded prior to the war in Lebanon in order to protest the official policy in the territories. In June 1982 it changed its name and goals to protest the war in Lebanon. It was composed of Communists, extreme leftists, and some professors at Tel Aviv University, including some who regarded themselves as anti-Zionist.

Soldiers against Silence—Founded a month after the start of the Lebanon war, when three officers and a pilot who participated in the bombing of Beirut met at a journalist's home in Tel Aviv and declared they were not prepared to die in such a war. A few weeks later, their action seemed to serve as an incentive for a spontaneous demonstration drawing some 15,000 people.

No to the Ribbon—Composed of a group of reserve soldiers who had fought in Lebanon and who urged those who had also served there to reject the campaign ribbon issued by the government.

Protest Vigils in Front of the Prime Minister's House—A group of individuals, also members of other protest movements, stood in front of Begin's house holding a placard with the number of war casualties, changing as the number grew, in order to keep the Prime Minister "informed."

Peace Now—The biggest and the best organized group during the war in Lebanon. Its roots go back to 1978 when reserve officers sent a letter to the Prime Minister urging the government to make peace with Egypt. The group was not active during the first three weeks of the Lebanon war either because most of its members, dedicated fighting reservists, were in the army or because it supported the strategy of the campaign that included a limited fight against the PLO terrorists. It called on the government to withdraw from Lebanon but required its people to perform reserve service and protest in democratic ways as civilians. Its activities culminated in urging the government to establish a commission of inquiry following the massacre at the Sabra and Shatilla camps. This brought almost half a million people into the streets and resulted in the dismissal of the Defense Minister. During the Intifada, the movement urged the implementation of peace talks with the Palestinians and initiated various talks and meetings between Palestinians and Israelis. Throughout the two conflicts Peace Now activists and supporters emphasized that they were "part of the national consensus and took positions that were publicly Zionist" (*Davar,* 18 August 1988).

Although they warned the public about the moral dilemmas faced by the soldiers serving in the territories and did not advocate refusal of military service, they could empathize with the moral distress facing the soldiers who took this position (Linn 1991). The thrust of their opposition against refusal sprang from the fear that such action would legitimize and pave the way for ideological objection by the right (those who may later protest withdrawal from the territories if and when a peace agreement would be achieved). They also feared that close contact to Yesh Gvul (the refusers' movement) would obscure the legitimacy of Peace Now in the eyes of moderate Israelis. The labor party Minister of Defense who suppressed the Intifada (Rabin) was not sharply criticized by Peace Now either. In both conflicts, some reservists who decided to refuse military service were identified as exmembers of Peace Now who claimed that its conventional modes of protest were quite anemic (Linn 1989b). During the Intifada, Peace Now demanded direct talks with the PLO.

Yesh Gvul (there is a limit)—Began as a protest against service in the territories shortly before the Lebanon war. It came about on the first day of the war and evolved into an ad hoc movement pertaining to Lebanon, advocating refusal to serve there as the right moral action. Its members were mainly reservists, some of whom prior to the Lebanon war had refused to serve in the territories. A letter signed by both reserve officers and men, which was sent to the Prime Minister and the Minister of Defense, contained the policy of the movement:

> We (15) officers and (71) soldiers in the reserve ask you not to send us to Lebanon as we can no longer handle it. We have killed and been killed too much in this war. We conquered, bombed and destroyed. Why? Today it is clear to us: through the use of war and military force you try to solve the Palestinian problem. But there is no solution to this type of problem. You are trying to force a new arrangement on Lebanon and to kill and be killed for the Phalanges (the Christian forces allied with the IDF, R.L.). You lied to us! You spoke of 40 km and you came 40 km from Damascus and entered Beirut. And still another bloody road awaits us: conquest, resistance, oppression. Instead of *peace for the Galilee*, you brought us war without end. For this war, these lies and this occupation there is no national consensus. Bring the soldiers home! We swear to defend the peace and security of the country of Israel. We are committed to this oath. Therefore we entreat you to allow us to

perform the reserve service on Israeli soil, not in the Land of Lebanon. (*Ha'ir*, 9 July 1982)

Of the sample of 36 reservists who refused to serve in Lebanon during the first years of war, approximately half of them were members of the movement (Linn 1989b). Following the war in Lebanon there was a split in Yesh Gvul regarding the refusal to serve in the territories. Some claimed that service in Lebanon was not analogous to service in the territories. Others, argued that there was a direct link between the two assignments and that they would refuse. On 31 December 1987, at the beginning of the Intifada, 165 reservists declared in a petition that they would "refuse to take part in suppression of the uprising and insurrection in the occupied territories." They argued that this suppression "illustrates the price of occupation and the absence of a political solution," and that they could "no longer bear the burden of shared responsibility for this moral and political deterioration" (*Jerusalem Post*, 1 January 1988). In another letter distributed to soldiers returning from the service in the Intifada it was stated:

> The Palestinian uprising and its brutal oppression is further proof of the urgent need to end the occupation and to obtain a political agreement between ourselves and the Palestinians. . . . We, the reserve soldiers in the IDF, choose to object conscientiously and publicly announce that we will not take part in the oppression of the uprising. . . . Remember you have the right to ask to serve inside the Green Line. Remember that according to military law, your duty is to refuse to obey any flagrantly illegal command. (*Yediot Acharonot*, 31 December 1987)

In the eyes of movement activists, the refusal to take part in the occupation was a form of civil disobedience destined to break the current deadlock between the nations and lead to talks with the Palestinians. A Major, who had signed the petition said to the press:

> I am not part of the general refusal to serve in the territories but I would refuse to take part in actions of oppression in which I have to put my finger on the trigger." (*Yediot Acharonot*, 31 December 1987)

On May 1988, the Yesh Gvul organization issued a "service booklet" advocating the right to refuse in the territories combined with practical advice (*Davar*, 10 February 1989). The booklet was delivered to reservists only (as its policy was not to encourage young people to refuse, though they supported those who made such a decision). This action resulted in the decision of Israeli legal advisors to order an investigation of Yesh Gvul members. During the Intifada, Yesh Gvul deviated from its general focus on reservists and approached young recruits in high school warning them not to volunteer to join spearhead units in the IDF—the *mistaravim*, who actively fight terrorists and inciters of Palestinians, calling these units illegal and immoral (*Chadashot*, 30 October 1992).

Zav Kria ("call up order"; also "appeal")—Founded over a year after the Intifada started by a group of dedicated reservists who wanted to draw attention to the indifference surrounding the Intifada and the fact that militarily the army was not preparing itself for war. In terms of morality, they wanted to point out that it was impossible to act against civilians in accordance with IDF norms: "There has been enough shooting and weeping. We want to return to being an army of defense" (*Jerusalem Post*, 28 March 1989). These reservists often protested in front of the office of the Minister of Defense.

Dai Lakibush (end the occupation)—A small peace movement in the early stages of the Intifada consisted of (1) members of left wing organizations who participate as an expression of their broader political vision; (2) unaffiliated veterans of previous campaigns for peace; and (3) a wave of new activists. Politically, its members were mainly affiliated with the various communist parties, some with zionist left groups as well as the Civil Rights Movement. Its main objectives have been, in addition to the ending of the occupation, negotiations with the PLO as the sole representative of the Palestinian people, establishing of an independent Palestinian state alongside Israel, and the negotiation of peace in the framework of an international conference. They launched rallies and vigils against fresh acts of soldiers' brutality, showed solidarity with the Palestinians (visits to villages, etc.). Some of its members who were antizionist and Trotskyist were associated with a smaller coalition called "Hala Hakibush" (Down with the Occupation) that supported the demands of the Intifada without taking any stand on the resolution of the conflict (Kaminer, 1989).

The Twenty-First Year—Consisted of young academics and was named after a document entitled "the twenty-first-year covenant of the struggle against the occupation," which was signed by thousands of Israelis during the first weeks of the Intifada. The covenant was premised on the analysis that the occupation "has become an insidious fact of our lives. Its presence has not been confined to the occupied territories. It is, alas, among us and with us" (in Kaminer 1989, p. 238). It outlined a new approach to struggle against the occupation—spelling it out in terms of "refusal to collaborate" and "resistance"—and offered some suggestions such as boycotting goods produced by Israeli settlers in the territories. It organized a subcommittee that sent Israelis to serve as witnesses of the occupation in the hope that the physical presence of Israeli protesters might prevent some excesses by the military. Other committees have organized seminars for high school students on the problem of military service during the occupation. Like Yesh Gvul, this group made an appeal for personal moral responsibility and a striving for a new politics of refusal in the face of various "red lines." Two of the three drafters of the covenant, university philosophy lecturer Adi Ofir and literature lecturer Hanan Hever, also belonged to Yesh Gvul, and Ofir was jailed for refusing military service in the occupied territories.

v. Protesting through Holocaust symbols and metaphors (see chapter 7)

Ib. *Secondary Voice*—Individual and group protesting on behalf of fighting soldiers

Women against Silence—Wives of soldiers in Lebanon who protested several times in Jerusalem as the war continued.

Mothers against Silence—Formed three weeks after the war in Lebanon by mothers of fighting soldiers. Some 15,000 women signed a petition to "stop the madness" (Gilat 1988).

Parents against Erosion (Play on the word in Hebrew where erosion is the word *shchika* and silence is *shtika*)—parents of soldiers who served in the territories during the Intifada and who refused to comply with the collapse of values: "We are deeply concerned about the damage caused to the IDF as a result of its dealings with oppression rather than defense (*Jerusalem Post*, 2 May 1989). The group wrote letters to the Minister of Defense and met with him. The organization did not promote any political line nor advocate a specific solution to the situation.

Women in Black—Emerged in January 1988 soon after the Intifada originated. The group started its protest against the war and the occupation with weekly silent vigils. Dressed in Black, the women held vigils every Friday noon at busy intersections in the center of Jerusalem. Within weeks, similar groups began vigils in

Tel Aviv and Haifa. By 1990, there were more than twenty groups of women in black throughout Israel. Symbolic vigils were also held by women's groups in Europe and the USA. The group consists of women who hold different political opinions.

II. Exit

IIa. *Internal Exit*—refusal of military service

i. 'White' refusal (see chapter 4)

ii. 'Gray' refusal

Unlike the White refusal (public and direct), Gray refusal is defined within the Israeli culture as opting out of service without being committed to prison. The number of reservists using avoidance of duty through the employment of a variety of counterfeit excuses—such as contrived illness—is not known. The estimated number of soldiers and commanders in the field suggests that there are ten times more gray refusers than white refusers. These numbers, however, have never been studied by army officials or social researchers. The relatively easy path open to gray refusers (if they are successful in releasing themselves) lies in the fact that their mode of objection does not pose a moral threat to the army or the public. In the words of this Intifada white refuser who was imprisoned five times:

> The gray refusers are not challenging the army or the ones who judge them. However, when a career officer has to judge a white refuser like me he must question himself: "How can I continue to do my job if his moral concerns are just?"

The phenomenon of gray refusal has not been studied in Israel. There is sometimes documentation, however, of reservists who have been caught when released from service through false medical documents or through succeeding in bribing the unit. For example, on 1 January 1992 the public was informed that a general who exempted reservists from service following a generous contribution to his unit was court-martialed (*Chadashot*).

As a form of criticism, gray refusal does not seem to attract those who wish to assume a connected position. By demonstrating the willingness to pay the price and be public for their moral choice, some white refusers hope to be regarded as assuming a connected position. Thus, while it seems justified to place the gray refuser under the rubric of *Exit*, the placement of white refusers within this category is more problematic.

It must be emphasized that reservists who tend to voice their moral concerns in public were gradually regarded by the army as (moral) "trouble makers." Very often, they were granted permission not to serve on morally controversial missions and sites when called for the reserve (*Chadashot,* 17 March 1989). The increased load of service, however, seems to have followed a decrease in the ability of the IDF to morally justify this unequal share of the burden. This scenario caused some paradoxical situations when combatants from an elite unit who were repeatedly drafted were advised to consider the reserve duty as *voluntary* service (*Yediot Acharonot,* 16 June 1991).

Since the beginning of the Intifada, more and more gray refusers have made their actions public. One of these reservists explains his motivation in taking this stand:

> My refusal is 'gray' but it is public. . . . I can call the thing by its name. It can be said that I am evasive and only taking care of myself. . . . But in our society, which piles so much on you, this is a legitimate act. (*Yediot Acharonot,* 15 September 1989)

Another form of gray refusal is the high incidence of transfer of old reservists from fighting combat units to rear units. This move reflects the accumulating frustration experienced by the Israeli soldier. This thirty-two-year-old sergeant entrepreneur in an armoured unit who fought during the war in Lebanon reflects upon his feelings during the Intifada:

> I am frustrated because . . . we do not know what we are fighting for. . . . Fighting in order to defeat them—I agree. If we are fighting in order to give them a state—I agree. Fighting for nothing—I don't agree with. It started in the Lebanon war—to this day I don't want to die for Shamir or the generals. . . . I am not going to sacrifice myself for any of them . . . Therefore I lowered my medical profile . . . but I don't feel good about it because I let down my friends who remained there. . . . I am not fully at peace with my decision but I live with it. (Rosen and Hamerman 1990, p. 200)

A similar trend was observed during the interview days prior to a reserve service in the territories. On these days soldiers with ad hoc problems can ask to be released. Since the outbreak of the Intifada, these ad hoc problems seem to have increased. One reservist describes: "The commander days turned into a company happening. Only the wives and kids were missing." Some battalion commanders responded to this trend with letters sent to the soldiers prior to their reserve duties in which they tried to raise some feelings of moral guilt because of the low motivation. Others conclude their letters: "There will be no release." (*Yediot Acharonot,* 15 September 1989).

IIb. *External Exit*—rejection of life in Israel

i. Emigration (in Hebrew *yerida*—literally *descent*)

In a country that gives any Jew upon his or her arrival in Israel immediate citizenship and as one that depends heavily on the commitment of its citizens to defend it, there is a strong cultural condemnation of those who choose to leave and settle elsewhere. They are called *yordim* (descenders) a label with a negative connotation (Sobel 1986; Levine 1986). General Ran Goren, the IDF Chief of manpower, viewed the reserve service as the main reason for this exodus:

> The continuous and heavy burden results in burn-out and descent because the reservists are exhausted by the strain of the Intifada . . . and from a national point of view, lowering the amount of the reserve service should be a priority." (*Yediot Acharonot,* 30 March 1990)

The Israeli reservist often sees a close tie between his inability to cope with the physical and/or moral burden of the service and his conditional stay in the country. During the Intifada, a dedicated reservist from the artillery unit made this analogy:

> After the tour of duty, I reached the conclusion that I didn't want to be in Israel any more. . . . I don't want to wear the uniform. This was a uniform I was once proud to wear. . . . I never believed I would reach the stage where I would hate my uniform. . . . Today I don't see myself as belonging to this country. I don't want to be here. . . . (Rosen and Hamerman 1990, p. 35)

Emigration as an extension of refusal seems to be a familiar path of exit among morally distressed reservists:

> I thought about refusal . . . but I know that if I decide to refuse, I'll descent as well. That is to say, I won't refuse and stay in Israel because there are certain rules for living here. . . . I am ready to sacrifice my life . . . and one who cannot cope with this rule of self-sacrifice must not live here. (Rosen and Hamerman 1990, p. 57)

For some reservists, emigration is an action that is a by-product of their criticism. For others, it marks the starting point of moral criticism a safe place from which they can allow themselves to take a position as moral critic. A reserve psychiatrist reflects about the burden of reserves service:

> Our burden is indeed heavy, it is a Damocles' sword of sorts, constantly hanging over our heads, influencing every minute of our lives . . . no one knows just how many men have emigrated from Israel without being able to openly admit—even within those periods of great stress—the personal cost to such a victim. (Levy 1990)

From the United States, a reservist, a poet who wrote a childrens book entitled *Father Goes to the Reserves*, responds to his critics:

> In Israeli society, the reserve is a monster. A modern and real Dracula. . . . The reserve is a monster for national and personal morale, it paralyzes millions of productive work days. A monster for Dads who are obliged to leave their homes, families and activities and deal with degenerate army work." (*Chadashot*, 10 January 1992)

Emigration thus means not only a departure from the Israeli "siege mentality" (Bar Tal and Anteibi 1992), it also guarantees the individual freedom from the "next term in the reserve unit" (Student 1991).

It seems, that for many dedicated reservists, emigration is an easier mode of exit than refusal. To some extent, refusal might be seen as an exit within the system. Unlike emigration, the detachment of the Israeli refuser from his unit is not conceived as a total one, at least from the refusers' point of view. In both conflicts, many asked to remain in touch with the unit in various ways. Yet, even when claiming to leave the unit only selectively and temporarily in order to voice their moral concerns, the Israeli refusers are positioned by the public on the exit track. Thus, very often the decision to descend is easier for the Israeli reservist than to become a refuser, since this moral position is more clear than the one who selectively refuses. By positioning himself on the exit track, the Israeli reservist knows he might be facing the risk of losing his credentials as a moral critic in his country, for which he wanted to fight. So, he will think twice before he makes this move, as this Intifada refuser explains: "There are moments when I tell myself that I am descending from this country—but on reflection I realize that I have not descended. It seems as if there are still more ordeals that I am capable of swallowing. . . ."

ii. Suicide

There has been an increase in the number of successful suicide attempts in the Israeli army since the war in Lebanon and the Intifada, but no study regarding its link to the moral confusion has been published. Some reservists see the increased rate of suicide as the manifestation of the moral deadlock in which the soldiers find themselves (*Chadashot*, 5 May 1990). Ego resilience, the nature of the war, and the support system available during and after the war have been documented as affecting specific outcomes of war experience (Elder 1987; Elder and Clipp 1988, 1989; Elder and Caspi 1990; Elder, Gimble, and Levy 1991; Noy, Nardi, and Solomon 1986). Though there has been an increase in the number of successful suicides in the Israeli army since the war in Lebanon and the Intifada, the possible link between the existing moral confusion and the ego resilience of the soldiers has not been studied. In general, suicide cases number approximately thirty per year, one-fourth of these cases are reservists. According to IDF figures, two-thirds of the suicide cases are soldiers in compulsory service, the second group consists of reservists, and the remainder—less than 10 percent—are career officers. Army officials argue that the suicide rate is no higher than the rates for the comparable age group in other Western countries (Rothberg and McDowell 1988; Rothberg and Ursano 1987). None of these democracies, however, requires their underpaid civilians to perform reserve service in face of existential military threats that increase in their moral complexities.

A hidden connection between a state of moral distress and suicide is found in the case of Lieutenant Ofer Michaeli. Michaeli was stationed with his battalion at Jebalia refugee camp where the Intifada erupted on December 1987. Michaeli's infantry Battalion with its fifty-four reservists were drafted on November 22. After having undergone two to three days of training, they were sent to guard the refugee camp of Jebalia with its 50,000 inhabitants. In a visit by the high-ranking command a week before the Intifada erupted, soldiers complained that "there are two armies around here—one has to suffer the consequences of being ill equipped, and uninformed. The other is the army of the career commanders who come for short visits and talk about restraint" (*Yediot Acharonot*, 4 December 1992). On the first morning of the Intifada, when the army failed to send additional forces to the area, Lieutenant Ofer Michaeli was sent with three other soldiers to disperse a demonstration of thousands who were attacking their military stronghold. During the course of the action Michaeli was chasing one of the stone throwers to his house and was trapped there with his people. He shot in the air. One person was killed (the first Palestinian victim of the Intifada). The battalion commander was not in the area. When the high-ranking commander arrived after the demonstrators had retreated, his first question was, "why did you enter into the house?" He was told, "these were the instructions—to chase and catch every stone thrower." The soldiers were informed by General Mordechai, head of southern command, "I don't want to hear of any more shootings here." Michaeli was removed from the IDF. He was forced to remain in this exit position as a form of punishment. He was not allowed to return to reserve service in spite of his request to do so (and despite the fact that an IDF investigation found Michaeli's response to be adequate). Soldiers tried to protest on his behalf by writing letters to higher authorities, but they were not answered. On 5 January 1990, Michaeli made a suicidal dive in the blue cave in the Red Sea and was never found.

Two years later, following an inquiry into the mistreatment of an Arab who was captured during a severe riot in the Intifada, the investigated reservist wrote a suicide letter to his brother who was about to be inducted into the IDF:

> I hope you will be a good soldier and succeed in your service. I believe that part of your assignment in the territories will be to suppress a troublesome population of one kind or another. Unfortunately, the one who is hurt is the one who is forced by the system to do what he must not do. (*Chadashot*, 20 August 1989)

Fearing their expected grim future, high school graduates wrote a letter to the Minister of Defense protesting the excessive suicide rate. In their letter they claimed that there is a relationship between suicide and the activities soldiers have to pursue in the territories against their conscience (*Ha'aretz*, 4, December 1989).

The account of this reserves psychiatrist sums up this section:

> In Israel, you always find yourself before, during and after a war. Thus, in 1985 we were "after the war in Lebanon." In 1990 we were "during the uprising in the occupied territories" and perhaps before the war with Iraq. No one can predict if and when the characteristic Israeli situation will change . . . a young, healthy and more or less sane male recruit is expected to retain a uniform for thirty-seven years. . . . He may emigrate from Israel . . . or he may be manipulated for decades by the military machine, for more as

> well as for less justified security needs of the country. . . . I am a forty-five-year-old Israeli. Twenty-seven years have passed since I was drafted, or drifted, into the army and completed compulsory service. I have passed through several wars and served in the reserves—nothing impressive by Israeli standards. I have ten more years of military duty to serve. Time will pass, I shall, or shall not, manage. (Levy 1990, pp. 247–248)

Conclusion

Though trained to choose loyalty as a pattern of response to pressure, since the war in Lebanon, the dedicated reservist is tempted to consider the possibility of refusal. However, in Israeli society, with its emphasis on moral connectedness, he may dare to do it only as a form of voice, not as exit, because he may not want to lose his moral identity to which the army is central. One writer reservist portrayed the reserve service as the "iron tongs" of the Israeli entity (*Yediot Acharonot*, 5 July 1991).

It seems that since the war in Lebanon, a growing number of Israeli reservists has dared to challenge the habitual ingrained loyalty to reserve duty. By positioning themselves in the *voice* or *exit* tracks, these reservists force themselves to review not only their present dilemmas but also the morality and the necessity of their participation in previous wars that they considered just.

The following chapter examines the voice of the Israeli reservist when encountering Holocaust metaphors and symbols during service. This protest is wide in scope and necessitates a chapter of its own.

Notes

1. The official duration of the War of Attrition (provided by an IDF spokesperson) is 8/3/69 to 7/8/70. However, many view the start of this war as being right after the 1967 war.

All vanishes except the memory.

—Albert Camus

7

Criticism and Culture

From Collective Memories to Voice

Critical thinking requires the use of imagination, "seeing things from perspectives other than our own and envisioning the likely consequences of our position" (Barnet and Bedau, p. 4). In this chapter we argue that the collective memories of the Holocaust serves as a central perspective for the Israeli civilian in uniform; that fighting and refusing soldiers often construct their criticism within the metaphoric system of the Holocuast.

Since an individual's decision to join a military enterprise is not performed in a social vacuum, his moral reasoning and action cannot be understood detached from the historical self (Broughton 1987), his desire to preserve the values of a given society (Shinhar 1989), and his "imaginative rationality" (Lakoff and Johnson 1980, p. 193).

Though only 25 percent of the subjects in this sample had parents who were Holocaust survivors, most (65 percent) indicated they often used the Holocaust as their moral frame of reference. This chapter examines the formative role of the collective experience of the Holocaust in the construction and understanding of common civil and military phrases in times of war and threat.

It will be argued that Holocaust-related metaphors create a reality in which some Israeli soldiers tested and judged their moral claims when facing morally ambiguous situations. They are being used in times of moral confusion when Israeli soldiers question themselves as to how to behave in a morally correct way when constraints may swing moral actors into positions similar to those played by victors and victims in the Holocaust. Although the individual Israeli soldier could not by himself change the reality of war, he is capable of questioning the situations and of reexamining his moral threshold, particularly in terms of his sensitivity to the words and phrases used to define the phenomenon.

Even if Holocaust-related metaphors are not viable, one's own moral claim is to be judged against them. It is argued in this chapter that, by using such metaphors, Israeli soldiers were able to generalize beyond their immediate situation in a particular morally conflicting experience in their attempt to make sense of their lives in some larger perspective. The use of Holocaust metaphors and symbols not only provided the soldiers with guidelines for the present situation, it also allowed them to locate themselves in the collective memory of their community and enabled them to voice their criticism from a "connected" position. The key metaphoric themes to be discussed in this chapter are:

It is good to die for our country
Tohar haneshek (purity of arms)
Shooting and crying
Cog in the machine
Camps
David and Goliath

It Is Good to Die for Our Country

The road to Lebanon passes by a statue of a lion under which appears the inscription "It is good to die for our country." The lion is located at the most historic prestate site in Israel, Tel Hai. Tel Hai (Hill of Life) was established in 1917 in the northern Galilee, a few meters from the present border between Israel and Lebanon. In 1920 a few Jewish settlers bought the small bindery there from Arabs. During a period when the area was under French military control, a mob of Arabs attacked Tel Hai, mortally wounding the military commander, Joseph Trumpeldor, who was reputed to have said: "It is good to die for our country." Every year, on Tel Hai Day, Israeli youths from all over the country make a pilgrimage to the site, which has come to symbolize the valor of the Jew in combat.

Until the 1982 war in Lebanon, this symbol was never challenged. Although the war in Lebanon was originally labeled the "Peace for the Galilee" campaign, aimed at destroying terrorist infrastructures, it was not seen this way by many Israeli soldiers. For the first time the Israeli soldier was obliged to find within himself the willingness to fight and be killed in a nondefensive war. With the prolonged stay on the Lebanese soil, the Israeli soldier found himself challenging Trumpeldor's proposition as he was passing by the statue on his way to his assigned service in Lebanon. This was the first war in which the Israeli reserve soldier questioned what he had never questioned before: "Why is it good to die for my country?"

Whereas any soldier is afraid of death, this question does not seem to focus on fear but on the unwillingness to die in vain. As noted by Walzer (1977), a soldier may die in vain even in a meaningful war. Often there is greater likelihood that a soldier will not fear a meaningless death if the war is aimed at protecting fundamental values, national independence, communal freedom, and people's lives. From the individual's point of view, a just war is a war protecting one's home. During wartime, home is not only a physical location but a metaphor—a metaphor for which a soldier is ready to die. One selective conscientious objector from the war in Lebanon explains:

> After a few days of fighting we reached a quiet place deep in Lebanon, and this was the first time I had had the opportunity to think. I asked my commander "Hey, can you tell me what are we doing here exactly?" . . . And he said, "I am asking myself the same question.
>
> The Chief of Staff said to the soldiers who were blockading Beirut that they were protecting their *home*. . . . I had just bought an apartment and invested a lot in its reconstruction. I hadn't yet fully paid for it. As I finished the reconstruction I was recruited *to fight for my home*. . . . Was it a symbol or a fact? As I was fighting, I gradually reached the conclusion that indeed I have a home but I was not sent to protect it.
>
> When the commander ordered us further on, I was already a few miles ahead of my comrades within my thoughts . . . I knew that I didn't want to die far away from my unpaid home. [emphasis added]

The Intifada brought an additional dimension to the fight for one's home. In their fight, some Palestinians not only want their share of the territory, but view it just as the first stage toward the liquidation of the Jewish state. "Dying *for one's home*" (real or potential) thus became a metaphor for the Arab side as well. Interestingly, since 1967, Israel has been flooded by Palestinian construction workers. Literally, they build homes for Jews whose homeland they would want to destroy. The emotions around this issue are presented by the Palestinians' propaganda in a straightforward manner. One example:

> To throw all the Jews out of the country, to kill them . . . so that their heads will roll like gravel along the roads . . . the country is all ours . . . we have to continue to build it so that we shall take it all built." (*Chadashot*, 3 April 1988)

Another version of this propaganda has to do with a direct reference to Hitler as siding with their long-term cause, by hanging, for example, his picture on the wall (reported to the author by a fighting soldier who served in the West Bank at the village of Beit Furick).

During the Intifada, the newspaper *Ha'aretz* called the attention of its readers to the words of the youngest survivor of Auschwitz in response to the threats by the Arabs:

> Unlike any other country, Israel cannot afford a defeat. When Arab leaders talk about "Erasing Israel from the map and throwing the Jews into the sea," these words are not simply rhetoric in our ears. We listen to them literally. Any other way of understanding them would indicate deafness or blindness and suicide, considering the lessons of our history. (*Yediot*, 13 March 1989)

For the average Israeli soldier, however, the fight for one's home must be compared to the prestate situation when Jews were killed like "sheep." For the Israeli, this awareness of the Holocaust is in tune with Trumpeldor's maxim: although people die, they do not die like sheep, but for their homeland (Aini 1992, Hendel 1991, Miron 1992). Some Israelis not only live by Holocaust metaphors before a battle, they often find themselves responding to such metaphors after experiencing a victory. For example, following the 1967 Six Day War, one Israeli soldier said:

> It is true that people believed that we would be exterminated if we lost the war. . . . We got this idea—or inherited it—from the concentration camps. It is a concrete idea for anyone who has grown up in Israel, even if he personally did not experience Hitler's persecution, but only heard or read about it. (quoted in Young 1989, p. 136)

"Not in vain"; the manner of death of the individual soldier has become a crucial issue within the Israeli fighting culture. It seems to repeat itself in each war as a response to the homeless passive Jewish figure in the Holocaust without a place to hide or equipment to actively defend his life. When referring to the Holocaust, the context of a passive mode of death is clearly present. For example, Israeli leaders refer to the 1973 Yom Kippur war, where many soldiers were trapped in their positions and died without fighting, as a "Holocaust."

This metaphor also occurs in writing. A journalist discussing the "Holocaust" aspects of the 1973 Yom Kippur War quoted one bereaved father who wrote at that time to the press:

> When the Major told me that my son had died I said, "He didn't die." He told me he fell. I said: "He didn't fall. An Israeli soldier does not fall, he dies standing." (*Yediot*, 20 September 1988)

During the Intifada, after it was announced that an IDF paratrooper had been "murdered" in Nablus (when an Arab youth whom the soldier had been reluctant to shoot for moral reasons dropped a building block on his head), a combat soldier wrote this to the press:

> Armed IDF soldiers fall when carrying out their military mission, they are not "murdered". . . It does not matter where it occurs . . . in the territories or on the border. . . . Therefore I protest as a reservist at the words of the Minister of Defense regarding the commander who "fell" on the border and the paratrooper who (was "murdered" R.L.) in Nablus. The IDF soldier who falls while protecting the country deserves to be treated with honor and not with pity. (*Ma'ariv*, 27 March 1989)

In September of 1989, the mother of a soldier killed in the Lebanon war applied to the Supreme Court six years after her son's death for an order to change part of the inscription on his grave from "Peace for the Galilee" to the "Lebanon War." The Ministry of Defense's citation on the headstone was: "Fell in the line of duty in the Peace for Galilee Campaign" (a formula mostly used for soldiers who die in accidents; otherwise, the phrase used is "fell in combat"). She argued that it creates in those who see the word "peace" in the name of a war a feeling of being deceived, as in Orwell's *1984*. She made her appeal, she said, because of the suffering she endured whenever she saw the "lie" carved on her son's grave and, still more, because it seemed to be directed against her, as if (in her words) the Ministry of Defense was saying: Not only did we take your son to fight in vain in an unjustified war and against your will, and not only did your son die in this war, but even after his death and on his grave, we impose our concepts, ideas and beliefs (*Ha'aretz*, 28 September 1989). In supporting her claim she presented an example from the case of soldiers killed by terrorists who infiltrated an army base near Tel Hai. The original format "Fell in the line of duty" was later changed to "Fell in fighting for the defense of the northern settlements."

For the post-Holocaust generation in Israel, death need not be equated with being a victim and Trumpeldor's statement does not seem to be outdated. A 1989 play was entitled *"Tov Nabut Be'ad Artzeinu"* ("It is good to club for our country") as a pun on *"Tov Lamut Be'ad Artzeinu,"* which is the Hebrew version for Trumpeldor's phrase "It is good to die [*lamut*] for our country."

The word for "club" in the pun, *nabut*, is in fact an arabic word that has moved into Hebrew slang. When some soldiers face insoluble moral dilemmas, being equipped for this purpose with a "club" they tend to relieve their frustration regarding this new policing job in the play on words concerning the word *club*. In Arabic the word is *nabut*, which has moved into Hebrew slang in the following examples:

A crack combat unit that was instructed to use clubs called itself "*Sayeret Nabut*" (*Ma'ariv*, winter 1988), which means "club patrol." This phrase is a play on the name *Sayeret Haruv*—an elite infantry unit with a fine reputation during the seventies.

This struggle with a new moral language seems to bring the Israeli soldier into a new moral position from which he is forced to reassess the myth upon which he grew up. The words of one refuser may serve to sum up this section:

> I guess German soldiers also thought that it was good to die for their country . . . and I believe that if the doctor tending Trumpeldor at Tel Hai had listened carefully to his last words he would have heard: "It is worth *living* for my country."

Tohar Haneshek (Purity of Arms)

The concept of *tohar haneshek* evolved during the prestate clashes between the Arabs and Israelis. It refers basically to the idea of keeping the weapon "pure" by preserving its use for definite cases of self-defense. In its broad sense it implies the preservation of "Humanistic norms in combat, refraining from unnecessary bloodshed, and avoiding, at all cost, harming civilians in general and women and children in particular. It further means avoiding damage to sacred buildings, treating POWs in a humane way and totally refraining from looting, raping and other atrocities" (Gal 1986, p. 239).

The ideal moral code is translated into practice in two ways. First, before sending soldiers into battle, IDF commanders are taught not to expect blind obedience but are required to provide soldiers with the moral logic of their mission. Soldiers are further taught that manifestly illegal commands should not be obeyed. Second, IDF commanders traditionally adopt a "follow me" policy: by leading their soldiers, commanders not only set an example of personal bravery but also fulfill their moral responsibility. With the traditional Israeli logistics of "few against many," these concepts of "purity of arms" and "follow me" mean more Israeli casualties but, nevertheless, were regarded by army officers as one of the most solid sources of strength of IDF soldiers. As stated by Colonel (Res.) Meir Pa'il, "Purity of arms does not detract in the least from the fighting ability of our soldiers" (Hardan 1985).

Within the IDF moral tradition the concept of purity of arms means that it is worth risking one's own life without exception for the sake of moral principles, such as not hurting the innocent. Yet, there are some situations where the translation of this idea into practice is problematic: How do you keep arms pure by extra self-sacrifice when the action may still entail innocent casualties due to terrorist strategies? Israeli soldiers seem to have turned to their collective memories for guidance, as this refusing soldier relates:

> When I was young I didn't pay enough attention to the meaning of the instructions I received in military training such as "to *purify* the target," to "*select* the right people," "to *clean out* the area of terrorists"—but coming to think about it now we cannot use these phrases any more—even with good reason. Prime Minister Begin's words about the "final solution" of the terrorist problem in Lebanon show why you cannot engage the Israeli soldier in this war.

To employ the idea of purity of arms during the Intifada is an even harder task. For example, in order to lower the number of casualties among Arab rioters during the Intifada, the army was ordered to disperse demonstrations by nonlethal means: tear gas, clubs, rubber bullets, plastic bullets, and the like. These methods, however, sometimes take victims on both sides; the injured civilian as well as the soldier who did not intend to kill. Safra, an Israeli writer, reflected on the concept of purity of arms when analyzing moral dilemmas of the Intifada:

> What has changed now? It is very easy for the victim to be moral. That is how for thousands of years Jews could have clean hands and drown in rivers of blood. Since our establishment as a state, we have been coping with the dilemma of how to preserve our existence and remain humane. In these days of the Intifada this dilemma is becoming razor sharp. There is a kind of inequality in the insoluble moral questions that have no remedy in the relations between us and our neighbors; we will always be guided by arguments of justice. That is why we invested in the invention of the craziest idea of all—rubber bullets. (*Yediot Acharonot,* 5 May 1989)

The moral confusion was manifested in the official language used in the Israeli media: When reporting about soldiers killing terrorists along the Lebanon border—the reference is to "our" soldiers whereas in the territories, reports are phrased somewhat more abstractly: "The forces" returned fire; "troops" returned fire; "the army" responded with fire; "there was" firing. One combat soldier sums up this moral split: "When I shoot in the territories I am a criminal but on the Lebanese border I am a hero" (*Yediot,* 27 January 1989).

The humane commands issued for dealing with the violent populations in the territories did not change the hopelessness of the situation: even the most morally mature soldier might err in judging when and how far to follow the command and its parts, namely tear gas and clubs; rubber, plastic and live bullets; at a distance no closer than 70 meters; to be fired only by officers; aimed only at the legs, and so on. On the other side of the arena, the demonstrating Palestinian youngsters are familiar with these regulations and tease the soldiers by showing their chests knowing they will not be shot at if the legs are hidden.

This newly invented means of dealing with the rebellion of a civilian population also became a symbol to which the soldiers responded. While the nonlethal ammunition might be the most just, its use might also be the most damnable. A kibbutz soldier writes bluntly to the press: "There is no purity in the club and no morality in tear gas" (*Yediot*, 3 January 1989). Another soldier reported finding the words *stop the occupation* carved on the club he was issued (*Davar*, 27 January 1989).

During the Intifada the Holocaust becomes a central metaphor for both the left and right wings. Professor Yehoshaya Leibovitz, who publicly and vigorously advocated refusal to serve, expressed his frustration by calling the troops who are obliged to rule in the territories "Judeo-Nazis" (*Yediot*, 5 February 1988). Right-wing settlers—interrupted while trying to build a memorial for a friend killed by Arabs—called the officials who tried to stop them "Nazis" (*Chadashot*, 2 June 1989). This most extreme expression, employed by individuals from both sides of the political map, must make us aware of the limited vocabulary the Hebrew language has to describe the present moral dilemma. The writer Uri Bernstein called our attention to this lack:

> The Hebrew language is intimate in its nature: it never had arrogant inscriptions like the Assyrians . . . the brutal victories of the Pharaohs or the heartless accounts of the Crusades. We have no experience in tyranny. We have no words for it. We have always had the language of the victim, the persecuted, tortured, or subject to injustice. . . . And now the language has no power. It cannot describe injustice from the perspective of the rulers. (*Yediot*, 5 May 1989)

The struggle for words also implies a struggle for moral order. Most notable was the conflict over the definition of the Intifada, which has never been declared officially as a war. Frustrated soldiers and/or officers are often heard to say (particularly after a bloody event) that "They (the politicians) do not understand that this is a war." (*Yediot*, 19 May 1989). Instead, various terms are applied: *disorder, rebellion, uprising,* which indicate tactical confusion in this military scene. Soldiers often see it as a moral drama: Yossi Levi was an Israeli soldier attacked in Tel Aviv by an Arab from the territories who wanted to kill him, but failed. Levi later said "I have nothing against him since both of us were like actors in the drama of our lives in this part of the world" (*Ma'ariv*, 9 April 1989). The attempt to preserve the concept of purity of arms is a subplot within this main drama. We hear of a combat medic attacked by an Arab in Ramalla who tried to stab him to death: he fought back, and then tended the Arab's wounds after the fight. This (morally) no-win situation is best described by one journalist in an article entitled by a play on words summing up the moral quandary "Shalom to the soldier now" (*shalom chayal achshav* where the word *shalom* means "peace" as well as "hello," *chayal* means "soldier," and *achshav*—means "now") (*Davar,* 19 February 1988).

The phrase *shalom achshav* is the Hebrew for Peace Now, a protest movement consisting of reservists who objected to government policy during the war in Lebanon but did not advocate refusal as the proper mode of objection (see chapter 6). Most intriguing is the fact that throughout the numerous wars the cry for Peace Now remained without an echo; no influential Arab Peace Now movement exists, and the refusal of an Arab soldier to serve in his army out of moral concerns for the lives of innocent Jews has not been documented. Thus, from this individual position even the peace-seeking Israeli soldier has (painfully) to realize that the call for peace remains unanswered, floating in the air. Nor does the desire to remain a moral soldier in a morally problematic situation make the soldiers morally effective. For this reason, there seems to be three possible meanings for the phrase *shalom chayal achshav*:

1. Hello to the Peace Now soldier
2. Peace to the soldier who is serving now
3. Hello to the soldier who is serving now

This wordplay with a linguistic figure points out the no-win situation of the soldier. It further seemed to imply that neither the Peace Now soldier nor the refuser can win in the moral complexity of the existing situation:

> If the soldier is trapped in an enemy alley he can refuse to serve in this alley, but the alley cannot refuse to remain an alley—and this transforms the individual soldier into the sole one responsible for his (immoral R.L.) actions." (*Davar,* 19 February 1988)

If purity of arms is not an obvious position of connectedness or an action of self-sacrifice on behalf of the community and its members, it must manifest itself in another form: the preservation of one's own moral individuality by raising a moral voice. The silence of the world during the Holocaust becomes a vivid point in the collective memory of the Israeli who would not want to find himself or herself in this moral position when history comes to judge. This view is reflected in the first writing on the Intifada and its moral turmoil by Avi Valentine (1989). In his book *Sahid* (Arabic for "saint"), he describes a fictitious assembly camp for Arabs, on the gate of which the Jews have hung a startling sign stating "Silence Serves Everybody" (p. 9).

The Chief Education Officer of the IDF during the first phase of the Intifada, Brigadier-General Dagan, who resigned his office for not being able to practice what he believed, offered a more optimistic outlook:

> I prefer the concept of "morality in fighting" rather than "purity of arms," because purity signifies something absolute and without exceptions. . . . I am proud that our youth do not accept things as they are but ask questions. (*Chadashot*, 30 April 1989)

If purity of arms cannot be translated into self-sacrifice, then what is left is at least the obligation to speak out, and it is still conventional wisdom that the weight given to the moral voice of a combat soldier is higher than to that of a nonfighting citizen who protests (Sprinzak 1977). This realization probably shaped the decision of some morally puzzled mothers of soldiers during the Lebanon war to organize a protest group they called "Mothers against Silence" (*shtika* in Hebrew), whose major purpose was to bring the soldiers home. During the Intifada, both fathers and mothers established a protest movement called "Parents Against Burnout" (*shchika* in Hebrew; note the play on words). Their idea is to prevent their sons from becoming refusers on account of the degradation of means to control the violence:

> We *refuse* to accept the fall in the values upon which we have educated our children. . . . Service in the territories has shaken the *moral immunity* of the soldiers and affected the motivation of the best of our youth to serve. (*Chadashot*, 2 May 1989)

A reservist, both of whose parents were Holocaust survivors, found it impossible to maintain purity of arms in the territories; he wrote to a member of the Knesset:

> The first week of service in the territories was like a nightmare for me. At first I tried to behave as I had in Lebanon—to try and choose for myself what was right and what was wrong, or as I defined it then, "to walk between the drops." . . . This time the "rain" is too heavy and it is impossible "not to get wet" (*Yediot*, 24 January 1989).

Through the rain, we observe this soldier operating on a different premise to purity of arms. He witnessed events and raised his moral voice by sending a letter to a member of the Israeli parliament. By so doing he has succeeded not only in maintaining moral integrity but also in encouraging others to assume a connected position of voice.

Shooting and Crying

Within Israeli society soldiers' tears have traditionally symbolized both moral dilemmas and their resolution in its various wars. In the Six Day War, the paratroopers who united east and west Jerusalem, expressed their relief by crying into the stones of the Wailing Wall—the last relic of the Jewish temple after its destruction by the Romans in 70 A.D. Following the 1973 Yom Kippur War, Israeli troops were sent to disperse demonstrations by youths in the occupied territories, mainly with tear gas. Some Israeli reserve soldiers found themselves obeying the orders but simultaneously resisting them. In a letter of protest sent to the press they described the insoluble moral conflict of their service as a situation where they were, literally, shooting and crying. During the Lebanon War, the same generation of paratroopers found themselves crying once again—this time when questioning their senior officers as to the moral meaning of their prolonged stay (Linn 1989b).

Apart from the Intifada, over which there was again a moral controversy, the younger generation of paratroopers is involved in another war with a high level of public consensus. Such soldiers patrol the Lebanon borders to prevent the continuous and persistent attempts of terrorists to infiltrate Israel. Mourning dead comrades who fell in an engagement while on such a patrol, the soldiers again use the language of tears. A senior commander (a Holocaust survivor) consoles them, saying

> You can cry. . . . Only those who are able to cry now, know how to fight. To weep is a sign of mourning over a friend who was killed, it is not a sign of weakness. It is a sign that though we have to be fighters, we remain human beings. (*Ma'ariv*, 2 May 1988)

When forced to fight among civilians (Israeli Vietnam) or against them (Israeli Algiers). The only option faced by the individual soldier is to shoot and cry: to shoot because this is the only way the individual soldier who finds himself surrounded by a violent mob can save his life; to cry because he knows that it could probably have been avoided. A soldier who refused to serve in Lebanon explained:

> One of the major arguments against disobedience in the army is that if we care about the situation we should change it from within—that if you go to serve in the occupied territories or in Lebanon and treat the people well, this is your contribution to the change. I cannot accept this argument because when young children begin throwing stones at you, you cannot just stand up and say "Just a minute, calm down." Instead, you begin to run wild even though you don't want to . . . and then come the unfortunate shootings. (Linn 1989b, p. 33)

The only moral resolution in this uncontrolled situation is the option of "not shooting and not crying" (Linn 1989a); if not for present functioning, then at least for future moral harmony. One Lebanon refuser explains:

> I always believed in making changes from within. . . . I could never see myself as a refuser. But after all these years of "shooting and crying" you reach a stage in this inner war when all the conventional modes of protest make you a full participant in these actions because *you commit them* even though you protest later. What would you say to yourself years from now: "I was screaming against the Lebanon war but I went there?" (Linn 1989b, p. 34).

In this emphasis on "years from now" Israeli collective memory is at work. Encountering a German aged over sixty, many Israelis often experience an involuntary question: Where was he in those days of the Holocaust?

To some extent, Israeli soldiers seem to fight their moral confusion with a growing sensitivity to the moral language used in the conflict. Most notably are the descriptive phrases that revolve around the metaphor of shooting and crying (*yorim uvochim* in Hebrew):

Yorim umochim (shooting and protesting). This refers to the moral struggle of combat soldiers who are instructed to shoot rubber or plastic bullets to disperse violent mass demonstrations but not to use live bullets (so as to prevent unnecessary killing). There is a dual moral complexity in this order. First, the rubber and plastic bullets are less accurate and therefore may easily injure innocent bystanders, such as children. Second, rubber and plastic bullets can kill if they strike soft parts of the body. Can you shoot without protesting the shooting?

Yorim veotmim (shooting and blocking up). This combination refers to the morally controversial task assigned to soldiers serving in the territories, namely to block up the house of a suspected terrorist after a terrorist action. Although this is done only after the terrorist admits the act, the fact that the house is blocked up before the trial is morally problematic.

Yorim umecharbenim (shooting and defecating). This is how soldiers in the rebellious towns in the territories describe their physical and mental feelings when they are instructed to man positions for long hours on roofs of houses in strategic positions that obviously lack sanitary facilities (*Jerusalem Post,* 21 February 1989; see also chapter 6)..

The foremost expression of the moral tradition in military life is found in a renowned book published following the 1967 war entitled "The Seventh Day—Soldiers Talk about the Six Day War" (Shapira 1971), for which the Hebrew phrase is *si'ah lochamim,* meaning "talks among fighters." In the book, army officers coming from Kibbutzim describe their inability to become conquerors of new territories they did not originally intend to capture during the 1962 war and of a population whom they did not hate. In this book, one soldier says:

> Those who survived the Holocaust . . . those who have listened to stories know that no other people carry with them such haunting visions. And it is these visions that compel us to fight and yet make us ashamed of fighting. (pp. 38–39)

Analyzing the Holocaust events as metaphors and symbols and the way that Israelis respond to them, Young (1989) reaches the same conclusion:

> This movement between past and present persecution, between the compulsion to fight and the shame of fighting, exemplifies Israel's own ambivalent need to remember the Holocaust and to forget it. It is simultaneously the reason for the Jewish life in Israel—for the state itself—and that which incites empathy in them for the newly defeated enemy. (p. 137)

Moral debates and dilemmas of soldiers in Lebanon and in the Intifada are often compared to the *si'ah lochamim* (talk among fighters). Kibbutz soldiers and officers who wish to sustain some order of priority regarding the identification of moral dilemmas and the mature ways of coping with them were trying to repeat history and express themselves in another version of *si'ah lochamim* updated to 1989. A book entitled *Talks with Soldiers 89* describes the moral pain of the individual soldier made victim through the fact of his being a conqueror, a position in which he can find no moral solace. The moral aspect of the Intifada dilemma is evident from the name given by the press to the confusion of fighting soldiers as it emerges in conversations; such discussions are called by soldiers "talks among oppressors" (*Chadashot,* 20 January 1988). Soldiers of the 1989 talks are sons of those who were interviewed in the 1968 talks. It is the talk of the generation whose parents thought (after the 1967 victory) they had fought the last war. One of the kibbutz participants in the 1968 talks sums up the situation:

> You ask me where the generation of the 68 fighters' talks is today? This is a generation without anything very significant to its credit. . . . This is a generation that meets the generation of the Intifada oppressors on the lawn at the kibbutz. . . . The younger generation is in a much more difficult situation than we were. All the national symbols that we had, such as national liberation and human rights, belong to the other side now. Our sons' generation is using the clubs and on the other side they are hoisting flags. . . . A good education in my opinion should lead them to refusal. . . . The situation in which they have to function is impossible . . . either they shoot or they cry. (*Chadashot,* 6 June 1989)

Facing the growing numbers of unsolved dilemmas (most notably how to respond in a moral way to the stone throwers), the reservists tend to name themselves "stone feeders." This is manifest in the moral dilemmas presented in the the 1989 booklet. Unlike the well-advertised 1967 book, the 1989 book was distributed only to ministers in the government (*Yediot Acharonot,* 18 April 1989).

Cog in the Machine

Probably more than any other culture, the post-Holocaust generation in Israel is sensitive to the phenomenon of blind obedience to authority. The chilling simplicity of Eichmann's statements that he was "just obeying orders" and was "just a cog in the machine" is a warning light to any Israeli system, including the IDF. In her book, Hannah Arendt (1963) skillfully conveys the frightening message that Eichmann was not a monster but a normal human being. Theoretically he could have obediently sent food parcels to the concentration camps if so ordered.

Although discipline is a central pillar to any army, the moral foundation of the IDF requires anything but blind obedience. The IDF soldier must be as fully informed about the moral foundation of any military action he is obliged to perform. The soldier is responsible for the morality of his action and must face a court-martial if he has carried out a manifestly illegal command (Straschnov 1994). Most of all, what makes army discipline flexible is the transition back and forth between civilian and army life and "the predominance of the reserve corps within the IDF . . . [which] affects the 'civilization' of military discipline" (Gal 1986, p. 233).

The closer military operations are to direct contact with civilian populations, the greater the risk that an individual soldier may lose sight of the moral code of combat. One concerned mother—a Holocaust survivor—voiced her worries regarding the intensity and nature of the missions imposed upon the IDF soldiers: "How many wars will our boys fight before they will become animals?" (Eilon 1983, p. 231, cited in Gal 1986).

The moral complexity of the assignment increases when soldiers face an uprising conducted by people who take advantage of the IDF moral code by committing the most vulnerable individuals (women and children) to violent acts against Israeli soldiers and civilians. Paradoxically, the IDF moral code was clear not only to the IDF soldiers but also to the Arab inhabitants of the territories who could watch on television the trials of soldiers who transgressed.

Combat soldiers serving in the territories were ordered to "search for listed individuals," to "select" and "deport" suspected terrorists, to "maintain order," and to "subdue." These were not neutral commands but fairly familiar to soldiers from their collective memory of the Holocaust who, therefore, ironically, often named themselves *Kalgasim*, meaning "shock troops" (*Ma'ariv*, 14 October 1988). As noted by Young (1989) "What is remembered of the Holocaust depends on how it is remembered, and how events are remembered depends in turn on the text now giving them form" (p. 1.).

A physician who was called for reserve service at a PLO prisoner camp resisted his mission arguing "My name is Marcus Levin and not Joseph Mengele, and by reason of conscience I refuse to serve in this place" (*Al Hamishmar*, 19 September 1988).

The use of Holocaust events, names, and metaphors as a frame of reference against which one's moral confusion is judged, seems to repeat itself over and over. For example, a captain in an armored unit, a son of Holocaust survivors, reports after a service in the territories:

> In the battalion the soldiers named our company the "Auschwitz squad" or "Demianjuk" because of our liberal use of tear gas in response to stone throwing. (*Ha'aretz*, 31 July 1989)

It is important to note that the sensitivity of the individual Israeli soldiers to the Holocaust-related metaphors never exists in a vacuum. Over the border Arab propaganda has labeled Israelis as "Neo-Nazis" (Linn and Gur-Zeev, 1995). This tendency increased after the 1967 war, but, quite surprisingly, any analogy coming from this source had little impact compared with the self-imposed Holocaust-related labels used by Israeli soldiers. Although tear gas is widely used around the world for dispersing violently demonstrating mobs, its use within Israeli society impinges directly upon moral values and, therefore, stimulates the resistance of the best soldiers.

When the individual soldier feels that he is losing his cultural and personal sense of identity—turning into a cog in the military machine—he may refuse his assignment:

> I am not one of those who went to the war like a *cog in the machine.* I was not happy about this war, but I could not reach a balanced conclusion at the beginning of it. . . . It was so confusing, you are called out in the middle of the night. . . . Your animal instincts are raised. . . . I travelled all through the night to Lebanon. . . . Maybe it is a cynical way to mobilize so you will not see the turmoil of the battles. . . . It was hard to be clever. . . . After all, if it had been a war with Syria, I would have gone! (Linn 1989b, p. 117) [Syria was considered the most fanatical and uncompromising enemy of Israel and most Israelis would treat an attack by Syria very seriously and with less debate than a preventive war against terrorism whose effectiveness is disputed.]

It seems that resistance to blind obedience is not only the function of the individual's moral competence (Kohlberg 1973) or his ability to reassess authority situations (Milgram 1974) but also in a form of the lesson of history experienced by the individual's parents or their generation. The story of this Holocaust survivor, Mr.

Ronen, illustrates this point. Mr. Ronen's son was severely wounded in the 1967 war. His second son, a dedicated combat soldier in the IDF, refused to serve in the territories during the Intifada. In his writing to the press (*Ha'aretz*, 30 January 1989) entitled "The Courage to Be Alone," Ronen, a historian who specialized in the Holocaust era, writes:

> Bratislava, Slovakia, April 1942: Over months, trains packed with Jews are going east. Nobody knows exactly what their destination is. In spite of this, every day Jews attend the deportation. . . . One young person decided not to obey. . . . Though he himself does not know what is the destination of the trains. . . . He helps others to escape to Hungary which is relatively safe . . . he is often imprisoned for his illegal acts.
>
> Bendin, Poland, 8 August 1943: Last week 20,000 Jews were sent to Auschwitz which is close by. The campaign is not over yet as there are a few hundred Jews awaiting deportation in the Ghetto . . . a dozen rebellious Jews are sitting in one of the corners . . . two girls are more salient than the others—their bodies and clothing leave no doubts as to the type of interrogations they underwent by the Gestapo. . . . They both want to die . . . but suddenly one of them said: "No, I won't go to Auschwitz, I will jump from the window even if I am killed."
>
> The Golan Heights, 10 June 1967: A young tank officer, the son of the man from Slovakia and the woman from the Bendin Ghetto takes command after his commanders and friends were killed . . . disobeying the illogicality of . . . few against many . . . when rescuing a friend from a burning tank a bomb explodes and his eyes darken. . . . There is no surprise—those who do not follow logical orders are entitled to get harmed.
>
> The West Bank, 16 January 1989: Some soldiers shoot and cry . . . others shoot and don't cry . . . some obey orders even if they are manifestly illegal. . . . A combat soldier who has already fought in two wars, a brother of the wounded soldier from the Golan Heights and a father of three kids, decides to object to a command which permits him to shoot at women and children. . . . He is punished and sent to jail . . . but prison is a familiar place to him from the family history . . . this is a family which is used to not obeying . . . he never heard in his family the words "we did not know" . . . "there was no choice." . . . This is a family where the father does not lower his eyes when he is asked by his son: Daddy, where were you at that historical moment when the lights were not shining?

Camps

The prison camp is a powerful symbol within the Jewish/Israeli culture. According to Young (1989) it displays the split personality of the young native-born Israeli, who is not sure who is the victim and whom he is guarding:

> Having carried the memory of his people's past victimization into battle in order never to be victimized again, the Israeli discovers the source both of his strength and of his weakness as *victor*: the same figure of victimization that motivated him as a soldier also compels extraordinary sympathy for his defeated enemies, now grasped in the figure of his own people's defeats. In fact, as long as the dual memory of Jewish martyrs and heroes remains the predominant ideological trope in Israel, her soldiers cannot lose their sense of identity with the victims. (pp. 136–137) (emphasis added)

The PLO prison camp in Lebanon, Ansar, seemed to include all the possible paradoxes of the war and proved to be the last straw for many soldiers, particularly the experienced ones (Linn 1989 b). In the words of a refuser whose parents did not experience the Holocaust:

> Ansar was the final catalyst. This was a different type of war. It was purely against civilians. I had never before known such a war. After two months of fighting, with a break of four days, I came back home, and found another draft waiting for me . . . this time to Ansar. I wanted to refuse but I couldn't cope with refusal. . . . My commanders are actually my friends and I knew that they would have to substitute for me . . . so I decided to go. We came in . . . it was like a *concentration camp for me*: wire fences, signs and piles of mud. . . . All the associations came into my mind. I told my commander that I was refusing. . . . He asked me "What is the difference between manning a checkpoint, and serving in Ansar?" It was hard to explain to him that this was the edge of my moral boundaries. I was proud that I could refuse. I told nobody about it. My name is not on the list of refusers. I felt contempt for myself before refusing. (Linn 1989b, p. 39)

As the first prison camp in which Israeli soldiers had to guard terrorist youth, Ansar became symbolically a moral frame of reference against which they made their decision as to whether or not to refuse. Thus Ansar became an emotional and moral turning point:

> Before my refusal my commander tried to persuade me to go, indicating that he would let me serve in Lebanon, not in Ansar. It became a kind of dichotomy, that Ansar is bad and Lebanon is good—but not for me. I said to myself that it would be better for me to be in prison than to guard at Ansar. (Linn 1989b, p. 39)

In an interview with the press, one refuser summed up this issue of Ansar:

> The name Ansar has a kind of emotional meaning for me, a very frightening one. In this word there is all the evil of the war. (*Ha'ir*, 22 April 1983).

Interestingly, or cynically, the prison camp of the Intifada still bears the name Ansar. Again it remained the last straw for many soldiers and the highest cause for evasion of service. One reservist wrote to the press that the tragedy is that "we have become a nation of prison guard" (*Ma'ariv*, 22 September 1989).

During the Intifada, however, the prison camps were much closer to home than in Lebanon. They are stationed in the territories. Some are even located *within* the Green Line. The prisoners were not child terrorists but children who threw stones. For some soldiers who were fighting in Lebanon the analogy to the Holocaust became the incentive for avoiding service during the Intifada:

> During the war in Lebanon, *I refused* to consider the option of *refusal*. . . . I said to myself—this is a war, though it is stupid, I have no choice, I have to go . . . My real problem started in Ansar . . . after a few hours there I knew I was going to refuse. . . . When the Intifada started I knew I would refuse . . . this is not a war—this is an oppression. . . . I cannot escape the analogy with the Holocaust though my parents weren't there . . . I saw myself as a potential victim of this situation . . . I think it is going to happen to us . . . and the Holocaust experience cuts through my experience in the Intifada—I know there can be no analogy to the Holocaust but I cannot escape the thoughts about the issue of my contribution to this situation of helplessness, a child facing the mighty.

There seemed to be a growing understanding that moral criticism is primarily the *refusal to remain silent* in face of injustice. This change is clearly seen in the following report of a reservist who was stationed in the Ansar prison within the Green Line. Ari Shavit writes:

> The unjust analogy with those camps of fifty years ago won't go away. It is not suggested by anti-Israeli propaganda. It is in the language the soldier uses as a matter of discourse; when A. gets up to

do guard duty in the interrogation section, he says: "I'm off, late for the inquisition." When R. sees a line of prisoners approaching under the barrels of his friends' M16s, he says with quiet interest "Look. The *aktion* has begun." And N., who has strong right-wing views, grumbles to anyone who will listen that the place resembles a concentration camp. M., with a thin smile, explains that he has accumulated so many days in reserve duty during the Intifada that soon they will promote him to a senior Gestapo official. And I, too, who have always abhorred this analogy, who have always argued bitterly with anyone who so much as hints at it, I can no longer stop myself. The associations are too strong . . . But then I realized that the problem is not in the similarity—for no one can seriously think that there is a real similarity—the problem is that the lack of similarity is not strong enough to silence once and for all the evil echoes, the accusing images.

What is happening here is that an entire population of our reservists—bank clerks, insurance agents, electronics engineers, technicians, retailers, students—has the task of imprisoning another entire population. Their tile layers, plasterers, lab workers, journalists, clergy, and students. . . . And you are a part of it. You comply. . . . *And you are part of this process* . . . and suddenly (you cannot say) . . . "I didn't know."

Yet, only one out of sixty of us refuse to do guard duty in the interrogation section. Only four or five look troubled. Most of the rest get accustomed to it very quickly.

Are we shock troopers? No. After all we (the reservists) do not want to be here. We don't like this work . . . and when we stand (in a check up) quite tired, distressed, and miserable, with the rotten webbing with the coats that do not warm us . . . it is hard to complain about us, for we are also the *victims*. . . . I estimate that several hundred young men at least must do reserve duty in this internment camp each year. . . . Thus after forty months of Intifada, more than ten thousand Israeli citizens in uniform have walked between the fences . . . and the country has been quiet. Has flourished . . . and although there is no basis for comparison—and in truth there is no basis for comparison—I begin to understand how it was with some of those other guards who stood in other places, over other people, behind other fences.

After forty months of Intifada and after the war in Lebanon . . . it seems that we have been *educated* to behave in this way. Otherwise it is hard to understand how smooth things are going here (in prison). How good we are at walking in between the written and the oral Bible. How come the inner contradictions in this place don't blow out the Israeli. (*Ha'aretz*, 3 May 1991)

Being imprisoned owing to one's Jewishness or national aspirations is a strong collective memory for the average Israeli. So is the idea of being a refugee, for many of the ancestors of Israeli soldiers were refugees. However, unlike the Arab states that consistently refuse to grant Palestinian refugees citizenship, using them as the symbol of their holocaust (Linn and Gur-Zeev 1995), the State of Israel marked the end of the historic status of the homeless Jew. Even if most Israelis tend to cling to the words of their first president, Dr. Chaim Wiezmann, that within the list of injustice done in this world, the creation of the state of Israel was the least of smaller injustices, the individual soldier still has a concrete problem when he encounters the individual refugee, owing to his unique situation of both occupying soldier and citizen who often wishes his ancestors had no part in the creation of this injustice (Morris 1989).

Since 1967, there are continuing personal contacts between Israelis and Palestinians who have worked in Israel. Under these conditions, it is possible that the Israeli employer of a Palestinian when called to do his army duty could turn out to be the combat reservist in charge of a Palestinian camp. The need to disperse demonstrations sometimes further takes the soldiers into the homes of the refugees; prior to the Intifada many soldiers never set foot in them. The physical and emotional preoccupation with various types of camps seems to attenuate the moral strength of the Israelis, who are not "trained" to be camp guards or to exercise these collective memories. One Intifada refuser presents the dialogue between the prisoner and the guard in the book by Jorge Sempsrum, Le Grand Voyage (1968), as a justification for his action:

> I refused since I did not want to be on the wrong side of the moral struggle—as in Sempsrum's book where he describes his guard: "He is there because he did not feel the need to be in another place . . . because he is not free." (pp. 46–47)

Camp is a memory, a reality, and a symbol Israelis live by (Lakoff and Johnson 1980). They cannot remain indifferent to this metaphor. The Israeli novelist Avi Valentin (1989) described a fictional work camp built by the Israelis. In his *Sahid,* one of the Arab workers says:

> The Jews had used up all their colors . . . yes, this is exactly what happened to them . . . blue is the color of the workers who take the first train (to work), khaki is the color of the soldiers, black,

> white, red, and green, have been banned (by the authorities), since they are our colors, so what is left? Yellow. Yes. This is exactly what happened and this would not have happened if *the Jews had not been sensitive to symbols and colors, but they are.* . . . Therefore they do not allow us to wear black, white, red, or green, but they don't mind if we wear yellow. Isn't it funny? That's why I liked to wear yellow. I liked it since I felt *right*. Right as the Jews did once. (p. 22) (emphasis added)

Within the Jewish-Israeli culture, yellow is not an innocent color because it was the color of the yellow star Jews were obliged to wear during the Nazi occupation. The Intifada, seems to have become a war of moral colors.

David and Goliath: The Miserable War against Children

Children are always the saddest victims of wars. One aspect of Israeli historical awareness deals with the 1.5 million children taken from or with their mothers to the gas chambers, or who died as they fell from speeding trains, thrown out by frantic parents on the off chance that they might survive. Within Israeli culture the sanctity of children is central: they are not used as a shield nor as front-line soldiers. In the Muslim world, the concept of the holy martyr is common and children are promised by their elders that they will reach the gates of Heaven if they die in war. During the Khomeini regime in Iran, such children were called "heaven's key children"; They also are now called Shahid (saint) by the Palestinians. During the war in Lebanon, these children were equipped with Soviet RPG missiles; in the Intifada, they are equipped with building blocks, stones, knives, Molotov Cocktails, and the like. (Interestingly, the Molotov Cocktail was always a symbol for heroism for the Israelis since the Holocaust and, more recently, since Israel's war of independence in 1948–1949, during which Kibbutz defenders miraculously succeeded to blow up a Syrain tank that was about to enter the Kibbutz).

Victimized children always mark the epitome of evil, and for the Israeli it is reminiscent of the Holocaust. There is no shortage of examples: on 15 May 1974 PLO terrorists infiltrated an elementary school in the Galilee town of Ma'alot, demanding the release of Arab prisoners. When their demand was not met they murdered twenty-four school children and wounded sixty-two others. Most typical of the Holocaust experience was an attack by terrorists against a home in the Galilee town of Naharia. The father and his four-year-old daughter were taken to the beach and murdered, while the mother who was hiding in the cellar of the house tried to stifle the cries of her two-year-old baby and accidentally suffocated him.

PLO terrorism against Israeli civilians reached its peak on 11 March 1978, when two buses were hijacked near Tel Aviv: parents tried to save their children by throwing them from the windows onto the highway. The incident ended with thirty-three dead and eighty-two wounded. The analogy to the Holocaust was not hard to draw. A week later the IDF launched an attack in Lebanon to destroy the PLO bases. The campaign was called the "Litani operation" after the small river that marked the boundary of the territory invaded. When explaining the rationale for this limited retaliatory attack, Prime Minister Menachem Begin quoted the Hebrew national poet Bialik: "The spilling of the blood of a child the devil has not yet invented"—lines from a poem written following a 1904 pogrom in the town of Kishinev in Russia. Ten years after the Litani operation, Peace Now activists use the same lines to protest the intolerable actions the soldiers are forced to take in the territories (*Chadashot*, 29 January 1989).

When the Israeli soldier is sent to fight (children) in the Intifada, he is likely to lose on moral grounds from the outset. In response to this situation, the Israeli novelist, Aaron Meged, wrote to the press:

> Since the "child-crusade" when a mad Frenchmen brought hundreds of children to the Mediterranean shore, promising them that he would divide the sea and bring them to the Holy Land, the result of which was that they all were killed or sold into slavery, there has never been such a horror in any people or land as that which is happening now across the Green Line (the pre-June 1967 border), where adults send boys and girls aged eight to nine and fourteen to fifteen to the front line, every day, while they hide at home or go to work in faraway places. . . . At the same time, many of their people are being killed in Lebanon . . . and no one is crying . . . not here and not in the world. . . . These words are not stated in order to justify beating, wounding and killing (by IDF soldiers—R.L) unless in self-defense or to protect lives, but to protest against the stirring songs in praise of the pure innocent Intifada heroes and against the IDF soldiers (who are viewed in these songs) as *child killers with an appetite.* (*Yediot,* 5 March 1989)

Many soldiers know not only that they cannot *win* this war but that they cannot even *fight* it. An Intifada refuser explains how he reached his decision to disobey:

> After the incident in Nablus (where a paratrooper was killed by a building block), the soldiers realized that the building blocks were not a joke. A friend of mine saw a four-year-old child about to drop a heavy block that had been put there for him on a roof under which an IDF patrol was going to pass. Standing orders allowed shooting at a building if the lives of the soldiers walking below were threatened, but my friend told me he just could not do it, and the decision was a matter of milliseconds. He became so concerned that he started shouting at the kid "Hey, Hey." The kid was surprised and dropped the block just before the soldiers passed. . . . My friend told me that he would never do reserve service in the territories. . . . He moved to Australia.

The poet Chaim Beer reflects on the soldiers' moral distress:

> We are learning to take our breakfast with information about a prisoner who had died from a beating; to drive to work with the knowledge of a four-year-old girl whose eye was injured (accidentally—R.L.) by a plastic bullet; to go to bed with our language corrupted beyond repair—for example, a youngster *met* his death tonight, as if from the morning he had been *looking for his death* and in the evening he finally found it. (*Yediot*, 5 May 1989)

Yehoram Gaon, a famous Israeli folk singer who often sang to audiences of troops in his reserve duty and did not advocate refusal, said in an interview with the press (*Ha'aretz*, 14 July 1989),

> The Intifada is the worst war we have ever had, since it hurts the IDF directly. In our previous wars, the IDF was damaged physically, but this time it is being damaged mentally. It has transformed the soldier into something else, not a soldier who defends his homeland. It is not by accident that a distinction is made between a soldier and a storm trooper. When women and children are facing you—that is a different war. (*Ha'aretz*, 14 July 1989)

This use of children and women as the spearhead of the war (which is also forbidden by the Geneva Convention)—causes even extreme leftist Israelis, who strongly support the Palestinian cause, to question it. At a meeting of educated women from both sides, the Israelis bitterly complained to the Arabs about the "exploitation of Palestinian children in the process of the Intifada." (*Ha'aretz*, 12 September 1989).

The concern about children also manifests itself in other public events. At a Children's Day celebrating the anniversary of the founding of a kibbutz in the Negev, the first prize was given for a song composed by young members of the settlement called "David and Goliath"; the lyrics were, in part:

> Dudi you wanted to be like David / Red headed and nice eyes, And always with a smile / In an alley at Nablus you forgot everything and turned into Goliath / A ten-year-old child was standing in front of you / With a stone in his hand and there was no way out. / You did not think for a second, you cocked your rifle—and now you are also the victim. Chorus: Two mothers are weeping at home now. / Two lost their children. / One a hero of his nation and the other is a shadow of himself. (*Ma'ariv*, 20 October 1989).

The renowned Israeli lyricist, translator, and satirist Dan Almagor seems to portray the moral crisis of some Israeli soldiers. His highly patriotic songs are still sung by Israeli soldiers and others. Since his son-in-law left the country after reserve service in Jericho, and he and his wife (Almagor's daughter) joined Amnesty International, Almagor turned down an invitation to write songs for the fortieth anniversary of Israel's independence and joined the extreme left protest movement, advocating refusal. This is one of his writings:

> The cry of kids, the cry of the eye or blood of a small child, will be heard when the day comes, in the opening trial. And when the trial opens against the transparent box, we will all sit in there. What was it our national poet (Bialick) said after that exceptional case (the Kishinev pogrom) Stand up, and leave this killing city.

Since his moral crisis, Almagor has not stopped drawing analogies between Israel and Germany. He says,

> It is clear to me that this is the worst association, the most provocative statement, that if my words have any echo, everyone will attack me for using this analogy. I did it deliberately. There is no doubt that the Holocaust was the greatest obscenity in human history and I don't dare to think, not even for a moment, that we could ever do what the Nazis did, that is, mass extermination with gas chambers. I know that every word such as gas, Nazis, glass box, etc., immediately creates antagonism. . . . I also made use of other symbols that are so sacred to us from our childhood. . . . The fact is, that when I see all these kids with hands tied after the soldiers arrest them in a demonstration it reminds me of a visit to Ger-

> many during the war in Lebanon. The mayor of a small town showed me the little museum they founded in memory of the Jewish community that had lived there. We were standing there, facing an innocent picture of Jews being lifted onto a truck. The mayor pointed to the driver, and said that it was him. He also identified other German citizens standing near the truck and smiling. Apparently, nothing particularly terrible was happening. . . . But when I visited headquarters in Nablus and saw those kids I said to myself, "One day when the Palestinian state is established, *these kids will remember me*. . . . I love this country . . . there are fine things here. . . . But I will also *be standing in the glass box*. This would be the first box in which I would be standing . . . now that I have written all that, I can *look my daughter in the eyes*" (*Kolbo*, 16 December 1988).

In summing up this section it is worth recalling that long before these two morally problematic wars occurred, the Israeli Prime Minister Golda Meir said,

> We will always be able to forgive the Arab leaders for killing our children, but we would never be willing to forgive them for causing us to kill their children.

Conclusion

This chapter attempted to delineate some of the leading metaphors and symbols in the lives of the Israeli soldiers. For this generation, the Holocaust is a metaphor and a symbol—a historical event where Jews were herded as sheep into carefully designed gas chambers without the ability to resist, having no homeland to go to nor the physical power to flee. For them, the Israel Defense Forces are a necessary reality as well as a metaphor for defending against becoming sheep, to the point where "it is good to die for this country." By refusing, they are objecting to the possibility of becoming sheep once again by blindly dying for a country where 'shooting and crying' is not a chosen action but an unfortunate and troublesome necessity.

The slightest deviation from the pure notion of self-defense, even as in the case of a preemptive strike against terrorists or the need to disperse violent demonstrations of children, seems to become an existential threat to the individual soldier's moral identity. He fears that he is heading toward a position where he might call himself a Nazi, and become a "cog in the military machine." In encounters with civilians, and particularly with children, the idea of self-defense is no longer clear and the individual soldier remains a morally naked Goliath. The Israeli soldier does not seek children to capture or to kill; they are there, in the battlefield, used as a shield by a rival familiar with the moral code of the IDF and following a different moral code of its own. Even though unfortunate killings can happen to any army in the world, the Israeli soldier cannot allow it to happen to him. For him, it is an action that can be devised only by a Nazi. If he does not want to become a Nazi, he is left in the vulnerable but moral stand of a sheep. In the life-threatening situations in which he has found himself in the Intifada, he cannot be Goliath nor can he remain David.

Although these metaphors point toward evil as well as toward good, soldiers who adopt them seem to try and identify with the good: They will not be a cog in the machine, nor do they seek to become Goliath.

It is important to note that what soldiers tend to remember and use of the Holocaust depends on how they remember it, and how they remember it depends on the metaphors they use as a frame of reference. In their unsuccessful and unwilling process of adjusting to the new military realities, Israeli soldiers seem to open another frontier—one that struggles with language to summarize the past and to bring them to a new approach in which they will be able to deal both with themselves and others in a morally defensible way (Segev 1990). The words of one Israeli soldier, who opposed the war in Lebanon, yet decided not to assume a separate position and not exit himself from the military service, end this chapter:

> My mother was imprisoned in Auschwitz seeing her family gassed while Germans orchestrated music. She argues that the only revenge she has is the fact that she is still alive, bore two kids (my brother is a pilot and myself, a commander in the armored division), who are capable of defending themselves. . . . I am morally troubled when the assigned military missions involve contact with civilians . . . but I see no resemblance to the Germans—if we make them partners for analogy, the Israeli soldier gives them too much credit.
>
> If I decide to refuse I have to think how to present it to my mother. . . . Though she is the one who educated me to be concerned about human lives, she is well aware of the fact that freedom does not exist by itself but rather needs to be defended. If we

> are not willing to be slaughtered like sheep once again—the Israel Defense Forces are a living dream for her—I do not know how I am going to tell her that I may decide to refuse military service.

This chapter has focused on collective memories as one source of soldiers' moral guidelines for action (Young 1989). Yet, as has been noted by Cohen (1971), a man's belief about the moral character of his own act is surely not the only court before which that act may be judged. While a reflective conscience is a necessary court and a very important one, it is not a sufficient one. The audience would want to know whether the individual was acting conscientiously, and whether this way of acting might have moral and/or political motivation. The following chapter utilizes Cohen's model for identification of the motivation for selective disobedience.

In Israel, refusal is the most political action a person can take outside the parliament. . . . I think that every political protester holds a moral component but not every moral refuser holds political components.

—An Intifada refuser

8

Refusal and Motivation

From Moral and Political to Personal

"To tell us again that war is hell, is not to tell us why one should be justified in demanding for himself an immunity in advance" or the right to dissociate himself from the fighting soldiers (Melzer 1975, p. 54). A full understanding of selective conscientious objection requires an appreciation of the motivation of the disobedient. For this, argues Cohen (1971), we must go beyond the analysis of the objectively performed act, inquiring into the subjective and, hence, murky sphere of the character and aims of the actor. Particularly in times of war, disobedience, even if claimed to be morally motivated (a claim that requires examination), is a prima facie wrong and the burden of proof rests upon the disobedient. As the act of disobedience is reflectively performed, the subject is well prepared to specify those other moral components in the situation that obliged him to refuse. The deliberate form in which the disobedience is performed suggests that it is not an accidental act but rather a function of a long process of self-doubts.

A number of intertwined motivating principles are likely to lie behind the most honest and scrupulous acts of civil disobedience, and some motives will be unconscious or unclear even to the law-breaker. According to Cohen (1971), "determining the 'real' motivation in a particular case is therefore a messy and uncertain business" (p. 22). Yet, this should not discourage the judge, as "often one can arrive at some fair judgment in this matter usually with the candid help of the protester himself" (p. 22).

In this chapter, Cohen's (1971) work on civil disobedience provides a framework for the classification of selective conscientious objection. Cohen (1971) has argued that moral and political motivations serve as the two major categories for inquiry into the refusers' motivation. Whereas these two categories cannot be separated, they can be distinguished. Thus, he explains, "some acts and decisions take place within an essentially political framework, being addressed primarily to the whole community in view of its common concerns. Other acts and decisions are more specifically personal, being undertaken by a man for himself, out of chief regard for principles and values that he accepts as governing his conduct. These latter often have political import—import for the whole community—just as the former have moral import. But in being differently conceived and differently aimed, the two kinds of acts may reasonably be distinguished from one another, the first called political, the second moral." (p. 58). In line with Cohen, disobedience for political reasons is much more common. It is disobedience specifically addressed to the members of the community at large and intended to influence their subsequent conduct. The reason for seeking such influence may be deeply ethical, of course, but the objective for the protest is the change of law or government policy. The effectiveness of such politically motivated disobedience must be judged by the extent to which the process advances the envisioned change: "Its justification may depend upon the likelihood of its having such political consequences" (p. 58).

According to Cohen (1971), morally motivated disobedience is less ambitious, has a limited objective, and is more specific in intent. Indeed, the morally motivated disobedient would also wish for the change or elimination of some policy, but his disobedient act is not so much aimed at effecting a change as it is a public statement of his inability to comply in good conscience. It is the refuser's response to a direct conflict between his personal ethical principles and some legal obligation that he is supposed to fulfill. It may or may not have some tendency to produce a desired political change: "The basic considerations for him are not the results to which the disobedience leads but the principles upon which it is grounded" (p. 59). Consequently, the morally motivated refuser may or may not disobey in public. As his disobedience is a concrete outcome of some ethical convictions, its tactical function is secondary at best. The criteria for identification of moral versus political motives in line with Cohen's work are presented in table 8.

Table 8. Motivation for Disobedience

Political
1. Wishing the action to be public
2. Referring to the action as essentially a tactic
3. Worried about the appeal of the action to the members of the community
4. Having an external goal the changing of policy
5. Emphasis on the action's effectiveness
6. Focus on the act
Moral
1. The action may or may not be performed in public
2. Priority for ethical conviction
3. Less ambitious than political action
4. More limited in object and more specific in intent than political action
5. Emphasis on the principles rather than the result
6. Focus on the actor

Note: Constructed from Cohen, 1971.

Table 9 provides another set of criteria identified in the narrative of the Refusers during the Intifada (on top of the moral and political reasoning). We labeled it as "personal" motivation.

Table 9. Motivation for Personal Disobedience

1. The action may or may not be performed in public
2. Referring to the action as essentially a tactic
3. Not worried about the appeal of the action for the members of the community
4. Limited in object—to remove oneself from the dilemma situation
5. Focus on the actor

The following narratives portray three types of motivations for refusal according to the above schemes.

The morally motivated refuser. We were in the Gaza Strip in April 1988. As a commander *you* are responsible for the people's motivation, you have to be able to convince them that what they are doing is important. I don't think that you have to refuse in all situations . . . but in my context at the time when I refused an additional service like that, I found it justified. There was no specific reason for this refusal—I just felt I wouldn't be able to do it again . . . for example, . . . there were riots and three Arabs were killed . . . not by soldiers from our unit. The next day we were there on one of our patrols, and they had a memorial. People were praying. We passed by, we reported to the high command that there was a gathering of praying people. So we were told to wait. Many more forces were brought to the place and there was an order to disperse the demonstrators . . . so somebody shot tear gas and there was a mess. They dispersed and half a minute later the Brigadier came in and said—it is okay. They can continue to pray quietly. There is no need to disperse them . . . so they were allowed to return . . . meanwhile you hear on the radio that we should be on alert. Why? Because there was a fear that there would be more and larger riots. Why? Because an old man was killed by the gas that we were shooting . . . there is fear that his funeral would bring about riots . . . it was not any kind of flagrantly illegal command, nothing special, somebody made a mistake, said we should disperse demonstrations, accidentally there was an old man there, maybe he was even sick, and the gas hit him, nothing deviant, nobody "broke bones" on purpose. But for me, a man was killed, and we were informed "By the way, a man was killed—try to avoid it next time so there will be no riots" . . . there was another case, when we were chasing two people hoping to catch the one who threw the stones. We saw somebody rushing into a house. It was clear to me who was the one . . . but the one next to him was also hit with a rubber bullet while we were chasing them, he wasn't hurt severely. We caught the one who had thrown the stones and he said "it wasn't me." I was 99 percent sure that he was the one. This was so frustrating . . . the commander, who is my friend asked me: what do you think? I said to him—I can swear that this is the guy . . . finally we released him and I suddenly found myself in a situation where I myself said "he probably didn't do anything." If I decided not to refuse but fight within the system, there are two options—not to disperse the demonstrators . . . or to do this job but avoid thinking about it in conscientious terms . . . then I will not be frustrated and be able to do my job. I feel that if I was a simple soldier I would not refuse . . . a soldier can always volunteer and guard the back yard or stay in the kitchen and he can afford not to know the end result of his actions in the field. I think that there is a limit to my ability to contribute morally while I am in the field. After all when these people are forced to leave the country (transfer) and I am in the field all that I will be able to do is to lift them *gently* onto the truck. I am sure they will not be thrown onto the truck . . . so what? I am also sure that in the concentration camps there was a soldier who gave soup to a person before he was gassed. I was assigned to be a platoon commander and I felt it was beyond my ability . . . my refusal is very much a hesitant one. I said, "I want to do my reserve service with another battalion . . . who would not be my soldiers so I would not feel the same commitment as I feel to them." I couldn't be loyal to the missions we had in Gaza, I thought they were immoral—but I had to behave as a commander and motivate my soldiers. I don't object to serving in the territories . . . but personally I felt that in this place I could not command my soldiers . . . my refusal is very personal. However, when I hear that someone has refused I am not sorry about it. I don't think this should be a political refusal since the situation is changing all the time . . . all I can say is "only do the moral thing." I was considering refusal in Lebanon . . . but there, it was also an issue of fear. What made it easy for me to refuse here is the fact that it is definitely not out of fear . . . when I met my battalion commander after prison he said to me, "since you were not there, there was a mess in the company. The officer that substituted you just killed somebody . . . its a pity that people were killed. If you had been there this would not have happened."

I had a long talk with the Brigadier . . . they seem to understand my desire to move to another battalion, but they didn't want me to refuse—this is just a pain in the neck for them. The soldiers didn't understand my action. After prison, they were serving along the border with Jordan. I would have gone to this service, but meanwhile I had been expelled from the battalion. One of the people in my company was killed. I went to the funeral . . . this was my hardest time . . . actually I felt I had deserted them. I am ready to serve again in the territories, but not as a commander. If you serve in the army you are helping the occupation anyhow since you are easing the burden on other frontiers.

The politically motivated refuser. My crisis started in the 1973 war . . . we were rescuing the paratroopers from the Chinese Farm.

Then I crossed the Suez canal and later was granted a forty-eight-hour leave to get married. . . . I was almost killed by our forces. . . . Our Deputy Chief of Staff . . . (General Barak, the second Chief of Staff during the Intifada, R.L.) was responsible for this friendly fire. It fills you with some strange thoughts about your military leaders and their abilities. Then came the Lebanon war and once again, I was in the brigade that was bombed by our own forces . . . this is my war folklore. Friends were killed in both cases. I already had doubts regarding this "pretend war" but nevertheless I went (to Lebanon). . . . I could see how we tricked the Syrians to start a war with us . . . already then I said "I refuse" but the best thing that happened to me was the realization that they were already protesting in Tel Aviv . . . it was a bad feeling to realize that it was so easy to start a war. . . . I see refusal as one step forward beyond my innocence. I know that many do not refuse like me but say "I'll go to the field and see—if there is something bad, I will refuse," so I say to them, "but imagine that suddenly there is an alert and we are taken regardless of the fact that you were promised to be in the kitchen . . . and there is social pressure and when each one is in webbing can you say "I am refusing"? It is easier to refuse when you get the draft at home . . . my stay in prison brought me into political activism . . . this activism brought me more into the extreme. . . . I knew that if I did not become an activist after my prison term, then it meant that I had done it in vain. On the contrary, I intentionally published my refusal story in the press and therefore I felt much better during this time. One of the reasons that I became politically active in Yesh Gvul (There is a Limit) is to help others overcome their hesitations regarding the prison term . . . not to vanish while they are there . . . not to be forgotten. . . . I knew that I was not going to go to Gaza.

I was invited to a motivation discussion with the commander a day before the draft . . . he is a manager of a factory . . . and we had a "deaf talk," he said, talking from his own sphere of metaphors, "what if every *worker* would stand up and do what he wants?" and his other argument was "we particularly need moral people to be there." I said to him "no"—I am refusing and that is that. I can always say yes.

During the trial the judge said to me: "after two weeks they are through with the reserve, but you will get another draft that will get you another prison term." After my prison term was over, my platoon commander came and told me it was awkward to jail me once again—after all, we had already served seventeen years together and had witnessed some wars together . . . he advised me not to refuse but to come with them arguing that *"we are doing searches but we remain polite soldiers."* I told him—I am not entering into houses . . . so he gave me an alternative service. . . . I don't know what would have happened if they had thrown stones at me . . . it is worse than prison. My company commander said, "with your refusal you leave me alone." After my second prison term, he called me again and told me that he was depressed, and unable to accept what he was doing: hitting women, and some other commands . . . the third time when I had to go I called my commander to tell him that I was not coming to the reserve. He said over the phone: "for me you are sick, so be well." And later he found me a unit that does not do reserve service in the territories. I am not ready to go to the territories, neither in peace time nor in times of war. My refusal was originally a moral one but I try to make it a political issue for Yesh Gvul.

The personally motivated refuser. As a medic I was very lucky. I always managed to convince the authorities to send me somewhere else. During my compulsory service I decided that I would be a cook or a medic. Not because of the territories—during my army service I served in the territories . . . my refusal came out of my political studies at the university, my contact with Arab students, etc. I did not take part in the Yom Kippur war. I did all that I could to take no part in it. I also tried to leave the army using the excuse of a medical profile. I had a great fear of war—just pure fear.

I was shocked to realize that I had to decide which army I would join, the conquering one or the humanist one. From one reserve service to another I tried to walk between the drops. I had the opportunity to meet the IDF career officers with all the medals on their shoulders that turn them into entities without dilemmas. I don't blame them, this is a transformation they go through which enables them to survive.

One time I provoked them and entered a room full of them dressed in civilian clothes thinking that perhaps they would throw me out. A day later they told me that they do not need people like me in the Army. But I was stubborn and to this day I insist on going to the army not because I like it but because I see it as my civil obligation and I am only there because I have been drafted, and for no other reason. If it were left to me I would not spend one single day in the Army and if I had the power to do so I would release everyone that I could. I do not like the idea of there being an exception, as an ideology. During the war in Lebanon I did not go, I simply fled. My unit took part. I was scared. I decided I was not going . . . at the same time I had recently returned from abroad (after three years) and I made every excuse I could so that the authorities couldn't find my address . . . and when I finally went to register (knowing that my unit was having an exercise) I was told it was too late. I acted very surprised and said I hadn't known. They wanted to send me somewhere else but I used every trick I could think of and finally came with a suitcase full of books and asked them to send me to prison. They didn't know what to do with me so finally they put me in the headquarters as a medic. I will never forget someone coming to me sick, he was about twenty-seven or twenty-eight and he wanted me to give him pills so that he could get better quickly and get back to Beirut. He said it was pretty rough there and he wanted to get back to his unit. I was shocked. I thought does he really want me to give him pills so he can get healthy just to die there? But I never said it to him as I wanted to keep a low profile. Well, the reservist returned to his unit after I had given him all the antibiotics. [Then] I began to panic at the terrible conflict I felt. Here I was working in this tragic theatre and I felt so many values overflowing and with such contradictory feelings, I realized I couldn't go on. I changed my address so they wouldn't find me. Only at the end of the war when there was a military exercise I attended it and I was tried for not attending previously and was punished by having to pay a fine. Then Yesh Gvul started but in a way I was marginal for them since by the time they started I was already a long-term refuser. In a way I felt a bit detached from them. The great shock is that suddenly you have to withdraw from the focus of belonging to this society, that is to say, all that you have created before and the social network you have established and the individual derivatives—you have to abandon them all. I had returned from Europe with some intellectual and emotional assets that were automatically incorporated into the vacuum that was created in the Israeli entity and I had felt fulfilled but after I refused I felt completely alone. I crossed the border of refusal long ago—my only concern was the isolation. I had emotional fears and also hopes that I would not be involved in conflicts.

I think that in order to refuse one needs to have an independent way of thinking. When you refuse you know exactly which camp you are leaving, but you do not know the camp you are going to.

Discussion

Whether holding, or perceived to be holding, a separate or connected position of criticism, the identification of the motivation behind the action of disobedience is crucial for the assessment of the punishment. If public debate is raised, all would want to know whether this specific action was indeed selective conscientious objection and not political transgression, or rebellion. Within such a public debate, the intention of the law breaking would be taken into consideration and this in turn would affect the level of punishment. In this chapter we tried to distinguish between moral and political motives for selective conscientious objection and suggested the possibility of having a third category—the personal one—which is neither moral nor political but pragmatic. It is important to note that pragmatic refusers often presented morally or politically mature concerns and therefore need not be regarded as inferior to the moral or political refusers. On the contrary, we can look at these refusers as manifesting a new form of moral or political frustration; as if they say—we are well familiar with the moral and political reasoning for refusal, however, it is not *worth* using them as a form of justification. The presentation of personal or pragmatic reasoning is sometimes a protest against the use of moral or political reasoning in face of an indifferent government, army, or general public. In a way, the personal form of protest is a form of psychological retreat, as explained by this Lebanon and Intifada refuser: "The Intifada is a late PSTD (Post Traumatic Stress Disorder) of the Yom Kippur war which marked the end of the carnival atmosphere that dominated the country since the 1967 war—people did not come out with the feeling that we won, nor with the feeling that we lost. They came out with the feeling that we were fighting in vain . . . I do not exclude the possibility that the Israeli Secret Service shot the consul in London so we would have an excuse to go to war against Lebanon . . ."

It seems that the Intifada refusers are not ready to take a position of either/or regarding the motivation of their refusal. They often claim that their action incorporates a moral and political dimension. An Intifada refuser sums up this chapter with his insight:

> During the war in Lebanon there was a far-reaching question regarding the political aspect of the refusal: What if everybody does it? The response: Then we would not be in Lebanon. With the

> growing political objection to the war, the wave of refusers increased. The meaning of refusal in the Intifada is more complicated and I don't know what is the relationship between it and withdrawal . . . it is hard to believe that if everyone refused we wouldn't be in the territories. I don't see a linear connection between refusal and getting out of here . . . during the war in Lebanon, nobody believed it could take years. These days a refuser knows that the response to his act can take many years. That is why I believe that refusal is more conscientious now than it was during the war in Lebanon. Maybe the right definition in the present situation of refusal is as follows: *We are refusing out of conscientious reasons but we are being imprisoned out of political reasons*—we are political prisoners, conscientious refusers and victims of the system.

Though the identification of motivation is important for the assessment of the punishment, the judge would not be provided with the entire picture if he based his decision on these categories only. After all, an individual might be a philosopher in his reasoning and highly moral in his self-presentation, all of which may convince us that he is morally motivated in his principles. Yet we know nothing about the sincerity of these moral arguments. Even if the unprecedented action of selective refusal won some consensus as to the personal courage it demanded, the high level of moral maturity, moral consistency, and the like, it would be inadequate to allay the legitimate suspicion entertained by their immediate social circle and society at large: Is the objector a loyal citizen? Or is he a coward hiding behind moral principles? How sincere is his moral struggle? Can it be measured at all?

Most often this clash is not accidental. When it is followed by an act of disobedience against the law, the disobeyer's claim of moral maturity, consistency, and integrity are important and necessary, but not sufficient. The credibility of the justification for his act must be carefully examined. This examination is the focus of the following chapter.

In sending my friends to the territories without me . . . I solve only my problem. Not only I am not there to help them but I am sending the message that what they are doing is wrong. This was not an easy decision . . . with our obligation to doing reserve service, and the close relationship we have in the battalion where I have quite a central role makes it very difficult.

—An Intifada refuser

9

Refusal on Trial

From Morality to Credibility

Combatants' understanding of principles of justice does not guarantee that these principles are honestly held or believed, particularly when one's own life is at stake as in a war situation. These principles might be used as an excuse for not doing one's own duty, as a cover for fear, or even for revolutionary plans. These principles may place an extra risk and greater likelihood of casualties on those who are left in the unit and obliged to carry out the burden of the refuser's conscience. As has been noted by Cohen (1971), "If in obeying his conscience another man is obliged to do what he believes—in good conscience—to be morally wrong, the genuineness of that conflict must give us a pause" (p. 212).

Credibility refers to the weight given to admissible testimony. This characteristic is a crucial factor in any decision regarding the veracity of the witness' testimony (Feeney 1987). It has a special weight in decision making regarding a combatant who refuses to perform a specific mission or obligation in the name of moral convictions. It is thus a crucial dimension in the attempt to evaluate the claims and actions of selective conscientious objectors, particularly if we believe that "the principle of respect for persons does not require respect for the insincere conscience" (Childress 1982, p. 215).

The validation of a deliberate choice to refuse is not only the responsibility of the objector but also the duty of the community. At some point, as has been noted by Walzer (1970), the objector may have to stand alone and defend his personal integrity against his fellow citizens. "But this is hard to do and we ought not pretend that it is (morally) easy. Nor ought we make it easy" (p. 130). Walzer

(1977) suggested we examine the combatant's credibility in line with the following three questions: How did the refuser reach his decision? How honestly did he confront his obligations? How seriously did he weigh the alternative course of actions and consider their likely consequences for others as well as for himself?

How Did the Refuser Reach His Decision?

Fear is the major obstacle to fulfilling one's own obligation, particularly during war time. Greenwalt (1989) writes:

> If a soldier has self-interested reasons, including fear and likely deprivation, to avoid particular military duty, it may be impossible or highly difficult for him to decide if he is also conscientiously opposed to serving as well. For an outsider to try to make that judgment can be a daunting task. (p. 16)

The question is, What makes a particular individual incapable of overcoming his fear? There seems to be an interesting connection between the experience of fear and one's own concept of morality and justice. It might be argued that, with the growing moral suspicion regarding a military conflict, soldiers may cease to find within themselves the willingness or the ability to overcome fear. Support for this is evident from the reasoning of this Lebanon objector:

> I guess that if there was no punishment many more people would have refused to go to Lebanon. When I was drafted there was a man who shouted, "I don't want to come back in a coffin." We should not be ashamed of the fact that we are afraid, even during the most just war. However, there are more chances of overcoming this fear when the war is just. But here we couldn't—at least I couldn't.

Following the legitimization given by the Lebanon refusers to the talk about fear, the Intifada refusers further elaborated on its relationship to their refusal, using their experience in the Lebanon war as a frame of reference:

> During the Lebanon war, I learned to appreciate people who fear. . . . Now, during the Intifada, I believe that Israeli society would talk with its enemy after recognizing that fear is humane.

Another Intifada refuser added:

> During the war in Lebanon there were many reasons to be afraid. If I refuse these days to serve in the territories, everyone would know I did not do it out of fear.

With the increase of violence, the conventional notion of fear emerged among the Intifada refusers as well, as this refuser related:

> I cannot say that service in the territories is not frightening. I would like to meet the person who doesn't believe it's scary to drive a jeep with fifty kilograms of sharp metal potentially landing on your head. Anybody would be scared.

If they sensed that the motivation for refusal was fear, the strategy often used by the IDF commanders was to provide the soldier with alternative and less frightening military service within the war zone. This Lebanon Selective Conscientious Objector (hence, SCO) reported:

> Before the trial the commander called me for a talk. I told him that the war was unjust and a big mistake and that I wasn't going to Lebanon, and finally that I didn't want to die. He told me that if the reason was fear then we could both cope with it and he would put me in a bunker where I wouldn't have to go out and fight. I think there was something in what he said. When I came to think about it, I realized that it was indeed fear that prevented me from going to Lebanon. It was not the fear of dying but the *unwillingness* to die for an unjust war. I think I didn't want to die for Arik Sharon (the Minister of Defense).

Another way of managing the soldiers's fear was to refer the soldiers to a psychologist. One objector, for example, was instructed by his commander to talk with a psychologist while the whole brigade was in Lebanon, before the commander would consider his release. The soldier refused, as he recalled:

> Lebanon became such a scary area that the commander probably first wanted to make sure that a soldier like me would be able to set foot there, maybe later he would change his mind. I told my commander that there are many psychologists inside the Green Line and that if he has to send me to a psychologist, I can go to one here.

Were combatants' decisions to disobey reached alone, or did they mark an accommodation to an existing norm of refusal? The data suggest that 83 percent of the Lebanon SCOs and 79 percent of the Intifada SCOs were the only refusers in their unit. At the same time, 78 percent of the Lebanon SCOs and 67 percent of the Intifada SCOs insisted on returning to the same unit upon their release from prison. The more attached the soldier was to the unit, the harder it was to translate refusal into action. Here are the words of one Lebanon SCO:

> The worst part of the refusal was going to the commander, going to the unit and coping with the prison. . . . I am really attached to the unit, the people, and the commander persuaded me not to refuse. The commander is really my friend. He didn't want to put me in jail . . . we went through the same hard times during the Yom Kippur war and other campaigns and suddenly you find yourself on the other side. . . . And what happens after prison. You come back to serve with the same people and you still believe that if Syria attacks us tomorrow, you should go with them to fight, to protect your country without hesitation. But how would they accept you?

It must be emphasized that in both conflicts many commanders often took upon themselves the role of convincing the potential SCO to continue to serve even if they were not at peace with the ongoing military policy. Yet, given the apolitical nature of the IDF, even morally puzzled commanders during the two conflicts were trying to do their best to convince the soldiers to remain in the unit. The ordeal of these commanders has never been studied.

How Honestly Did the Refuser Confront His Obligations?

If an Israeli reserve soldier wants to evade his service, he can do it in various ways: lowering his medical profile, going abroad at the time of the service, or arranging for a special release due to business difficulties. Refusal can be just another tactic in this endless list. An Intifada refuser elaborated on this topic:

> I decided that since I couldn't lower my medical profile nor did I want to leave the country and because my reserve would start in a month, the only option I had was to refuse. Later on I found a medical complication that lowered my medical profile to the point where I was released from the army. If there is a way I will volunteer. I can no longer agree with the way things are being handled and so I have detached myself from the system.

Thus, it was the role of the commander to judge whether refusal was not just another tactic to evade service. IDF commanders (who often knew the reservists prior to this crisis), indeed tended to test the refusal against the soldiers' record of fulfilling obligations. Accordingly, a dedicated soldier was more likely to be defined as credible by his commander. If found credible, he was entitled to light punishment, as the story of this Lebanon refuser indicated:

> The major knew me very well. He knew that I didn't want to go to Lebanon for moral reasons and that I was willing to pay the price. He was willing to release me since he knew that I was a dedicated soldier, but the problem was that he had other soldiers as well: How would he know that those who refused after me did it out of moral reasons? And this is indeed a very hard question, and I really understood him. So, I sent him a letter. He opened it and said; "Okay, I will release you." This is what he thought about me as an individual. But I knew that he is also a battalion commander and he has hundreds more people under his command, and there is no way to hide it when he is asked where I am . . . and when he faced all the constraints he decided that he could not favor me over the others and that he could not give up in my case though I knew he wanted to respond to my request. But then there might be the possibility that all the battalion would refuse and he would also have to believe that they are sincere and he would pay with his position. Finally instead of forty days in prison he gave me fourteen.

Sometimes there might be a gap between the refuser's and the commander's assessment of credibility. This Intifada refuser gave one example:

> I think that people know when their military participation is their way of protecting the country. I think that the Brigadier who tried me should have seen me during the Yom Kippur war, when I volunteered to go to the Golan Heights even though we had been released from duty.

Those soldiers who did not hold some record of dedication were more prone to be labeled as not credible. The problem lies, however, in the gray cases, when the commander has little first-hand knowledge of the soldier's record of obligation fulfillment, as in the case of a new soldier in the unit.

Whether agreeing or disagreeing with the soldier, the IDF commanders seemed to follow Walzer's "not to make it easy" policy, as we learned from this Lebanon objector:

> The court-martial was the critical moment for me, I almost gave up . . . you're given the feeling that you are a traitor and a deserter of your country and that there is a war and that you come in the

> middle and say that you are not going in. It is a very hard feeling but I'm glad that I didn't give in to it. The Lieutenant Colonel who tried me twice gave me the chance to back down from my decision to refuse. But I was stubborn and in the end he said that he was sorry that he had to jail me . . . he made me feel that he understood. The fact is that he didn't use all his powers to sentence me to thirty-five days but gave me twenty-eight. Maybe he felt that there was something in what I said.

How Seriously Did the Refuser Weigh the Alternative Course of Actions and Consider Their Likely Consequences for Others as Well as for Himself?

In both conflicts, most of the politically motivated objectors knew ahead of time that they would not serve: "As soon as the war (or Intifada) started, I knew right away that it was not my war." Prior to their decision to refuse, politically motivated refusers tended to visit a prison and talk with exprisoners about their experiences or consulted with Yesh Gvul. Given the apolitical nature of the IDF, commanders were least tolerant to politically motivated refusers even if the refusers were not members of a political party. The worst case was the position of those refusers who were active in the communist parties. An Intifada refuser told the author:

> The moment my commander realized that I was refusing (knowing my political background) he gave me no opportunity to discuss the situation. I was immediately tried. The paradox is that the one who tried me was Yehuda Meir—the person who is today in jail. [see chapter 3]

Generally speaking, IDF commanders tried to assess the motivation of the refuser and his level of credibility prior to their decision about the punishment. In the case of the morally (versus politically) motivated refusers who were also dedicated soldiers, the commanders tried to convince them not to refuse and to stay in the unit, acknowledging that these soldiers were assets to their unit. Why dismiss them?

Morality, Credibility and Level of Punishment

There are four possible combinations of the refusers motivation (moral/political) and level of credibility (high/low): The first and the easiest to identify are the cases of soldiers who are morally developed and highly credible or not morally developed or highly incredible. It is more difficult to identify the morally developed person with low credibility (who may be articulate but far from genuine), and the less morally developed person with high credibility (the dedicated soldier who is not articulate and cannot convey his moral reasoning verbally). For the Israeli commanders it was relatively clear: because of the apolitical nature of the IDF, they tended to define the articulate refusers who held political views as being low in credibility.

The least verbally articulate (sometimes associated with a low socioeconomic background) but a "good soldier" with a record of participation in previous military operations, was more frequently found in the category of high credibility and low stage of moral development. Here is the reasoning of a credible Lebanon refuser with a low level of moral development:

> I told my battalion commander, "I don't want to go to Ansar [a prison camp for PLO terrorists]. It is more dangerous to serve there than to be in an IDF prison. In the Israeli prison it is more pleasant—at least I am *inside* and do not have to guard from outside.

In general, those identified as credible were tried by their immediate commanders. If identified as morally motivated, they received the minimum punishment. Those who were identified as noncredible, and/or deemed politically motivated, were often sent by their commander to a higher rank for court-martial. They often received the full punishment, which included repeated jailing, dismissal from the unit, and/or demotion.

During the Intifada, there seemed to be less tolerance of the phenomenon of refusal from the commanders' point of view (though more understanding as to what refusal means). This change is reflected in the fact that twenty-seven (57 percent) of the Intifada refusers were removed from the unit, compared to few similar cases during the war in Lebanon. Given the fact that 67 percent asked to return to their core unit following their prison term, removal from the unit seems to be an additional punishment. An officer who decided to refuse during the Intifada was subject to this harsh punishment and stated:

> The most difficult part of refusal is the fact that while you know where you are starting from, you do not know where it will end—how many times you will be in prison, what your future military

> status will be, whether your rank will be lowered, etc. I was removed from my unit by my commander. I can understand that the army cannot keep a company commander who wants to decide when he will function as a company commander and when he will not. If I decide that I will not serve in the territories, and once a year my unit has to serve there, the army cannot accommodate my decision not to serve there. I am now a commanding officer without soldiers. I have been separated from the unit with whom I have served fifteen years, this makes the punishment much harder.

The lack of tolerance is further seen in the tendency of some Intifada commanders to favor gray refusals over white ones. In one case, for example, a refuser who challenged his commander on moral terms was given the response, "I see that you are sick—so I release you." The negative attitude of the Israeli commanders to the politically motivated refuser did not appear to be a matter of personal dislike but was rather an expression of their concern with the broad implication of refusal. Within a democratic society, a political refuser may pose more of a danger than a moral refuser. The political refuser carries the message that those who do not refuse are immoral and that this is the way all moral people should behave. In some sense, this is a dangerous threat to the entire system of the law. In the case of the moral refuser, as long as he argues that he cannot perform an immoral action, it is enough if we are convinced about the genuineness of his claims (Gabison 1986).

Believing that due process is essential for the understanding of the refusers' motivation and the decision regarding the punishment, many commanders made extraordinary efforts to give the objecting reservists the needed time to present their case. An example of this is given by this artillery soldier who refused during the Lebanon war:

> Five minutes before the brigade was to go to Lebanon and everybody was on the bus, the Major told me: "Now you stay five minutes alone, without anyone, and you make the final decision, and you have to know that after this I will have to sentence you." I told him, "I don't need these five minutes; I'm not going with you and that's it. I don't need even one second." But he said, "No, you take another five minutes," and I guess he was right from his point of view, because even though my thoughts were consolidated by that time, this was a very hard process. Those five minutes seemed forever. I guess he wanted to be at peace with himself, that he'd done all he could in order to convince me to go to Lebanon. I'll appreciate it for the rest of my life . . . and this is one of the major rea-

sons that I wouldn't want to leave the battalion. After prison, he phoned me at home and asked me how I was feeling.

This Intifada refuser documented the same pattern:

> The Brigadier wanted to find out why I had taken this action. After a time we were having a philosophical argument, he would quote one philosopher and I would quote another. Finally he offered me the chance to withdraw my decision, throw the form in the garbage and return to my unit. I said no and then he scolded me for my refusal and for abandoning my friends who were now left to do the dirty work. I also talked for two hours to my company commander who tried to convince me that if I served I would not have to have contact with women and children.

Finally, it is important to note that within the Israeli scenario, very often there are several military activities. Thus the selectivity and credibility of the refusers can be tested in more than one battlefield. The following story of an Intifada refuser is an example:

> When I came out of prison I had decided to refuse a second time if I was called to serve in the territories. But it was at the time of the emergency before the Gulf War and I could not refuse at that point. I had prepared my daughters to expect another term of imprisonment for me but I could not justify refusal on the eve of the Gulf War or dictate to the army where I would serve. I could see no reason to break the law under these emergency conditions.

The Punishment

Compared with other countries, the penalty imposed on Israeli refusers was mild (fourteen to thirty-five days). But within the Israeli context, the refusers' real punishment could be judged as more severe.

In financial terms alone the refuser was deprived of his regular salary during the period in prison. With a mounting inflation rate of 200 percent to 400 percent during the war in Lebanon, this financial punishment was insignificant, especially for those who served two or three terms of imprisonment and did not know how long the army would keep calling them.

This source of economic pressure did not exist during the 10 percent inflation rate of the Intifada; yet once a soldier was imprisoned, he could not escape the fear that he would be forced to refuse again if presented with another draft. In one case an Intifada refuser was imprisoned five times in a row and, after spending five months in prison, his business almost collapsed. Some soldiers were not allowed to return to their core unit after prison and others were relegated to the ranks.

The morally motivated soldier was very often accused by the public of being a political anarchist. This charge reflected the unfavorable reaction of Israeli society to the emergence of refusal, and sometimes affected the decision makers at his workplace regarding his loyalty.

The blurred distinction between military and civilian life also contributed to the punishment. In Israeli society, for example, hiring practices are often based on the applicant's military record. Even though refusal was a more familiar mode of moral resolution during the Intifada, only 46 percent of the Intifada refusers voluntarily reported their imprisonment in their workplace. Many people work in security-related organizations and might be subject to suspension. In one example, an officer who worked as a scientist in a company that had connections to the Ministry of Defense was fired after he came out of prison. Another source of difficulty had to do with the political orientation of the refusers' employers (even though they may have evaded service in different ways). An example was presented by this Intifada refuser:

> The head of my division at work is a Likud person. The news of my imprisonment was published on television and one day while my [civilian work] division was at lunch someone said, "Lets send some food to him" (meaning me). My boss asked where I was and the person replied "in prison." My boss called me for a discussion and wanted to fire me saying that a person who did not believe in the IDF could not be a salesman in this institution and is not a normal human being. After some discussion we reached a compromise where he asked me to put in writing that as long as I work for the company I wouldn't refuse. I put in writing that I believed that the people of Israel must do their best while serving in the army and that I was willing to follow army regulations. I wrote it in a way that it could not be directed against me in a different way. Because it was not a legal statement I don't think he will be able to fire me if I refuse. This was a concession I was willing to make and perhaps next time my name will not be published.

This hostile attitude also existed in places that were not necessarily right-wing oriented. Another Intifada refuser explained:

from his obdurate position. In so doing they conveyed an implicit attitude of some respect for his action.

Commanders also realized that they would not be able to carry out their mission with a rebellious soldier. Therefore, they attempted to ascertain his feelings and show him how he could function in line with his moral concerns. If all this failed, they finally did try him, so as to prevent others from believing that this might also be a means of release for themselves.

It might be speculated that by not hurrying the soldiers to court-martial and by not exercising their full punitive powers, the commanders conveyed to their superiors their own hidden objection to the war and/or their criticism regarding an assigned mission with which they were not totally in accord.

The Impact of the Punishment

Though most refusers did not find the prison term easy, they acknowledged that it was a mild penalty (without taking the related punishments into account) that enabled them to act upon their principles and remain dedicated soldiers:

> I am glad that the punishment was as mild as it was. First, it showed me the moral strength of the IDF who were not scared of a wave of refusers in spite of this light punishment. Second, it made me act upon my moral principles. I guess that if the punishment were more severe, I would do what I could to cheat the army and avoid service and not be punished.

Another benefit of mild punishment was the opportunity to examine the implications of being disobedient. As this Lebanon refuser tells:

> I think that it is quite dangerous to go to prison and I wonder if all the refusers thought about it ahead of time. You are going to sit among military lawbreakers and this is a well-defined group of people. Throughout my time as an officer in the artillery many of these were my soldiers, whom I tried to help, etc. And now I was in jail with them since I was also fighting against the IDF, a fight I chose. And they also had a fight with the IDF, and suddenly I found myself in favor of any deserter, etc. I am afraid to think how (paradoxically) we (the refusers) would all have supported these people if the stay in prison had been longer.

An Intifada refuser reached another conclusion:

> While I was in prison I met a border patrol soldier who asked me why I was in prison. When I told him I refused to guard Ansar he said I must be a leftist and that while he was on border patrol they had liked to hit the leftists . . . when he realized what he had said he elaborated: No, we never hit the leftists, only the Peace Now ones. I told him I was with Peace Now. Interestingly, it didn't bother him that I refused. It didn't bother me that he used to hit leftists. We had a common world, a common interest, we both came from a world in which you hit each other.

Over all, most of the refusers were not angry for being punished. Seventy-three percent of the Intifada refusers considered their own punishment as justified and fair. They seem to be capable of seeing the difference between the individual case and the entire system:

> I have no complaints about the army. I think that the army is treating refusers in an exemplary way. They are trying to handle the many refusers in different ways. I don't believe that this policy is organized from the top. I think the commanders are very sensitive to preserving the cohesiveness of the units and that they try to find any solution no matter how crazy for the refuser.

In a certain sense, performing an action such as selective moral or political disobedience not only arouses society and forces it to collectively define its moral boundaries, but it also marks the boundaries of the actor's moral competence: "I thought that I would change the world but I did not." Yet, even if they failed in this respect, there was still a feeling of strength, as this Intifada refuser explained: "I think that refusal is the strongest instrument the small citizen has."

Most wanted to believe that the action of refusal had been constructed from a connected position as one of them explained: "I don't regret my action although it has caused me a lot of pain. I *used* the army *against* the army since I am *for* the army."

The main ideal of criticism as I conceive it is to use all that there is to use.

—Burke 1957

10

Criticism in the Making
From Emotion to Cognition

Israel's military preparedness rests heavily on the reserve force's availability for deployment in times of emergencies. The reservist's loyalty to this type of service was traditionally ascribed to his moral motivation—his belief in his right and necessity to fight a defensive and just war (Gal 1986). This belief was dramatically shaken for some when the "Peace for the Galilee" campaign was transformed into a war in Lebanon and eventually into an "Israeli Vietnam"; and not long after this when the Israeli reservist was sent to suppress the Intifada—to encounter the "Israeli Algiers." In both of these new types of military conflicts soldiers encountered numerous morally no-win situations (Inbar 1991). These conflicts gave rise to various forms of criticism, among which selective refusal to serve in the military conflicts was the most extreme and least studied so far. This type of criticism during the Intifada has been the focus of this book. The Intifada refuser has been viewed as a "graduate" of the Lebanon war, even if he was too young to serve there. Even if he did not participate in the Lebanon war, he has been regarded as a reservist who was functioning within the postwar "Lebanonization" process of Israeli society.

Assuming that "a way of standing is also a way of seeing or not seeing" (Burke 1965, p. 13), the study of selective refusal to military service has followed two distinct views of criticism, those voiced from a separate perspective and those voiced from a connected perspective of civil disobedience. From the separate position perspective (Kohlberg 1984; Rawls 1971), the moral critic is examined by objective measures and criteria, and the focus lies on the independent, rational, mature, and consistent modes of moral thinking and action of the critic. From the connected position perspective (Gilligan 1982; Walzer 1988), the moral critic is seen as a unique person searching for a unique way to conceive himself and his position in relation to others; both positions have been studied through in-depth interviews. These perspectives, however, do not always correspond to the subjective perception of the moral actor. Even if studied and/or judged from the separate position, the refuser might consider his action as springing from a connected position and vice versa. Table 10 portrays the separate viewpoint on relations between the refusers' moral judgement and action.

Table 10. Separate Perspective of Refusal

	I	II	III	IV	
Function	Position	Decision	Involvement in dilemma situation	nonmoral factors	
Cognition	Separate (moral stage)	single solution	active/ passive	courage	action
				(loose connection to unit, loner, commitment to political party, family, and cultural dictates	

The above table suggests that the emergence of refusal might be seen as being constructed by isolated individuals who rationally and publicly assumed a position from which they believed they would be better judges of the situation. We might interpret this position as springing from their view of the dilemma situation as demanding a linear mode of moral resolution since one of the two opposed actions can be judged as right (Kohlberg and Candee 1984, p. 62). The separate moral critic is required to be obsessed with singling out the most just claim of right as if moral conflicts are always resolvable. The hallmark of this autonomous and mature moral position is the (apparent) nonbiased individualistic outlook of the critic. In a way, this perspective assumes that each individual within a society has the privilege (not only the cognitive ability) of standing outside the system in order to maintain his ideal values of justice. In some way, this perspective questions the possibility of the Israeli SCO as holding thoughts and actions geared toward the saving or the protecting of lives by means of loyalty to the system of justice.

When we looked at the phenomenon of refusal from the connected perspective, we were able to see that even mature moral thinkers were not obsessed with singling out the most right claim of justice. Rather, they were most worried about the position they would assume in the face of an unresolvable moral conflict. Due to their attachment to the system and to some significant (real of imaginary) people within it (such as members of their units, Holocaust victims, etc.), their assuming of the moral position of refusal was a challenge to the socially constructed identity of the Israeli male. This identity reflects two lines of social and moral development: the morality of obligation and duties and the morality of belonging and loyalty. When we detached ourselves from the strict coding scheme for rational reasoning, we could hear and feel that the subjects' refusals were not constructed exclusively upon their moral wisdom. There were also salient and hidden voices of individual and collective moral feelings such as gratitude, guilt, shame, compassion, indignation, and the like. As they all grew up on the call to act beyond one's own duty as a moral ritual (Gal 1986), in a society that celebrates connection, belonging, and historical heritage (Ben Ari 1990; Levine 1986), the choice of 'exit' was initially seen as more of a temptation than a possibility, let alone a constructive mode of moral resolution. Yet when overwhelmed with the physical burden of service and an experience of moral alienation, they often found themselves (passively) being driven or (actively) self-directing themselves into this form of moral resolution. Whereas the separate position would not address the degree of self-involvement in the dilemma situation, the connected perspective would find it crucial for this moral experience and its understanding.

Like those who descend (emigrate), the refusers were aware of the fact that they might a priori lose their moral voice within Israeli culture. They were doomed to an experience of defeat because the fulfilment of their obligations was questionable (Fish 1984; Peleg 1989; Shokeid 1988; Sobel 1986). When considering the option of refusal, they suddenly figured out that they would not be able to exit without appealing to the morality of connection—letting themselves and the significant people around them test other aspects of their moral commitment to the group and values, and assess the degree to which the credibility of their personality would play a role in their moral struggle. They seem to have spread their action in a continuum of hope—those who had hope in the system combined their political concerns with their record of credibility. Those who had hope only in themselves combined their moral concerns with their record of credibility. Those who held the least sense of hope, both for the system and for the moral harmony awaiting them if and when they refused, often chose to present themselves as personally motivated and did not bother with the quest for perceived credibility by the audience.

The burden of the "connected" society, and the concomitant "connected identity," seems to perpetuate the refusers' desire to return to their home units, to redefine connection, and to fight for their credibility in terms of previous and future connections to their units. For some, however, refusal was primarily a resistance to this form of connectedness; an 'exit' from the obligation to be part of the whole which must sustain the horror of war (Almog 1992). *Exit* implies an attempt to connect one's self to an ideal society—to try and maintain one's secular conscience in a country in which only the religious conscience is respected. Table 11 portrays the connected perspective of refusal.

The table suggests that, from the connected perspective, the dilemma of refusal is being examined again and again at different levels of complexity, against different real and imaginary groups of audience. The connected refuser assumes a position by acting and talking in a different way to the people around him, through the voicing of his moral authority and his commitment to personal and collective history. His moral resolution entails an acknowledgment of moral ambiguity, of being caught between two images of self; simultaneously connected to a specific group of people, language, and personal and collective history, and separated when forced to choose the form of exit. The hesitancy of the subjects to assume a full-scale exit position suggests that we cannot sidestep their moral, social, and cultural context. We therefore examined common frameworks, metaphors, and rhetoric surrounding the memory of the Holocaust, which is central in the lives of Israelis (Breznitz 1983; Hasdai 1982; Lieblich 1983; Meyer 1990; Shaked 1986). One quarter of the refusers were the second generation of Holocaust survivors. However, the experience of the Holocaust seems to have had a profound effect at times on the emotional life of (almost) three-quarters of the subjects in this study. Should I guard Prisons? Shoot children? Follow orders? Act as a cog in the

Table 11. Connected Perspective of Refusal

MORAL ACTIONS/EMOTIONS/JUDGMENTS
PASSIVE/ACTIVE MORAL INVOLVEMENTS
CRITICAL DISTANCE
REAL/IMAGINARY AUDIENCE
MORAL LANGUAGE
MORAL STANCE
MORAL COMMITMENT
MORAL NARRATIVE
SHARED UNDERSTANDING
MORAL NARRATIVE
MORAL COMMITMENT
MORAL STANCE
MORAL LANGUAGE
REAL/IMAGINARY AUDIENCE
CRITICAL DISTANCE
PASSIVE/ACTIVE MORAL INVOLVEMENTS
MORAL ACTIONS/EMOTIONS/JUDGMENTS

machine? Is it good to die for my country? Is there another way to define the dictum of purity of arms? Does the connection to one's cultural collective memories and symbols require detachment from these objects in order to remove one's existential anxiety and live in moral harmony?

The Israeli subjects in this study were aware that the position of an SCO was not the mere action of disobedience but the need to undergo some process of external suffering on top of their internal moral pain: legal punishment, personal humiliation, being regarded as unpatriotic, financial loss, or something else. For the Israeli SCO, however, it seems that the (perceived) separate position of criticism that he assumed also entailed the pain of detachment as a form of punishment: an exclusion from the unit and/or the subjective feeling of exclusion from the community. The desire to return to the same unit suggests that the Israeli SCO tended to consider his position as a connected one.

In a way, this is not a surprise, given the context in which most Israelis grow up. As a small country under immense pressure, connectedness to the community is highly valued and marks a central ingredient in the Israeli moral identity. To some extent, criticism is a central part of this connectedness. It is one of the fundamental forms of self-assertion within Israeli society (Katriel 1985). However, criticism voiced from a (perceived) connected position may have provided the Israeli critics with the sense of rootedness and belonging that they needed. Considering the refusers' wish to return to their own units upon their release from prison, the connected perspective provided the refusers with the opportunity to reaffirm their sense of moral thinking, by negotiating their moral identity. We have come to realize that even within the connected position, they seem to oscillate between disconnection and connectedness. Even those who promised to detach themselves further by emigrating nevertheless believed they had first to try and refuse in order to preserve their ideal connected selves. Thus, it is not clear whether one's moral action is constructed in line with Kohlberg's (1984) premise—from "ought" to "is." Perhaps it can be better understood as an emotional and cognitive effort to move one's connected self from "is" to "ought."

It seems that what characterizes criticism since the war in Lebanon is not so much the quantity or numbers of those who assumed a position of refusal but the emergence of this position as a precedence, and later, as an option in the mind of the soldier. Never before has such a position been considered as an option by reservists, even in the face of growing moral doubts. Never before has it seemed that war activities that appear to violate moral principles require some of the most morally connected individuals to separate themselves from the shared understanding of their community.

Prior to the war in Lebanon, excluding oneself from the military setting as a form of criticism was traditionally inconceivable. The emergence of selective refusal marks a qualitative change in the sphere of criticism. The voicing of what seems to be a detached criticism, as has been documented throughout this book (mainly by civilians in uniform), has become more and more a part of the Israeli moral reality of wars. Not many individuals, however, refer to this form of detached criticism as conveying the notion of connection rather than separation. During the two conflicts discussed in this book, the voicing of connected criticism was wide in scope; it entailed delayed criticisms from previous wars and included Biblical analogies from David and Goliath right through to the Holocaust. Paradoxically, the refusers constructed a dramatic change in their sociomoral lives by creating a complicated scenario whereby, in order *to attach themselves to the community* in which they wanted to go on living and not to descend (emigrate) from the country (for which they cared but in which they could not act in line with their moral principles), *they had to detach themselves*.

It seems that the "insignificant number" of refusers is neither factual nor represents the moral pain experienced by larger number of soldiers, as many were granted to serve outside the war zone by sympathetic commanders or vanished from the scene via gray refusal. The low number of refusers is also due to the extraordinary efforts made for the most part by morally torn reserve commanders, who frequenty did seemingly impossible maneuvers to convince dedicated soldiers to remain in the units. With the growing alienation, this task became more complicated.

It might be argued that outbursts of refusal as a form of moral criticism among Israeli reservists mark a gradual process of burnout. This burnout would not only be a function of the accumulation of the reserves, but also of the realization of a moral dead end—that self-sacrifice can no longer serve as the most correct or most effective mode of moral resolution on the battlefield in times when peace agreements can be negotiated. The ability to publicly voice their moral feelings seemed to surprise the critics themselves, particularly those who knew themselves as dedicated soldiers since the 1967 war. Even those who had a history of rebellion in their civilian lives, or who were lone decision makers, had preferred not to opt out in earlier years in the face of injustice.

For these soldiers it took the war in Lebanon and/or the Intifada to take a stance. These military conflicts with the lack of national consensus, the cynical use and exploitation of the IDF soldiers (particularly its reservists), became a turning point for many. It took the soldiers' unrewarded as well as unbearable physical and moral load of service, and the lack of potential moral resolution to publicly voice their emotions and to threaten themselves and others with the position of exit.

What seems crucial is the notion of inclusion: whereas the objecting reservists who chose to refuse viewed temporary detachment as a prerequisite for performing a moral action that would enable them to renew their ties to their society, the nonrefusing soldiers viewed connectedness as the basis for moral action and change. As we were listening to the narratives of the critics from the connected position, we came to believe that the language of justice was not logical or prescriptive but rather rhetorical—there was no attempt to match reality to some abstract ideal. Instead it seemed to be a struggle to come to terms with the way the world was and to attack a particular injustice in a specific course of action. As has been noted by Solomon (1990), "our sense of justice is our persuasion to do what we can" (p. 16).

To exercise patriotism in the form of exit seems to be a painful moral resolution, particularly as the refuser is not sure how he will find his way back into the community and eventually to his identity. Because life and citizenship in Israel imply a concrete risk to one's own self, the preliminary response of others to exit of any kind (including emigration) is that the actor is regarded as selfish or egoistical (Shokeid 1988). Should the potential refusers remain morally selfless (doing things that contradict their moral convictions) or be regarded as morally selfish?

Some Israeli soldiers during the Intifada could not agree with the need to occupy, fight women and children, destroy without trial, or serve the religious or fanatic ideology of settlers. Their exit from the community was to some extent their way of voicing their moral concerns for the system, exhibited in their willingness to pay the price imposed on them by the system. Unlike the premise of the separate position (that the principled person would guide his action by tuning himself to the logic of justice), the refusers' experiences seem to have raised their concerns about the morality of particular others: their own army, the future of their children and a way to recognize their secular conscience and patriotism in their Jewish community.

During the war in Lebanon, objecting Israeli reservists could comfort themselves that exit was unfortunate, yet the most effective form of criticism and opposition to what they considered to be wrong decisions by a right-wing government. The refusers' position during the Intifada was more complex; the "moral suppression" and cynical use of the reservists was a result of a left-wing government, which was the political affiliation of almost all of the refusers. The Intifada refusers seemed to be less idealistic than their counterparts in Lebanon. The realization that the moral ordeal of the Lebanon refusers made no impact on the war generals seemed to cause the Intifada refusers to be less attuned to the moral or political considerations. Even when they had the ability to understand and present such considerations, they were not sure whether it was *worth* assuming such a position at all. Their moral distress seems to have led them to some sort of apathy and hidden or public gray refusal.

Table 12 summarizes the phenomenon of Selective Conscientious Objection by presenting its three central dimensions: (1) separate or connected position; (2) morally or politically/personally motivated; and (3) passive or active self-involvement.

The table suggests that the disobedient refuser might construct his action of disobedience from a moral, political, or personal motivation. The three motivating categories might be defined as degrees of "emotional engagement with others" (Solomon 1992, p. 92). In this way, a politically motivated refuser is more engaged with others than the morally or the personally motivated refusers. This table may show how some refusers can view their disobedience as taking place within an essentially political framework ("I am serving in an occupying army"; "if there were be 5000 refusers we would not be there"). Other refusers may view their disobedience as more morally specific ("Let them do their own war"), as geared toward the preservation of their their own principles. And others may view their disobedience as the most pragmatic tactic for preserving their own pragmatic beliefs. While we found some sort of "pragmatic realization" (everyday thought rather than logical thoughts) in each interview, refusers seemed to differ in their desire to present these considerations as central (Wason and Johnson-Laird 1972).

But the action involves not only the motivation but also the actual position of the self in the dilemma situation—as a responsible and apparently active self or with a passive mode of self-involvement. The active/passive dimension of the self may shift the focus of engagement to nonmoral dimensions. Moral and practical motivations for refusal seem to be less ambitious and more specific in intent than political motivations. The passive morally motivated refuser does not like the policy of his country and wants it changed. He would not try to convince other soldiers to refuse. He would try to preserve his principles by not serving, and let others "make their own war." The gray refuser would be personally motivated. He may decide to assume a passive form of self-involve-

Table 12. Dimensions of Refusal

Position	*Self*	*Passive*	*Active*
Separate	Motivation		
	Political	Affiliated to political party	Hunger strike, protest letters, and marches
		Membership in "Yesh Gvul" after refusal	Membership in "Yesh Gvul" before refusal
		No influencing others	Influencing others
		5000 Refusers Would Stop the Intifada	
Connected	Moral	"This is not my war. Let them do their own war"	Try to make changes within the system prior to exit.
		Ben Moshe, Bernard	Thompson, Eli Geva
	Personal	gray refusal	Public gray refusal

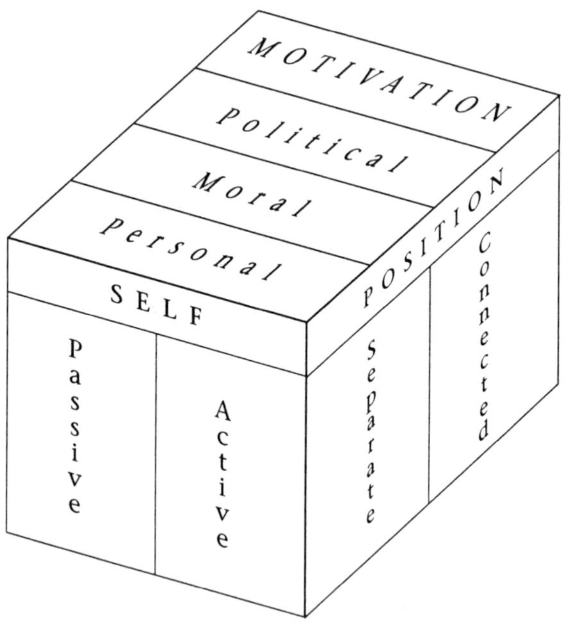

ment in the dilemma situation and the expected consequences. The personally motivated gray refuser who is actively engaging himself in the dilemma situation will make his action public. Yet, he is not morally motivated as he does not take it upon himself to pay the price for his disobedience. The active moral actor would be Thompson or Eli Geva—the one who would not fear risking his self in order to save others within the system, and who constructs his action in connection with the situation to try to avoid misjudgement of others regarding the evil he perceives in the field.

Whereas morally, politically, and personally motivated refusers would present rational justifications for their action, they would differ in the focus of their rationality. The political refuser would see himself as part of the whole and would try to find some logic between his actions and the system. The morally motivated refuser would search for some logic between his action and his set of principles. The personally motivated refuser would search for a logic between his action and his resulting benefits from it. This logic is often connected to the experience of the soldier—the most politically or morally motivated refuser may turn into a personally motivated refuser when losing hope.

Because they viewed themselves as loyal citizens of their country, the Israeli refusers had more than a legal obligation to obey the law. The moral duty of this obligation arose out of their role as citizens, particularly in a democratic country where they had the right to participate in making the laws of their community. None of the refusers in our Lebanon or Intifada sample was given a flagrantly illegal command. Yet, the Intifada soldiers seemed to fear these commands more than their counterparts in Lebanon, and therefore tended to consider refusal long before they actually served—as a sort of moral prevention.

Psychologically, however, this position raises a question regarding the refusers' nonmoral attributes. While we know the refusers had the lonely courage to disobey, they did not reveal why they could not rely on this courage for resisting the authority in the field while serving. Perhaps this is the type of strength that the objecting yet nonrefusing reservists believed they had in themselves when they did not hesitate to take upon themselves the risk of serving. Obviously, it requires further study.

Whether separate or connected, selective conscientious objection should be seen as an action that has been undertaken on the crest of passion. It is an act by a number of individuals who respect the law and are obedient to it. It requires a rational justification; but what is the right way to define rationality? It seems that politically motivated refusers were those individuals who were more capable than others to reason in terms of our conventional definition of rationality (Rawls 1971). Thus it might be suggested that the difference between the groups was not necessarily moral, political, or personal but rather the ability to control one's own moral emotions. To some extent, the morally motivated refusers as well as the personally motivated refusers were more affected (or allowed themselves to be more affected) by moral emotions. Unlike Rawls' and Kohlberg's rational view on the SCO, it seems that the Israeli SCO was less rational than hypothetically portrayed. Their moral language was emotional and contextual. Their personal feelings seemed to reflect their *care* about justice.

Rather than abstract principles, we may argue that the justice concerns voiced by the critics reflected a connected position—a way of participating in the world, a way of being with other people, a set of feelings, of affections and affiliations that linked them to other people; these other people were the family they left behind, their political party, their community at large, or even an abstract audience of people to whom they felt they owed an explanation, such as those who died in other wars or the survivors of the Holocaust.

And above all, we do not allow the dead to rise up against us.

—Orwell *1984*, p. 204

11

Refusal in Perspective

From the War of Attrition to Moral Attrition

Seven years after the beginning of the war in Lebanon, and in the second year of the uprising in the territories, the Haifa Theater staged a play written by Irwin Shaw in 1936 called "The Rebellion of the Dead." In the play six dead soldiers raise their heads during the funeral service and refuse to be buried. Their refusal to comply with the proper order of the war causes their General to appeal to their wisdom and their sense of duty: "Comrades, your country demands of you one more thing—that you lie deep in the ground."

While at any other time prior to the war in Lebanon Israelis would have regarded this play as anachronistic, now it evoked a reaction from both sides of the political map. One reader wrote to the press:

> The generals in this show are not our generals and their message is not to us. . . . The percentage of officers among our war dead is extremely high compared with other armies in the world and this fact must serve as an indication for our army. (*Kolbo*, 26 October 1989)

In defending the presentation of the play, the Israeli director stated:

> Every society demands some sacrifices from the individual and this causes severe conflicts. . . . I am not playing politics—I am trying to understand how a soldier feels in the grave. He feels deceived. . . . The war in Lebanon was the first war in which this type of emotion arose among some of the soldiers and the public, and this is a fact. (*Ha'aretz*, 12 September 1989)

Yoram Falk was the director of Sartre's play, "The Altona Verdict" (in Hebrew, "Nidonei Altona"). The play was written as an allegory on the French involvement in Algeria and the destruction of an entire generation of young people in France as a result. Falk had to stop working in the middle of rehearsals as he was sent to the occupied territories as a combatant reservist (*Yediot Acharonot*, 8 February 1988).

With the prolongation of the Intifada, Israeli press people as well as foreign crews were no longer enthusiastic to go into the field. Thus the moral ordeal of the Israeli soldiers was often documented from the point of view of Palestinian crews—who were taking pictures of the backs of the Israeli soldiers. When the faces of the soldiers were revealed they were seen as tired, confused, humiliated, and above all, lonely. Throughout the Intifada they remained lonely in the crowd, they were lonely when facing the mob in the territories, when watching the people bathe on the Tel Aviv beaches, and when the bathers question the soldiers why they have injuries from stones on their forehead. They were lonely when they were brought to trial. The Gaza Strip remained the no-man's land in the minds of the Israeli public as well as in the minds of the Palestinians, and Ansar became the prison of the individual's collective memories—a place where all who enter are immediately turned into victims.

Following the peace accord, a soldier from Jerusalem is called for by his parents, the Berman family, to help them in their business. Young Berman has been chasing youths who have been hanging PLO flags in the territories for three years. His parents are now sewing PLO flags and need his help in the family factory (*Ha'aretz*, 9 September 1993).

The writing of this concluding chapter was started on 14 May 1994; a day when the withdrawal from the Gaza Strip had been completed following the Peace Treaty with the PLO. The last place to be evacuated was the Jebalia Refugee Camp—where the Intifada erupted on 7 December 1987 (according to an IDF spokesperson). The military calendar shows that this month marks the twenty-fifth year of the War of Attrition—an unknown and forgotten war; even the day of its inception is not clear. While officially it is a war that lasted seventeen months from 1969 to 1970, it might be regarded as a war that started on the seventh day of the Six Day War. This is the war of my generation. As young conscripts we believed (like the reservists of those days) in what we were doing.

We believed we were keeping the 1967 administered territories, and the status quo, in the name of "peace for land." When our counterparts in the USA and Europe were marching against the war in Vietnam and/or the establishment, we were climbing to Tel Chai in the Galilee to affirm our moral motivation and oneness with Trumpeldor's slogan: "it is good to die for our country."

The compulsory service soldiers from the War of Attrition evolved in time into the reservists of the Lebanon war and the Intifada. The liberated territories were transformed into the occupied territories. At the time of this writing, some of these reservists are already parents of compulsory soldiers who knew only the Intifada as an Israeli war. These "graduates" from the Intifada are labeled among their peers as having a B.A. (Bogrei Intifada—"Bachlor of Intifada"—a play on words for the phrase "Intifada graduates"). Their parents cannot escape some similarities between the compulsory service their sons underwent in the Intifada and their own earlier compulsory service in the War of Attrition.

The Name. Both conflicts got their name from Arab sources. The War of Attrition was coined as such by Egypt's President Nasser. In his speech on 23 June 1969 he said: "We could not conquer the Sinai Desert, but we can put Israel under attrition and break its spirit" (*Bamachane,* 23 March 1994). To indicate its length or apparently the fact that the Six Day War was not only six days, Nasser used to refer to the War of Attrition as the 1000 days war. The media (mainly the radio since there was no television in those days) adopted this name. The name Intifada was coined by the Palestinians. The Israelis hoped to cling to terms such as *disorders* or *demonstrations* but gradually the media adopted the name Intifada. Though the Intifada was closer to Tel Aviv than the Suez Canal had been, the psychological distance from the people in the hinterland was identical; as if living Orwell's (1949) most frightening prophecy, in *1984:* "by becoming continuous, war has ceased to exist" (p. 164).

While sitting along the Suez Canal, the soldiers were convinced they were protecting Tel Aviv (*Bamachane,* 23 March 1994, p. 42). Similarly the Lebanese and the Intifada reservists were told they were protecting Tel Aviv when guarding Beirut and later Gaza.

Geva's lone public criticism regarding breaking into Beirut marked the beginning of a new era of criticism. While they appeared to be more morally vulnerable during the Intifada, it was the ability to use various modes of criticism and the option of refusal during the Intifada that made the Israeli reservists during this period more resilient in sustaining the numerous morally no-win situations. Having no name—the War of Attrition was first coined "the war after the war"—reflects in some way the reluctance of Israeli leaders to face the reality that the status quo of the Six Day War victory could not last forever. The Intifada was often regarded as the continuation of the 'Lebanese mud'. Whereas all could see that Israel had withdrawn from Lebanon, not all could convincingly confront themselves with the fact that the Israeli soldiers had succeeded in taking the Lebanon mentality out of their mind. (*Yediot Acharonot,* 12 December 1992).

War with No Heroes. The War of Attrition does not appear in the list of Israeli wars or in the army's official prayer for the dead. No medal was given to the participants of the War of Attrition. It seems that no medal is awaiting the graduates of the Intifada either. The War of Attrition was the first Israeli encounter with a gray and prolonged war that was being conducted far away without dramatic victories. Neither did the Intifada produce any heroes. Who is the new hero, the one who kills or the one who is sent to kill and succeeds in not killing despite the ambiguous or clear commands of how to (legally) kill and above what age and through which part of the body? Neither war had a victory song.

Trapped Soldiers. In both wars, the individual IDF soldiers were physically trapped: in narrow tunnels along the Suez canal (the Bar Lev strategic line) or alone in a narrow alley during the Intifada. They were often alone when posted in a (physical and moral) position on a Palestinian rooftop in the middle of a hostile Palestinian city. Whereas soldiers in both prolonged conflicts often asked, "What are we doing here?" the War of Attrition reservists were backed by the national consensus and their questions were answered with direct and confident slogans. The questions raised by Intifada soldiers received no clear responses. However they raised more questions.

Motivation. Since the War of Attrition was neither heroic nor well known, soldiers who were living abroad (either permanently or temporarily) did not return to fight in it. Nor did reservists return to fight in the Intifada. Both the War of Attrition and the Intifada were signified with a wave of patriotism by veteran reservists at the outset who volunteered as "tigers" to the bunkers, or as adjutant commanders to the units in the territories.

Censorship of Criticism. Criticism was not part of the public discourse during the War of Attrition, partly because it followed the dramatic victory of the Six Day War and the country was still obsessed with celebrating and developing a respect for the career officers and heroic fighters. It took the war in Lebanon and later the Intifada before some of the most sincere war heroes would admit that, being drunk on victory, their judgement during the War of Attrition was faulty (Peled 1993). Career General Yanush Ben Gal (1992) presents a critical view of his experience as a young officer during the War of Attrition:

> In spite of the high toll of that war . . . it was a lost and forgotten war, without landmarks and war heritages. . . . We were all obsessed with the glory of the Six Day War. The IDF was busy issuing new victory albums and transforming the commanders of the Six Day War into immortal beings. . . . The state of preparedness of the IDF along the Suez Canal was casual. . . . The IDF had underestimated the change in the Egyptian army. . . . The newspapers issued every noontime the pictures of the dead . . . many of the soldiers were broken . . . it is hard to imagine the surrealistic position that characterized that war. For example defecating into an empty sand bag, because of the fear to go to unprotected toilets outside the bunker where one could be caught in the shelling . . . many soldiers gave up going home on leave for fear of being hurt by mines. For the fighters along the Suez canal time lost all meaning . . . the longer the war was prolonged the greater we felt the gap between us, the fighters, and the high-ranking command. The frequent visits of high-ranking commanders merely increased the gap between us. They traditionally were obsessed with the ritual of checking the shooting slots that they believed would help us prevent the canal being crossed. . . . When a soldier complained about the incompatibility of the protective devices and the fighting requirements, he was scolded and we were instructed that in times of shelling we should go inside the bunker and play "dice." There was also a distance and dissociation from the civilian hinterland. We could feel it the moment we were given a day off. Once we went to north Tel Aviv and felt we had landed on another planet. The War of Attrition does not stand on its own . . . on the seventh day of the Six Day War we could already see clear indications. Even in those days—the signs were written in blood, but

> most of us could not or would not decipher them. We were blinded by our previous achievements, holding the wrong concepts and jealous of our rituals of superiority over the enemy. Those [critics] who were brave enough to warn us about the changes that had occurred in the Egyptian army and how their fighting ability had improved, were blocked by the sealed conception. They were regarded as crazy, prophets of doom and destruction. . . . The reason for the fact that we tried to remove the War of Attrition from our collective memory is to forget the tragic mistakes and lack of understanding that were so prevalent in the military and political policies. (*Yediot Acharonot,* 6 October 1992)

During the war of attrition, Jerusalem was apparently united. The Hebrew University was filled with some extreme left-wing activists who called themselves "Campus" and demanded direct talks with the PLO. Fifty-eight high school students signed a letter to Golda Meir (who was Prime Minister at that time) protesting the status quo of war. A reservist who was among the organizers reflected in 1994: (the power of the letter) "lay in its originality. For the first time in the country's history a group of students who were about to be drafted, protested the government's policy, and hinted at the possibility of not serving in the IDF. . . . Fifty-eight students succeeded in waking up the educational system that taught them up to that day that it was good to die for this country. . . . Alon, the Minister of Defense, called us in for a reconciliation talk that took over two hours . . . he wanted us to believe him (that he was seeking peace, R.L.), to believe Golda, and that we would return to the path of obedience. We came out very confused from this conversation. None of the signatories wanted to be excluded from military service and thrown out of the national consensus. Some of the signatories broke down under the pressure and published a note that advocated the government policy. Most of the signatories served in fighting units; another attempt to prove to the public they were still in the consensus. Years later the following generation of youth sent other letters of refusal to serve in the territories. These were not the same students or the same letters" (*Bamachane,* 23 March 1994).

The insensitivity to those who have to carry the burden of continuous service continued throughout the years. When "professional" Intifada reservists found themselves serving sixty days a year even after the peace accord, they desperately threatened to "bring the kids with us to the reserves!" if they were called again. High-ranking officials such as Amnon Shachak, the Deputy Chief of Staff, responded: "the IDF will be shortening the reserve duty in 1994 by 400,000 days. But the first one to get it is the *non fighters* (emphasis added). We are sorry because we see that there are small groups who are doing a lot of reserve service and many big ones that are doing very little or even nothing" (*Yediot Acharonot,* 31 January 1993). When nothing was changed, on 24 August 1993 hundreds of officers assembled in Tel Aviv and decided to create a charitable fund commemorating the death of three of their friends in Gaza. The officers' wives brought forward their complaint to the Chief of Staff arguing that "only a small group of reservists who serve in fighting units are doing their share . . . at the expense of their families and their income. (*Yediot Acharonot,* 24 August 1993). In response, the Chief of Staff promised them that the burden would decrease though the gap between the fighting units and the noncombatants would remain (*Ha'aretz,* 29 August 1993). This trend continues up to the time of this writing, when combatant reservists send letters that ask for an explanation for their heavy physical load (Israel TV, 1 June 1994). Other reservists send individual letters in which they say among other things that "the reservists are a cheap and readymade expenditionary force. Part of the problem is that the (career) commanders who recruit us are not obliged to submit a report regarding the use that is made of reservists. The result is that no one has an incentive to reduce using us" (*Ha'aretz,* 21 March 1994). Unknown (yet growing) numbers of reservists try their luck with gray refusal. Major General Uri Sagi, Army Official, admits he is not surprised since this "is a norm in the IDF" (*Jerusalem Post,* 14 January 1992).

Throughout the years and throughout the wars, the reservist continues to be the moral barometer of the Israeli society; when, for example, philosopher, Yeshyahu Leibowitz, was nominated as a candidate for Israel's National Prize, they protested and succeeded in removing the nomination. Leibowitz, was among the first to warn that the "seventh day" of the Six Day War will lead to moral deterioration. From the war in Lebanon, and more so during the Intifada, he became the moral pillar for some morally puzzled soldiers who were considering refusal. While respecting his right to voice his ideas regarding the Intifada, some reservists viewed his labeling of Israeli soldiers in the territories as "Judeo Nazis" as the last straw. And when, on the eve of his nomination, Lebowitz dared to compare the Israeli Mistaarvim (secret fighting squads) to the Hamas (Arab fundamentalists' squad), reserve officers sent letters of protest saying "even though they are identified with the left wing to the center politically, they also fight in the front line and are being stoned" (*Ha'aretz,* 22 January 1993). The nomination was cancelled.

Though doomed to serve in the reserves throughout their adult lives, Israeli reservists have never been informed of their rights. In February 1994, a booklet, which dealt only with the stage of recruitment and not the service itself, was first published but regarded as classified. It is not yet clear how the reservists will obtain a copy for their own information (*Yediot Acharonot,* 2 February 1994).

On the eve of the peace talks, Trumpeldor's slogan "it is good to die for our country" becomes the motto of the right winger who opposes this process. There are few cases of refusal among right-wing reservists settlers. They argue that a "soldier who agrees to relinquish the territories is like a kappo, those who cooperated with the Nazis" (*Yediot Acharonot,* 10 June 1993). Shlomo Goren, a former Chief Rabbi, issued a halachic (religious) edict ruling that it is strictly forbidden to uproot the settlements. In his words "one is obliged to give one's life in order to prevent the evacuation of the settlement" (*Jerusalem Post,* 11 March 1994). Attorney General, Michael Ben Yair, argues that soldiers should not refuse to remove a settlement if ordered to do so. At the same time he issued an order to the high command to try to find alternative military service for those (left wingers) who refuse to serve in the territories. (*Davar,* 10 May 1994).

When it comes to the Golan Heights, many left wingers and even some of the Lebanon and Intifada refusers seem to be flexible with their moral sanctions. On 5 January 1993, a group of twenty high school graduates sent a protest letter to the Prime Minister in which they conveyed their objection to a possible withdrawal from the Golan Heights and their refusal to evacuate citizens if asked to do so (*Ha'aretz*). In defending their position they said, "In the past we regarded the refusal of the left wing as a grave act, and we could not understand how a person could possibly disobey an order. Today we think we understand this feeling and the idea of refusal. We understand that a refusal violates the law, but there are some things that you simply cannot pursue."

Inevitably, the dilemmas surrounding refusal as a form of moral criticism provide Israeli society with another lens to examine its past and present. A filmmaker providing a renewed look at the establishment of the Jewish state brings into focus an inquiry into the motivation of some Hagana soldiers not to shoot at the ship *Altlena,* which reached Tel Aviv seashore with ammunition for the right-wing underground (*Yediot Acharonot,* 3 June 1994). Book critic, Tom Segev (1990) questions generals' autobiographies: "I want to see what he [General Peled] thinks of the limit of obedience." The story of Peled is a story of passivity (so typical of the general conformity to the army service). "I was called to serve," "I was ordered to fight," "I was sent," "I was appointed—a tin soldier" (*Ha'aretz,* March 1994).

Journalists entitle their articles "Vietnam and Gaza" (*Ha'ir,* 22 April 1994) and before the committee of inquiry over the massacre in Hebron, the IDF Chief of Staff, General Barak, continues to compare the situation to Algiers (*Ha'aretz,* 29 March 1994). Scholars make efforts to find similarities between Ireland, Algiers, and Gaza (Lustick 1994).

In the post-Lebanon and Intifada era, the Israeli is obsessed with travelling to Auschwitz and Dachau concentration camps. He is obsessed with making himself understand his roots as a victim. The new Sabra with his "secular conscience" of the nineties (Moskos and Chambers 1994), seems to have regained his inner strength not only from his being a new Jew as an Israeli fighter, but also from the Diaspora and the collective memories of his Jewish history. Both are shaping his past and his moral decisions. The tenuous gap between Memorial Day and Holocaust Day seems to disappear. The two memorials seem to merge. Even if the Jewish/Israeli critic decides to (temporarily) detach himself from the IDF, he is facing the dilemmas of moral connectedness—if not with the present or future, at least with the collective past. The journey to the past is not an independent one—the Israeli moral investigator is magnetized by the Holocaust, a stage upon which he was supposed to have been a successful player, one on which he views himself both as a victim and a spectator. He daydreams part of his reality:

> Saturday. I woke up late . . . the dining room is closed already so I am going to have to find food elsewhere . . . On the way, I see a group of reservists walking toward me. When they come closer I get a shock. They are speaking in loud German! Whatever they were talking about causes them to laugh. Just imagine the picture; in front of me and to my right, soldiers are talking in German, and on my left—a ramp that surrounds the compound, and behind it the straight fences lining up like rulers, the tents of the prisoners, the guard's towers colored in gray, and powerful searchlights. It is true that the soldiers are simply reservists, some from Jerusalem, and that those who are involved in killing the

imprisoned people are the prisoner's friends. But nevertheless it is shocking.

Later on I recollected that the night before, Friday evening, there were some reservists who were using Yiddish. So maybe these were the soldiers that I saw and heard on Saturday morning, and the Yiddish simply was transformed for me into German. But this is no accident, is it? After all, Yiddish is mostly German. So due to this incident in Ansar I have started thinking and questioning myself. Why is it that we recently have a growing tendency to develop study courses for the preservation of Yiddish? The language of a nation who was our most lethal enemy. (Shlomo Frankel, *Laisha*, 1 January 1990)

This imaginative rationality has been already experienced by Israeli reservists who fought in Lebanon. One of them reported:

I was going out for a twenty-five-hour break. I had managed to get a ride. The driver was a German journalist. We were stationed beyond Tyre, and he was in a hurry to arrive in Jerusalem before 7:00 in order to broadcast his program at 8:00 on the German TV. They will be seeing familiar pictures. The German adores us . . . he thinks that we are great and that we are showing the entire world what it deserves. His identification with us frightens me. We are not so similar to each other, but maybe we are. He asks me how it was in Ein Hilwe (a huge refugee camp, where there was the most bitter fighting against terrorists who used the population as a shield). I answer: "It was like the Warsaw Ghetto"—and then I see the smile on his face, coming out straight from the fridge. But I tell him there was one difference—the terrorists have more ammunition and guns than the Jews had in Warsaw. I don't want this German to include me in his dreams of the Third Reich, but I myself don't want to be taken to be a part in the Reich of Begin and Sharon. (Dudu, in Rosenthal 1983, p. 80)

And there are Intifada refusing reservists for whom the Holocaust is not a fiction or a part of their imagination but reality:

Both my parents were in Auschwitz. I never knew my grandparents. They all died in the Holocaust as well as my other relatives. My parents hold a record for Auschwitz. They were there for two and a half years! . . . they survived the "death march". . . . I grew up with stories of Auschwitz. . . . I don't like it when people use Auschwitz to justify the things they are doing from either the right or the left perspective.

A refuser who is second generation to Holocaust survivors hold a different perspective:

> Both my parents are Holocaust survivors who fought the Nazis. My mother committed suicide when I was three. I hardly knew her and remember very little. She came from the ghettos of southeast Poland, which not many people know about. There was a revolt there, a serious revolt, and my mother was a commander of the bunker and she was captured. She committed suicide on the anniversary of the revolt. I assume that such an event has an effect somewhere on the subconscious. My brother did his doctoral studies . . . on the topic of the Yudenrat. It is a topic that exists in our family . . . it is not a repressed topic. My father married again and I had a happy childhood on the kibbutz . . . but the subject of the Holocaust remained. I think that subconsciously the Holocaust had something to do with my refusal—the fact that such a dreadful crime had been committed by a cultured society, by ordinary people the same as everyone else, people who were eating, sleeping, making love, etc. We couldn't believe that they could do such things. . . . Maybe I won't change the world—but when refusing, I am doing the best I can so that the world won't change me. Then I will be able to look into the eye of my kids when asked, "Daddy, where were you in those days?" I always say that I was born in 1939 . . . that is how I feel.

The Intifada gave the Palestinians an audible presence, a voice within the language of conflict. It also brought the realization that the Israeli mind is mediated through the Holocaust. A Palestinian writes "Our pain is deemed to be forever filtered through the dark, larger than life muffler of the Holocaust, forever insignificant in juxtaposition" (*New York Times Magazine*, 28 April 1991).

But it is only when a comparison is made that one can realize that there is no comparison—a fact that has made the collective memories of the Holocaust so strong for the young Israeli, and the desire to protest evil inevitable (Linn and Gur-Zeev 1995). When a released Palestinian poet from Ansar camp complained that Ansar is like Auschwitz because the prisoners are given an opportunity to take a shower only once a week, the reporter answered him: "But we [the Jews] received one shower and that was it" (*Ma'ariv*, 2 June 1989), and he left his interviewee.

But you need not be the son of Holocaust survivors in order to implement the morality of the Holocaust into your moral dilemmas. As this Intifada refuser explains:

> I am a third generation of the Holocaust but in terms of feelings it is as though I am a first or second generation. It makes me angry

> that my people, my nation is put in a position where these considerations must be raised.

His fellow refuser echoes:

> Although my parents weren't Holocaust survivors I always find the connection. When you see pictures of twelve-year-old children with their hands tied, the memory of the Holocaust flashes into your head.

And a third one comments:

> All my generation are preoccupied with it. Everything that happens in this country has to do with the Holocaust. First of all there is the fear, the identification of everything as a forthcoming Holocaust. Arafat is identified with Hitler and there are other similar distortions. As a child I thought about the Holocaust a lot and tried to imagine how I would have behaved if I had been there. My fear is that the social processes that affected the Germans may be found here as well and that we have to be prepared to avoid such a psychological process.

Symbolically or accidentally, the trial of a suspected Nazi criminal (Damjanjuk) started the week the Intifada started. My generation, who grew up in the shadow of Eichmann in the glass box, were awaiting this trial as a testimony for their own children. The old Holocaust survivors were waiting for their last chance to bear witness, before no living evidence would be left. The Intifada removed the public attention from this trial. After seven years of Intifada and legal battles over the suspected Nazi's identity (a victor or a victim?), an Israeli lawyer managed to set him free on the grounds of false identity. Paradoxically, throughout these seven years, the struggle for clear moral identity was the concern of the Israeli soldier as well. Yet his moral drama seemed to be elsewhere, as this refuser explained:

> It might sound pathetic but a country that pursues Nazi war criminals and brings them to trial in Israel and accuses them of the crime of obedience to authority, should treat its own sons who refuse to obey orders they think are crimes against another nation in a better way. I don't want to exaggerate but I believe that some day we will be tried for our actions. I don't want to use the Holocaust as a component of my refusal to serve in the territories. I think, however, that it has an important role in my position, not a dominant one and not the most important, but enough to make me feel that I cannot say I am not responsible for my deeds.

This responsibility is clarified by this Intifada refuser who has no family connection to the Holocaust:

> I remember in 1969 a youth group consisting of Arabs and Jews was sent from my home town to Germany. Here you have the three ingredients of the conflict: Jews, Arabs and Germans! I talked to two German girls. They told me that Germany had two traitors: one was Hitler who brought Germany to disaster and the other was Willi Brandt who fled from the flag. The girls told me this thirty-five years after the Holocaust. So if you want to know how my refusal started we have to go back (to the construction of the moral position) to this sentence: "Either you are with one or the other, there is no possibility of being in the middle."

And this Intifada paratrooper who has been fighting in Israeli wars since 1967 and had no family connections to the Holocaust, nevertheless is haunted by it. It affected his decision to refuse during the war in Lebanon and twice during the Intifada:

> In the last ten years I am deep into the Holocaust. I see myself as a potential victim of that situation. I mean, I have some sort of apocalyptic vision that the Holocaust will get us one day. I guess I have read all that was written in Hebrew on the topic . . . and the Holocaust cut into the Intifada . . . this helplessness in the face of the mighty . . . we have grown up within the green line and the refugees were not in front of our eyes . . . and now we have a part in it whether we want it or not. I guess we are both victims. I am praying all the time that the refusers will remain a small group . . . because I don't want their action to be destructive . . . not to hurt the fabric of the IDF that is so important to our survival.

Yuval Neria, a hero and a symbol of my generation, provides a summary for this book. Born to parents who were born in Jerusalem and had fought there in the War of Independence, Yuval was severely wounded and won the highest medal for bravery for his fighting with an armored division during the 1973 Yom Kippur War. It was only sixteen years after the 1973 war that he managed for the first time to voice his criticism regarding his war experiences in his documentary novel entitled *Fire* (Neria 1989). In an interview about his book he told the press:

> It took time (for me to express my true feelings concerning the horrors of the war). . . . I didn't take part in any of the protest movements after the 1973 war. *I was without identity, I was living in a bubble.* My friends had died or returned to the army. The rumpus

over my decoration made me even more secluded. . . . In 1977 [before Egyptian President Anwar Saadat made his peace-seeking visit to Jerusalem R.L.] two friends and I wrote the famous "officer's letter" [calling on Begin to make peace with Egypt]. From this protest letter Peace Now was born. . . . I was still naive during the war in Lebanon, where I have already served as a battalion commander . . . defending it before everybody . . . at the beginning. The best recipe for driving someone mad is to have him go through this terrible war and then to give him a medal for bravery. . . . The medal was the greatest obstacle to my writing. . . . How could I talk out when I was a symbol? As a symbol I had to be exemplary . . . but a symbol is related to something very sad. . . . It did not fit the speeches, the talk or the cocktail party at the President's residence, when the five of us who had survived and won medals were there. I am sure that the Chief Education Officer knows what we are supposed to represent. But I didn't know. The award should attest to success, but to my generation it represents catastrophe. My parents always got the message across to me, without words, that the War of Independence was the last terrible war. . . . That is why I felt so betrayed. . . . You know through this book, I talked to my parents for the first time (*Yediot Acharonot,* 22 October 1989).

APPENDIX
KOHLBERG'S FORM B TEST*

There was a woman who had very bad cancer, and there was no treatment known to medicine that would save her. Her doctor, Dr. Jefferson, knew that she had only about six months to live. She was in terrible pain, but she was so weak that a good dose of pain killer like morphine would make her die sooner. She was delirious and almost crazy with pain and in her calm periods she would ask Dr. Jefferson to give her enough morphine to kill her. She said she could not stand the pain and she was going to die in a few months anyway. Although he knows that mercy killing is against the law, the doctor thinks about granting her request.

1. Should Dr. Jefferson give her the drug that would make her die?

1a. Why or why not?

2. Is it actually right or wrong for him to give the woman the drug that would make her die?

2a. Why is it right or wrong?

3. Should the woman have the right to make the final decision?

3a. Why is it right or wrong?

4. The woman is married. Should the husband have anything to do with the decision?

4a. Why or why not?

5. It is against the law for the doctor to give the woman the drug. Does that make it morally wrong?

5a. Why or why not?

---

*From Kohlberg 1984, pp. 644–645.

6. In general, should people try to do everything they can to obey the law?
6a. Why or why not?
6b. How does this apply to what Dr. Jefferson should do?

Dr. Jefferson did perform the mercy killing by giving the woman the drug. Passing by at the time was another doctor, Dr. Rogers, who knew the situation Dr. Jefferson was in. Dr. Rogers thought of trying to stop Dr. Jefferson, but the drug was already administered. Dr. Rogers wonders whether he should report Dr. Jefferson.

1. Should Dr. Rogers report Dr. Jefferson?
1a. Why or why not?

Dr. Rogers did report Dr. Jefferson. Dr. Jefferson is brought to court and a jury is selected. It is up to the judge to determine the sentence.

2. Should the judge give Dr. Jefferson some sentence, or should he suspend the sentence and let Dr. Jefferson go free?
2a. Why is that best?
3. Thinking in terms of society, should people who break the law be punished?
3a. Why or why not?
3b. How does this apply to how they should decide?
4. Dr. Jefferson was doing what his conscience told him when he gave the woman the drug. Should a law breaker be punished if he is acting out of conscience?
4a. Why?

Note: The description of the jury's role in the trial of Dr. Jefferson was dismissed in order to match the dilemma to the Israeli experience. The same was done in regard to the question of the death penalty.

REFERENCES

Aini, L. (1992). *Sand Tides* (a novel). Hakibbutz Hameuchad: Siman Kria.

Almog, O. (1992). The new pillar of fire. *Politica* 42/43, pp. 10–13.

Arendt, H. (1963). *Eichmann in Jerusalem: A Report on the Banality of Evil.* New York: Viking.

Bar-tal, D., and Antebi, D. (1992). Beliefs about the negative intentions of the world: A study of the Israeli siege mentality. *Political Psychology* 13, 4, 633–645.

Beeson, D., and Lowenthal, M. F. (1975). Perceived stress across the life course. In M. F. Lowenthal, M. Turner, and D. Chiriboga (eds.), *Four Stages of Life: A Comparative Study of Women and Men Facing Transitions.* San Francisco: Jossey-Bass.

Ben-Ari, E. (1990). Masked soldiers: The IDF and the Intifada. In R. Gal (ed.), *The Seventh War: The Effects of the Intifada on Tisraeli Society.* Tel-Aviv: Hakibutz Hameuchad (in Hebrew).

Ben-Gurion, D. (1953). *A Vision and a Path.* 2d ed., vol. 3. Tel Aviv: Isarel Workers Party (in Hebrew).

Ben Noon, C. (1992). *Civil Disobedience.* Tel-Aviv: Yaar.

Benhabib, S., and Cornell, D. (eds.). (1988). *Feminism as Critique.* Minneapolis: University of Minnesota Press.

Benvenisti, M. (1992). *Fatal Embrace.* Tel Aviv: Maxwell-Macmillan-Keter.

Berry, J. W. (1990). Psychology of calculation. In J. Berman (ed.), *Cross Cultural Perspectives.* Nebraska Symposium on Motivation. Lincoln: Nebraska University Press.

Blatt, M., Davis, U., and Kleinbaum, P. (1975). *Dissent and Ideology in Israel: Resistance to the Draft (1948–1973).* London: Ithaca Press.

Bilton, M., and Sim, K. (1992). *Four Hours in My Lai.* London: Viking.

Blasi, A. (1983). Moral cognition and moral action: A theoretical perspective. *Developmental Review* 3, 178–210.

Breznitz, S. (1983). *Stress in Israel.* New York: Van Nostrand Reinhold.

Brown, L. M., Tappan, M., Gilligan, C., Argyris, D., and Miller, B. (1989) Reading for self and moral voice: A method for interpreting narratives of real-life moral conflict and choice. In M. Packer and R. Addison (eds.). *Entering the Circle: Hermeneutic Investigation in Psychology.* Albany: State University of New York Press.

———, and Gilligan, C. (1993) Meeting at the crossroad: Women's psychology and girls' development. *Feminism and Psychology* 3, 1, 11–35.

Brown, R., and Herrnstein, R. J. (1975). *Psychology.* Boston: Little Brown.

Broughton, J. M. (1978). The cognitive developmental approach to morality: A reply to Kurtines and Greif. *Journal of Moral Education* 7, 81–96.

———. (1987). Piaget's concept of the self. In Polly Young-Eisenberg and J. A. Hall (eds.). *The Book of the Self.* New York: New York University Press.

Brynen, R. (ed). (1991). *Echoes of the Intifada.* Boulder, Colo.: Westview.

Burke, K. (1897). *The Philosophy of Literary Form: Studies in Symbolic Action.* New York: Random House.

———. (1965). *Permanence and Change: Anatomy of Purpose.* New York: Bobbs-Merrill.

Burnet, S., and Bedau, H. (1993). *Critical Thinking.* Boston, Mass.: Bedford Books of St. Martin's Press.

Candee, D. (1976). Structure and choice in moral reasoning. *Journal of Personality and Social Psychology* 34, 6, 1293–1301.

Childress, J. F. (1982). *Moral Responsibility in Conflict: Essays on Non-Violence, War and Conscience.* Baton Rouge: Lousiana State University Press.

Clarke, D. M. (1987). Acting according to conscience. In J. D. G. Evans (ed). *Moral Philosophy and Contemporary Problems.* Cambridge: Cambridge University Press.

Cochran, L. (1985). *Position and Nature of Personhood: An Approach of the Understanding of Persons.* Westport, Conn.: Greenwood.

Cohen, C. (1971). *Civil Disobedience: Conscience, Tactics and the Law.* New York: Columbia University Press.

———, Wolfsfeld, G. (1993). *Framing the Intifada: People and Media.* Norwood, N.J.: Ablex.

Cohen, S. (1991). Criminology and the uprising. *Tikkun* 3, 5, 60–96.

Colby A., and Kohlberg L. (1987). *The Measurement of Moral Judgement,* vol. 1. New York: Cambridge University Press.

———, and Damon W. (1992). *Some Do Care: Contemporary Lives of Moral Commitment.* New York: Free Press.

Curry, D. G. (1985). *Sunshine Patriots: Punishment and the Vietnam Offender.* South Bend, Ind.: University of Notre Dame Press.

Dupuy, T. N., Martell, P. (1985). *Flawed Victory: The 1982 War in Lebanon.* Fairfax, Va.: Hero.

Eilam, Y. (1991). *The Executors.* Jerusalem: Keter.

Elder, G. H. (1987). War mobilization and the life course: A cohort of World War II veterans. *Sociological Forum* 2, 449–472.

———, and Clipp, E. (1988). Combat experience, comradeship and psychological health. In Z. Harel and B. Kahana, *Human Adaptations to Extreme Stress: From the Holocaust to Vietnam.* New York: Plenum.

———, and Clipp, E. (1989). Combat experience and emotional health: Impairment and resilience in later life. *Journal of Personality* June, 311–341.

———, and Caspi (1990.) studying lives in a changing society: Sociological and personological explorations. In A. I. Rabin, R. A. Zucker, R. A. Emmons, and S. Frank (eds.), *Studying Persons and Lives.* New York: Springer, pp. 201–247.

———, Gimbel, C., and Levi, R. (1991). Turning points in life: The case of military service and war. *Military Psychology* 3, 4, 215–233.

Emler, N. (1983). Morality and politics: The ideological dimension in the theory of moral development. In H. Weinrich-Haste and D. Locke (eds), *Morality in the Making: Thoughts Action and Social Context.* Chichester: Wiley.

———, Renwick, S., and Malone, B. (1963). The relationships between moral reasoning and political orientation. *Political Personality and Social Psychology* 5,5,1073–1080.

Feeney, T. J. (1987). Expert psychological testimony on credibility issues. *Military Law Review* 115, 121–177.

Fish, N. (1984). "Israelis in America: Migration, Decision Making and Its Consequences upon Adaptation to the American Jewish Community." Unpublished doctoral dissertation, Yeshiva University.

Fishkin, J., Keniston, K., and MacKinnon, C. (1973). Moral reasoning and political ideology. *Journal of Personality and Social Psychology* 27, 109–119.

Freedman, R. O. (1991). *The Intifada: Its Impact on Israel, the Arab World, and the Superpowers.* Miami: Florida International University Press.

Fromm, E. (1981). *On Disobedience—And Other Essays.* New York: Harper and Row.

Gabison, R. (1986) The crime of the blue-white collar. *Politic* April 7, 28–30.

Gabriel, G. P. (1982). *To Serve with Honor.* Westport Conn.: Greenwood.

Gabriel, R. (1984). *Operation Peace for the Galilee: The Israeli-PLO War in Lebanon.* New York: Hill and Wang.

Gal, R. (1985). Commitment and obedience in the military: An Israeli case study. *Armed Forces and Society* 11, 4, 553–564.

———. (1986). *A Portrait Of The Israeli Soldier.* Westport, Conn.: Greenwood.

———. (1990). *The Seventh War: The Effect of the Intifada on the Israeli Society.* Tel Aviv: Kibbutz Meuchad.

Gamson, W. A., Fireman, B., and Rytina, S. (1982). *Encounters with Unjust Authority.* Homewood, Ill.: Dorsey.

Gans, C. (1992). *Philosophical Anarchism and Political Disobedience.* Cambridge: Cambridge University Press.

Gibbs, J. C., Widaman, K. F., and Colby, A. (1982). Construction and validation of a simplified, group-administrable equivalent to the moral judgement interview. *Child Development* 53, 895–910.

Gilat, N. (1987). "The sound silence: Parents against silence." Haifa University. Unpublished M.A. thesis.

Gilbar, G. G., and Susser, A. (eds.). (1992). *The Core of the Conflict: The Intifada.* Tel Aviv: Kibbutz Meuchad.

Gilligan, C. (1982). *In a Different Voice.* Cambridge, Mass: Harvard University Press.

———, Lyons, N. P., and Hanmer, T. J. (eds.). (1990). *Making Connections.* Cambridge: Harvard University Press.

———, and Wiggins, G. (1987). The origin of morality in early childhood relationships. In J. Kagan and S. Lamb (eds.), *The Emergence of Morality in Young Children.* Chicago: University of Chicago Press.

Glazer, P., and Glazer, M. (1977). War resisters in the Land of Battles. *Dissent* 24, 289–296.

Goffman, E. (1959). *The Presentation of Self in Everyday Life.* New York: Doubleday.

Greenwalt, K. (1989). Accommodation to selective conscientious objection: How and why. In M. F. Noone (ed.), *Selective Conscientious Objection: Accommodating Conscience and Security*. London: Westview.

Haan, N., Smith, B., and Block, J. (1968). The moral reasoning of young adults. *Journal of Personality and Social Psychology* 32, 255–269.

Habermas, J. (1990). *Moral Conscientiousness and Communicative Action*. Cambridge Mass.: MIT.

Hardan, D. (ed.). (1985). *The Moral and Existential Dilemmas of the Israeli Soldier*. Jerusalem: World Zionist Organization.

Hare, R. M. (1965). *Freedom and Reason*. New York: Oxford University Press.

———. (1981). *Moral Thinking: Its Levels, Methods and Point*. Oxford: Oxford University Press.

Harris, P. (ed.). (1989). *Civil Disobedience*. Lanham, Md.: University Press of America.

Hasdai, Y. (1982). "Doers" and "thinkers" in the IDF. *The Jerusalem Quarterly* 24, 13–25.

Heikal, M. H. (1975). *Road To Ramadan*. New York: Querange.

Hendel, Y. (1991). *Mountain of Losses*. Tel Aviv: New Library. (Hebrew)

Hersh, S. (1975). *My Lai 4*. New York: Vintage.

Hertz-Lazarovitz, R. (1993). Political Altruism: A case study. In S. Oliner and P. Oliner (eds.), *Embracing the Other: Philosophical, Psychological and Historical Perspectives and Altruism*. New York: New York University Press.

Hetsroni, A., and Holz, M. (1992). "All we were saying was give peace a chance: A study on hopes which are not fulfilled—The high school protest letters and their writers." Seminar work, Tel Aviv University, Department of Psychology.

Hirschman, A. (1970). *Exit Voice and Loyalty*. Cambridge, Mass.: Harvard University Press.

Horne, A. (1977). *A Savage War of Peace*. New York: Macmillan.

Horowitz, D. (1987). Strategic limitations of "A nation in Arms." *Armed Forces and Society* 13, 2, 277–294

Inbar E. (1991). Israel's small war: The military response to the Intifada. *Armed Forces and Society* 18, 1, 29–50.

Kaminer, R. (1989). The protest movement in Israel. In Z. Lockman and J. Beinin (eds.). *Intifada: The Palestinian Uprising against Israeli Occupation*. Toronto: Merip.

Katriel, T. (1985). "Gripping" as a verbal ritual in some Israeli discourse. In M. Dascal (ed.), *Dialogue*. Amsterdam: John Benjamin.

———. (1986). *Talking Straight: "Dugree" Speech in Israeli Sabra Culture*. New York: Cambridge University Press.

———. (1991). Between the promise land and the land of promise: Israeli emigration and Israeli identity. In I. S. Lustick and B. Rubin (eds.), *Critical Essays on Israeli Society, Politics and Culture*. Albany: State University of New York Press.

———, and Nesher, P. (1986). Gibush: The rhetoric of cohesion in Israeli school culture. *Comparative Education Review* 30, 2, 216–232.

Kelman, C. R., and Hamilton, V. L. (1989). *Social Psychology of Authority and Responsibility*. New Haven: Yale University Press.

Kimmerling, B. (1985). *The Interrupted System*. New Brunswick: Transaction.

Kohlberg, L. (1970). Education for justice: A modern statement of the Platonic view. In N. F. Sizer and T. R. Sizer (eds.), *Moral Education: Five Lectures*. Cambridge, Mass: Harvard University Press.

———. (1973). The claim to moral adequacy of a highest stage of moral judgement. *Journal of Philosophy* 70, 630, 646.

———. (1976). Moral Stages and moralization; The cognitive developmental approach. In T. Lickona (ed.), *Moral Development and Behavior: Theory, Research and Social Issues*. New York: Holt, Rinehart and Winston.

———. (1984). *Essays on Moral Development; The Psychology of Moral Development: The Nature and Validity of Moral Stages*, vol 2. San Francisco: Harper and Row.

———, and Kramer. (1969). Continuities and discontinuities in childhood and adult moral development. *Human Development* 12, 93–120.

———, and Meyer, R. (1978). Development as the aim of education. *Harvard Educational Review* 13, 123–170.

———, and Candee, D. (1984). The relationship of moral judgement to moral action. In W. Kurtines and J. Gewirtz (eds.), *Morality, Moral Behavior And Moral Development*. New York: Wiley.

Krebs, R. L. (1967). "Some relationships between moral judgement, attention and resistance to temptation." Unpublished doctoral dissertation, University of Chicago.

Lakoff, G., and Johnson, M. (1980). *Metaphors We Live By*. Chicago: University of Chicago Press.

Leming, J. (1974). Moral reasoning sense of control and social-political activism among adolescents. *Adolescence* 9, 507–528.

Levine, E. (1986). *Voices from Israel: Understanding the Israeli Mind*. New York, London, Toronto: Cornwall.

Levy, A. (1990). Yes Lady, your blood is redder than mine: Israeli men as victims. *Israel Journal of Psychiatry and Relational Sciences* 27, 4, 247–250.

Lieblich, A. (1978). *Tin Soldiers on Jerusalem Beach*. New York: Pantheon.

———. (1983). Between strength and toughness. In S. Breznitz (ed.), *Stress in Israel*. New York: Van Nostrand Reinhold.

———. (1989). *Transition to Adulthood during Military Service: The Israeli Case*. Albany: State University of New York Press (first published in 1987 as *The Spring of Their Years* [in Hebrew]).

Linn, R. (1986). Conscientious objection in Israel during the war in Lebanon. *Armed Forces and Society* 12, 4, 489–511.

———. (1987). Moral disobedience during the war in Lebanon: What can the cognitive developmental theory learn from the experience of the Israeli soldiers? *Social Cognition* 5, 4, 383–402.

———. (1988a). Moral judgement in extreme social contexts: Soldiers who refuse to fight and physicians who strike. *Journal of Applied Social Psychology* 18, 13, 1149–1170.

———. (1988b). Terrorism, morality and soldiers' motivation to fight: An example from the Israeli experience in Lebanon. *Terrorism: An International Journal* 11, 139–149.

———. (1989a). Hypothetical and actual moral reasoning of Israeli selective conscientious objectors during the war in Lebanon (1982–1985). *Journal of Applied Developmental Psychology* 10, 1, 19–36.

———. (1989b). *Not Shooting and Not Crying: Psychological Inquiry into Moral Disobedience*. Westport Conn.: Greenwood.

———. (1991). Holocaust metaphors and symbols in the moral dilemmas of contemporary Israeli soldiers. *Metaphor and Symbolic Activity* 6, 2, 61–86.

———. (1994). Conscience at war and the assessment of credibility: Theoretical and practical questions. *Politics and the Individual* 4, 2, 47–61.

———. (1995a). The claim for moral maturity, consistency and integrity among objecting Israeli soldiers during the war in Lebanon. *Applied Social Psychology* 25/5, 399–415.

———. (1995b). Resistance and motivation: Moral political or personal? *Social Behavior and Personality* 23, 1, 35–44.

———. (1995c). The moral dimension in nonevent transition—Israeli expatriates in Canada: A separate and connected critics of self and others. *Journal of Psychology and Judaism* 19, 3, 227–240.

———, and Gilligan C. (1990). One action two moral orientations: The tension between justice and care voices in Israeli selective conscientious objectors. *New Ideas in Psychology* 8, 2, 189–203.

———, and Gur-Zeev, I. (1995). Conquering the others' symbol: Holocaust dialectics in the Palestinian struggle for independence. *Metaphor and Symbolic Activity.*

Lissak, M. (1990). The Intifada and Israeli society: Historical, sociological perspective. In R. Gal (ed.), *The Seventh War: The Effects of the Intifada on the Israeli Society*. Tel-Aviv: Hakibutz Hameuchad (in Hebrew).

Locke, D. (1980). The illusion of stage 6. *Journal of Moral Education* 9, 103–109.

———. (1981). Cognitive stages or developmental phases? A critique of Kohlberg's stage-structural theory of moral reasoning. *Journal of Moral Education* 8, 3, 168–181.

———. (1983). Moral reasons and moral action. In H. Weinrich-Haste and D. Locke (eds.), *Morality in the Making: Thought, Action and Social Context*. Chichester: Wiley.

Lustick, S. I. (1994). *Unsettled States, Disputed Lands in Britain, Ireland, France and Algeria, Israel and the West Bank-Gaza*. Ithaca, N.Y.: Cornell University Press.

Lyons, N. P. (1988). Two perspectives: On self, relationships and morality. In C. Gilligan, J. V. Ward, and J. M. Taylor, *Mapping the Moral Domain*. Cambridge: Harvard University Press.

May, R. (1969). *Love and Will*. New York: A Delta Book.

———. (1979). *Psychology and the Human Dilemma*. New York: W. W. Norton.

Melzer, Y. (1975). *Concepts of Just War*. Leyden, Holland: Sijhoff.

Mergendoller, J. R. (1989). God and ill will: War resistance as a context for the study of moral action. In M. J. Packer and R. B.

Addison, *Entering the Circle: Hermeneutic Investigation in Psychology*. Albany: State University of New York Press.

Meyer, M. A. (1990). *Jewish Identity in the Modern World*. Seattle and London: University of Washington Press.

Milgram, N. A., Bar, K. (1993). Stress on wives due to husbands' hazardous duty or absence. *Psychology* 2, 180–190.

Milgram, S. (1974). *Obedience to Authority*. New York: Harper and Row.

Milstein, U. (1992). *The Outbreak of the War, the Yom Kippur War, the Airborne Forces, the Firing Line*. Tel Aviv: Yaron Golan.

Minuchin, I., and Minuchin, D. (eds.). (1985). *The Limits of Obedience*. Tel Aviv: The Yesh Gvul movement and Siman Kria.

Miron, D. (1992). *Facing the Silent Brothers: Essays on the Poetry of the War of Independence*. Jerusalem: Keter.

Mischal, S., and Aharoni, R. (1989). *Speaking Stones: The Words Behind the Palestinian Intifada*. Tel Aviv: Kibbutz Hameuchad.

Morris, B. (1989). *The Birth of the Palestinian Refugee Problem, 1947–1949*. Cambridge: Cambridge University Press.

———. (1994). *Israel's Border Wars 1949–1956: Arab Infiltration, Israeli Reltaliation and the Countdown to the Suez War*. Oxford: Clarendon Press.

Moskos, C. C., and Chambers, J. W. (1993). *The New Conscientious Objection: From Sacred to Secular Resistance*. Oxford: Oxford University Press.

Neria Y. (1989). *Fire*. Tel Aviv: Zmora Bitan.

Netanyahu, B. (1986). *Terrorism, How the West Can Win*. New York: Farrar, Straus and Giroux.

Noone M. (ed.). (1989). *Selective Conscientious Objection: Accommodating Conscience and Security*. Boulder, Colo.: Westview.

Noy, S., Nardi, C., and Solomon, Z. (1986). Battled and military unit characteristics and prevalence of psychiatric casualties. In N. Milgram (ed.), *Stress and Coping in Times of War: Generalizations from Israeli Experience*. New York: Bruner/Mazel.

O'Brien, W. V. (1986). Terrorism: What should we do? In S. Anzovin (ed.). *Terrorism*. New York: Wilson.

Oren, A. (1992). Private and general: The subjectivity of objection. Paper presented at the international seminar on conscientious objection, The Israeli Institute for Military Studies, Ceasaria, Israel, November 18–20.

Orwell, G. (1949). *1984*. New York: Harcourt, Brace and World.

Peled, Y. (1993). *Soldier*. Jerusalem: Ma'ariv Book Guild.

Peleg, M. (1989). The relationship of separation from love objects, and a severed national ideology, to depression, among Israeli immigrants in the U.S. (I). *Journal of Psychology and Judaism* 13, 189–223.

———. (1990). The relationship of separation from love objects, and a severed national ideology, to depression, among Israeli immigrants in the U.S. (II). *Journal of Psychology and Judaism* 14, 5–48.

Peri, Y. (1983). The rise and the fall of Israel's national consensus. *New Outlook,* August–September, 28–29.

———. (1993). Israel: Conscientious objection in a democracy under siege. In C. C. Moskos and J. W. Chambers (eds.), *The New Conscientious Objection: From Sacred to Secular Resistance*. Oxford: Oxford University Press.

Piaget, J. (1932/1965). *The Moral Judgement of the Child*. New York: New Press.

Pines. A. M. (1990). The Intifada and Israeli burnout. In R. Gal (ed.), *The Seventh War: The Effects of the Intifada on the Israeli Society*. Tel-Aviv: Hakibutz Hameuchad (in Hebrew).

Power, F. C., Higgins, A., and Kohlberg, L. (1989). *Lawrence Kohlberg's Approach to Moral Education: A Study of Three Democratic High Schools*. New York: Columbia University Press.

Rawls, J. (1971). A theory of civil disobedience. In P. Harris (ed.), *Civil Disobedience*. University Press of America.

Rest, J. (1979). *Development in Judging Moral Issues*. Minneapolis: University of Minnesota Press.

Rosen, R., and Hamerman, I. (1990). *Soldiers in the Land of Ishmael: Stories and Documents*. Tel Aviv: Am Oved.

Rothberg, J. M., and McDowell, C. P. (1988). Suicide in United States Air Force personnel, 1981–1985. *Military Medicine* 153, 12, 645–648.

———, Ursano, R. J., and Holloway, H. (1987). Suicide in United States military. *Psychiatric Annals* 17, 8, 545–548.

Rozental, R. (ed.). (1983). *Lebanon: The Other War*. Tel Aviv: Sifriat Poalim Publishing House Ltd. (Hebrew).

Ryff, C. D. (1984). Personality development from inside: The subjective experience of change in adulthood and aging. In P. B. Baltes and O. G. Brim (eds.), *Life Span Development and Behavior*. New York: Academic.

Scheissel, L. (1968). *Conscience in America*. New York: Dutton.

Schiff, R. L. (1992). Israel as an "uncivil" state: A reconsideration of civil-military relations. *Security Studies* 1, 4, 636–658.

Schiff, Z., and Yaari, E. (1984). *Israel's Lebanon War.* Trans. and ed. Ina Friedman. New York: Simon and Schuster.

———, and Yaari, E. (1990). *Intifada.* Tel Aviv: Schocken.

Segev, T. (1991). *The Seventh Million: The Israelis and the Holocaust.* Jerusalem: Maxwell-Macmillan-Keter Publishing House and Domino Press.

Shaked, G. (1986). The case for secularism. In E. Levine (ed.), *Voices from Israel: Understanding the Israeli Mind.* New York, London, Toronto: Cornwall.

Shalev, A. (1990). *The Intifada: Causes and Effects.* Tel Aviv: Papirus.

Shapira, A. (1971). (ed.). *The Seventh Day: Soldiers Talk about the Six Day War.* Penguin.

Sheleff, L. (1989). *The Voice of Honor: Civil Disobedience and Civilin Loyalty.* Tel Aviv: Ramot.

Shiffer, S. (1984). *Snow Ball: The Story behind the Lebanon War.* Tel Aviv: Yediot Acharonot, Edanim (Hebrew).

Shinhar, A. (1989). To be there: Protest songs of soldiers during the war in Lebanon. *Hetz* 1, 34–47 (Hebrew).

Shokeid, M. (1988). *Children of Circumstances: Israeli Emigrants in New York.* Ithaca and London: Cornell University Press.

Sivan, E. (1991). *The 1948 Generation: Myth, Profile and Memory.* Tel Aviv: IDF.

Sobel, Z. (1986). *My Grants from the Promised Land.* New Brunswick, N.J.: Transaction.

Solomon, R. (1990). *A Passion for Justice: Emotions and the Origins of the Social Contract.* Reading, Mass.: Addison-Welsley.

Sprinzak, E. (1977). Extreme politics in Israel. *The Jerusalem Quarterly* 5, 33–47.

———. (1986). *Every Man Whatever in His Own Eyes.* Tel Aviv: Sifriat Poalim.

———, and Diamond, L. (1993). *Israeli Democracy under Stress.* Boulder and London: Lynne Rienner.

Steenberger, B. N. (1991). All the world is not a stage: Emerging contextualist themes in counseling and development. *Journal of Counseling and Development* 70, 288–296.

Straschnov, A. (1994). *Justice under Fire.* Tel Aviv: Yediot Acharonoth.

Student, M. (1991). *In the Shadow of War: Memories of a Soldier and Therapist.* Philadelphia: Temple University Press.

Swirsky, S., and Safir, P. M. (eds.). (1991). *Calling the Equality Bluff.* New York: Pergamon.

Tappan, M. B. (1990). Hermeneutic and moral development: Interpreting narrative representations of moral experience. *Developmental Review* 10, 239–265.

Timmerman, J. (1985). *The Longest War: Israel in Lebanon.* New York: Knopf.

Valentine, A. (1989). *Sahid.* Tel Aviv: Am Oved.

Vine, I. (1983). The nature of moral commitments. In H. Weinrich-Haste and D. Locke (eds.), *Morality in the Making: Thought Action and Social Context.* Chichester, England: Wiley.

Wallace J. D. (1988). *Moral Relevance and Moral Conflict.* Ithaca, N.Y., London: Cornell University Press.

Walzer, M. (1968). Civil disobedience and "resistance." *Dissent,* January–February, 13–15.

———. (1970). *Obligations: Essays on Disobedience, War and Citizenship.* Cambridge: Harvard University Press.

———. (1977). *Just and Unjust Wars.* New York: Basic.

———. (1983). *Spheres of Justice: A Defense of Pluralism and Equality.* New York: Basic Books.

———. (1988). *The Company of Critic: Social Criticism and Political Commitment in the Twentieth Century.* New York: Basic.

Wason, P. C., and Jonson-Laird, P. L. (1972). *Psychology of Reasoning.* London: Batsford.

Yaniv, A. (1993). *National Security and Democracy in Israel.* London: Lynne Rienner.

Young, J. M. (1989). *Writing and Rewriting the Holocaust: Narrative and the Consequences of Interpretation.* Bloomington and Indianapolis: Indiana University Press.

Yousaf, M., and Adkin, M. (1992). *The Bear Trap.* London: Leo Cooper.

Zashin, E. (1972). *M. Civil Disobedience and Democracy.* New York: Free Press.

INDEX

L

M